Sixteen American Presidents

Sixteen American Presidents

DAVID K. E. BRUCE

THE **BOBBS-MERRILL** COMPANY, INC.
A SUBSIDIARY OF HOWARD W. SAMS & CO., INC.
Publishers · INDIANAPOLIS · NEW YORK

PREFACE

I HAD originally contemplated writing a series of essays on all the Presidents of the United States. In 1939 I had completed about half of this projected work, and the result was published that year in an English text covering the period from George Washington to Abraham Lincoln.

Thereafter, I have been occupied with various tasks which have not left me sufficient leisure for additional research and writing in this field. The present edition represents a thorough revision of the 1939 book which was entitled: "Revolution to Reconstruction."

The period of American history covered by this work includes the beginning of the Union of the American States and finishes with the preservation of that Union after a bitter struggle between the North and the South over the issue of the right of the Southern States to secede and to establish their own independent government.

Some of these sixteen Presidents of the United States were great men, some were mediocre. All of them were honorable and faithful public servants.

The position of the President under the American Constitutional system is a powerful one. He not only is the head of the civil government but is also the Commander-in-Chief of the armed forces of the nation.

The Federal Constitution provides for three distinct branches of Government—the Executive, the Legislative, and the Judicial. A President can exercise considerable influence over the decisions of the Congress. However, the Congress is very jealous of its prerogatives and its responsibility for initiating and freely debating legislation. In addition, it is sometimes under the control of a political party other than that represented by the President. In such event, the influence of the President in obtaining a favorable vote on legislation desired by the Executive is often thwarted.

The Federal Judiciary, independent of the Executive and Legislative branches, protects the liberties and interprets the rights of the citizens under the Constitution.

The separation of the powers of Government amongst three divisions, independent but coordinated, is a feature not only of the national constitution, but is likewise characteristic of the constitutions of the individual States of the Union.

This strict separation of powers has often proved baffling to Europeans, many of whom do not realize that the authority of the President is sharply defined and limited. When Woodrow Wilson, shortly after the first World War, unsuccessfully attempted to have his personal commitments in favor of the League of Nations ratified by the United States Senate, there was a great deception abroad, where it had been too often assumed that the commitment of a President would almost automatically be followed by the necessary constitutional approval.

In spite of this system of constitutional checks and balances, the occupant of the Presidential office exercises vast powers. Much depends on his prestige with his countrymen. It will be remarked by readers of these essays that those Presidents who enjoyed public approbation of their policies were usually able to implement them regardless of determined opposition and obstruction in Congress.

Therefore, the success of any presidential administration depends in large degree on the personality and character of the Chief Executive, and on his ability to engage the support and loyalty of the electorate.

I have attempted to portray these individuals informally, against the historical background of their respective epochs, with particular attention to their moral, social, intellectual and political traits.

DAVID K.E. BRUCE

Paris, July 1953

CONTENTS

George Washington

Born: February 22, 1732.

Married: January 6, 1759.

Elected "General and Commander-in-Chief of the Army of the United Colonies" on June 15, 1775.

Cessation of hostilities between Great Britain and the United States proclaimed: April 19, 1783.

Resigned his commission as Commander-in-Chief: December 23, 1783.

The Federal Convention met in Philadelphia May 25, 1787.

Draft of the Constitution signed: September 17, 1787.

Elected President of the United States: February 4, 1789.

Re-elected President of the United States: December 5, 1792.

Died: December 14, 1799.

GEORGE WASHINGTON

Over two hundred years have passed since the birth of George Washington. During that period many Americans have won public distinction, some as conquerors and some as political leaders, but only a few have, like Washington, combined the qualities of the soldier with those of the statesman. Although neither an extraordinary General nor an original political philosopher, he achieved unusual success in both these fields.

His task as a General was almost unique. At the outbreak of hostilities with England the Colonies had no central military organization, and Washington was bitterly opposed to the system of short-term enlistments that obliged him, at times, to witness the disbanding of one regiment and the recruitment of another in the face of impending battle. His troops lacked everything—food, money, muskets, powder, lead, clothing; most of his officers and men were deficient in discipline, and many in courage. He was environed by a civil population, one-third of which, it is estimated, was loyal to the British Crown. As the struggle progressed, he confronted cowardice, desertion, treachery, mutiny and attempted assassination. Amidst perilous conditions he believed himself threatened by a cabal composed of certain of his own subordinates, supported by influential members of Congress. Undaunted, he faced all difficulties.

Added to his responsibilities as Commander of the Army and of the Navy was the difficulty of securing effective co-operation from the politicians. The Continental Congress had advisory rather than executive powers; war supplies were drawn from the governments of the various Colonies, whose attachment to the common struggle varied greatly. To those in provincial authority Washington's letters were almost incessant; with them his influence was immense. His personal character was the Treasury and the Arsenal of the Revolution. He was the organizer of victory, the personification of the rebellion; probably no other man could have held together the pitifully inadequate colonial forces, or have attracted the determining assistance of France to the cause of independence.

The same dynamism of personality characterized his career in civil life. Washington's moral qualities aroused in those who knew him well a confidence and a respect akin to awe. When the security of newly gained freedom was menaced by the weakness of the Articles of Confederation, he insisted upon the need for a strong national Government. This resulted in his presiding over the convention that framed a Constitution later pronounced by Gladstone as "the most wonderful work struck off at a given time by the brain and purpose of man." Feeling ran high in many states as to the wisdom of ratification of this Constitution, but much of the opposition was silenced by the knowledge that Washington would be the Chief Executive. Unanimously elected first President of the United States, he was able to establish the machinery of a novel form of administration, and by his own prestige to guard it against partisan attacks until he had transformed a discredited Confederacy into a respected nation.

His fame, so expanded during his lifetime as to rob him of any semblance of privacy, has suffered no posthumous diminution. Exhaustive historical research has not impaired his high reputation as one of the noblest figures in history. As Jefferson said of him: "His integrity was most pure, his justice the most inflexible I have ever known, no motives of interest or consanguinity or friendship or hatred being able to bias his decision. He was indeed, in every sense of the words, a wise, a good, and a great man."

Had he never filled a high station he would have been a notable figure. He was the first horseman of his day, in an age when many Virginians were rather centaurs than humans. Striking in appearance, fastidious in dress, courtly in manner, dignified in bearing, skillful in field sports, hospitable as Timon of Athens, he was the ideal Southern cavalier. His temperament, deeply passionate, was restrained by an iron will. His personal courage was unimpeachable; indeed, it bordered on rashness. Something exalted in his character, a fine balance of accomplishments, temperance of judgment, unusual personal magnetism distinguished him from early manhood in a society that produced more remarkable political leaders, in proportion to population, than any since Attic times.

Although his position in Virginia was practically that of a feudal lord, he was thoroughly at home amongst frontiersmen and soldiers, and accustomed to hardship in many forms. He was not only one of the greatest landowners in America, but one of its most enlightened agriculturists. His interests were not, however, confined to the rotation of crops or to the manifold activities of plantation life, for his vision was rather continental than local. He forecast the westward march of settlements, devoting much time and money to water connections between Virginia and the lands beyond the Alleghenies. He was a tireless traveler, regarding his country in terms of empire when his fellows were content with the present boundaries of their states.

While his friends were still at school, he was making his living by surveying tracts of virgin land, sleeping out beneath the stars or in vermin-infested cabins, exposed to attack by marauding Indians, supplementing his meager provisions by shooting wild turkeys and deer. Play with wooden soldiers, casual instruction by his elder brother in European military matters, a few lessons with a rapier, a knowledge of woodcraft, formed his preparation for his first command.

Through political influence, he was appointed, at the age of twenty-one, District Adjutant General of the Virginia Militia with the rank of Major. Before his twenty-second birthday he had delivered a message from Governor Dinwiddie of Virginia to the French Commandant at Fort-de-Bœuf on the Ohio River.

At this period, the French and English alike were determined unjustly to despoil the Indians of the rich lands west of the Allegheny Mountains, extending from the Great Lakes to the Ohio. The French claimed this area by right of discovery, the English by right of treaty; the pretensions of the former were impertinent, those of the latter were fraudulent. The unsatisfactory answer of the French Commandant to the impudent demands contained in Dinwiddie's letter led to the outbreak of the French and Indian War, in which Washington played a prominent part.

His initial military skirmish was with a small contingent of French and Indians, whom his men surprised and defeated, killing their officer, de Jumonville, and some of his followers. "I heard the bullets whistle, and, believe me, there is something charming in the sound," was Washington's comment on this encounter.

There was some doubt as to whether the assaulted French were engaged upon a diplomatic or a hostile mission; it is now believed to have been the latter. At the time, however, after the scalps of the dead had been exhibited, and news of the event had been relayed to Paris, there was an indignant outburst against Washington.

Later that year he was promoted to a Colonelcy. His forces were soon defeated in an engagement with troops led by a brother of the late alleged Ambassador. Washington had chosen to defend a fort ill-suited to resistance, and after a spirited exchange of musketry he was obliged to surrender his position, but had the consolation of being allowed to withdraw his men. By one of the articles of capitulation he admitted the "assassination" of M. de Jumonville, a phrasing afterwards used to plague him and to lead to strictures upon his honor. Since the articles were written in French, a language unknown to him, and translated by a Dutchman who imperfectly understood either English or French, his offense in this regard was at least venial.

After the defeat at Fort Necessity he remained for some time on the frontier. Finally he resigned his charge, disgusted by the ruling that a colonial of any grade was outranked by all holders of a royal commission. He emerged from retirement at the invitation of General Braddock to become a volunteer Aide-de-Camp in that officer's expedition to take Fort Duquesne from the French.

This British campaign was ill starred from its commencement, but at last the marching columns got under way, laboriously hewing a path through the forest, progressing at the rate of about five miles a day. Braddock was an exceptionally brave General, but unused to conditions of colonial warfare. Washington, laid low by his lifelong foe, dysentery, made part of the campaign prostrate on a springless wagon. He was still weak and ill when the day of battle arrived.

After an arduous journey the long lines of infantry with their attendant baggage train and camp followers, male and female, debouched from the gloomy forest. The fighting columns crossed the Monongahela River, drums beating, bayonets sparkling, uniforms speckless, belts and gaiters freshly pipe-clayed, prepared for an easy conquest of the rustic fort standing upon the site of the present city of Pittsburgh.

The thirteen hundred British and colonial troops, meandering over a narrow, sunken road, were suddenly attacked by a force of approximately two hundred and fifty French and six hundred Indians enfilading the redcoats with a leaden hail from vantage points in nearby thickets.

In vain, Braddock attempted to rally his men and lead them in platoon formation. He himself fought with super bravery. Four horses were killed under him before he fell.

Meanwhile, two horses had succumbed under Washington, four bullets had pierced his uniform. His Virginians took cover in the woods, like ruffed grouse; whence they might have turned the tide had not many of them been killed by the mistaken fire of British regulars. A rout ensued.

Of Braddock's 1300 men, 456 were killed, and 421 wounded, while the victors sustained only thirty casualties. The General succumbed to his wounds, and was secretly buried in the forest road, lest his body be discovered by the Indians.

The tidings of this defeat reverberated. The impression spread throughout the Colonies that the redcoats were not, as hitherto believed, invincible. Washington's reputation for valor and resourcefulness was the only glory gained in the disaster; it was to be recalled in later years when a choice was to be made of a Commander for the Revolutionary Army.

Governor Dinwiddie appointed Washington Commander-in-Chief of the Virginia forces assigned to the protection of the otherwise defenseless frontier. He soon discovered that many of his militia were unreliable; amongst them he executed two, condemned by a court-martial.

Illness again racked him. While still convalescent, he joined the British General Forbes in another attempt upon Fort Duquesne. This campaign terminated when the French abandoned and destroyed Fort Duquesne. Soon afterwards, Washington returned to Mount Vernon; at the age of twenty-six, he believed his military career to be over.

Then ensued sixteen years of bucolic existence, perhaps the happiest of his life. Its peace was unbroken until he set out for Boston, in 1775, as Commander of the Armies of the Colonies in rebellion.

The story of the Revolutionary conflict was, as Washington expressed it, "a history of false hopes and temporary expedients." The American Army which the "Old Fox," as the British were to call its

General, found awaiting him at Boston was composed of about 14,500 soldiers out of a civil population of 2,000,000 whites.

In some companies, lieutenants and captains were elected by their men, and went to odd lengths to curry favor with these voters; frequently the higher appointments were made by Congress for political reasons. The unusual spectacle was afforded of a captain shaving a private on the parade ground, and many officers were to be arrested and cashiered for such offenses as poltroonery, or drawing pay and provisions for more men than they commanded. During the entire war the short terms of enlistment and the militia system were disruptive of efficiency. If Washington had not directed a devoted nucleus of men, who had contracted to serve for the duration of hostilities, he might at times have been almost entirely without troops; the largest number he had under his immediate orders on any occasion was twenty-five thousand against Howe's thirty-four thousand. During the height of the struggle, his followers numbered less than ten thousand effectives, and they were expected to cope with the flower of the British service. On the other hand, Van Tyne estimated that fifty thousand American loyalists fought on the British side.

It was reputedly said in the American Army that General Gates loved the militia because they would never bring him under fire. When their term of enlistment was over, militiamen were likely to return to their farms, there to assist in crop making, even when their presence was most urgently needed at the front. Nor did they hesitate to take away with them precious muskets and equipment; one souvenir soldier was detected carrying off a cannon ball to his mother, for her use in pounding mustard. The giving of bounties to stimulate enlistments led to many abuses, for not a few deserted to re-enlist. In 1778, a man was executed who had deserted and re-enlisted seven times under the allurement of bonuses.

Peculation and graft were common in contracts for military supplies. The civilian population produced a more than modest quota of turncoats and profiteers, while the Army was not irreproachable for frequent examples of drunkenness and cowardice. On some occasions, Washington's soldiers fled from the enemy not in squads but in battalions. Desertions attained the proportion of migratory tribe movements; the Commander-in-Chief once remarked bitterly: "We shall be obliged to detach one-half of the Army to bring back the other."

The death penalty was freely meted out. Two privates and a

corporal, deserters from the 1st Pennsylvania Regiment, upon being captured by fellow soldiers were told by the latter that one of them would be immediately killed. They drew lots for the sacrifice. The corporal, proving unlucky, was decapitated. His head, impaled upon a pole, and carried into camp by the two remaining culprits, was exhibited as a warning against similar enterprises. Such drastic punishments induced better order amongst the troops, but even at Yorktown desertion was still a serious problem.

The life of the American soldier was a hard one; a sense of patriotic satisfaction was too often his sole reward. His meager pay was generally in arrears. If he had been given any uniform whatever, it was probably destined to be worn to rags. The officers too were scantily equipped; some of them confected gaiters by skinning dead Indians. More than once the path of the Army was traceable by the blood-stained imprints of insufficiently shod soldiers. Food was often scarce. The conventional allowances of rum were belated. Antiseptics and anesthetics were, of course, unknown. Sanitary conditions in hospitals and prison camps were unspeakable. The sick and wounded faced greater danger from disease than they had from enemy action; in one Virginia regiment putrid fever killed thirty-seven out of forty privates in a single hospital.

Upon the outbreak of hostilities, the shortage of guns, powder and lead made Franklin's advocacy of the use of pikes, supplemented by bows and arrows, not untimely. Following the Declaration of Independence, the great lead statue of King George III on Bowling Green was melted by the Americans into bullets for the destruction of his soldiers, while the house roofs of Philadelphia and New York were stripped for the same purpose. Benedict Arnold's men who, on their march to Canada, had subsisted on broiled dogs, raw berries, boiled moccasins and cartouche boxes, arrived at the scene of action with only five rounds of ammunition apiece. In the summer of 1776, nearly one-fourth of the soldiers were without arms; the New York Convention ordered each unequipped militiaman to bring with him a shovel, spade, pickax or a scythe straightened and made fast to a pole.

Only Washington, whose personality tempered the adversities of famine, weather and war to his troops, could have surmounted the odds confronting the American cause. Despite difficulties of transport, the British Army was sufficient in numbers and equipment to have defeated probably any American General except him.

His own military shortcomings were numerous, but he was an

incomparable master of fighting men, inspiring them with his own deep passion for liberty. He neglected the use of cavalry, which would have been of the greatest service to him; his disposition of artillery was seldom happy; he blundered almost fatally on one occasion, his forces being saved from complete annihilation only by General Howe's lethargy. The battle of Long Island was so ill-conceived and ill-executed that the American Army was barely extricated from disaster by the witlessness of the British, coupled with a fog which made possible Washington's masterly retreat across the East River to Manhattan Island.

His only decided successes in the field were the minor but daring engagements at Princeton and Trenton, and the defeat of Cornwallis at Yorktown. This last triumph was the culmination of a skillfully planned campaign and investment. It was made possible by Washington's energy, initiative, and excellent tactics, as well as by the diplomatic manner in which he obtained the co-operation of the French marine and land units.

During the war, he was unassisted by any first-class Generals except Greene and Arnold. The former arrived late at his brilliant military maturity; the latter, though brave as a lion, became blackly perfidious, wringing from Washington the sad commentary, "Whom can we trust now?"

The close of the eight long and weary years of the Revolutionary War marked the end of Washington's active military career. When during the presidential term of John Adams hostilities with France appeared unavoidable, all eyes turned toward the retired warrior of Mount Vernon and he was named Generalissimo of the Republic's forces. Happily, a composition of the difficulties ensued.

Though Washington had little Latin and less Greek, his understanding was penetrating and sound. Few causes were dearer to his heart than the establishment of a national university. His favorite reading was of husbandry, politics and war. By assiduous practice he developed into a clear, forceful letter writer. He was diffident of speech in public assemblies; upon first taking his place in the Virginia House of Burgesses he attempted to express his appreciation of the attentions shown him upon his entrance into that body, but stammered and faltered, only to be lauded by the Speaker, Mr. Robinson, who said: "Sit down, Mr. Washington, your modesty equals your valor, and that surpasses the power of any language that I possess." Though he shrank from debate, he was influential in conversation. After the return to Virginia of its delegates to the first Continental Congress at Philadelphia, Patrick Henry upon being asked who was the greatest man at the convention, replied: "If you speak of eloquence, Mr. Rutledge of South Carolina is by far the greatest orator; but if you speak of solid information and sound judgment, Colonel Washington is unquestionably the greatest man on the floor."

In social discussions Washington was usually taciturn, but if warmed by a subject talked freely. His reputation for habitual austerity is unfounded; he was reserved and shy, but loved dancing, laughter and gay conversation. He liked the theater and went to the playhouse whenever an opportunity offered. He played cards often, also billiards, gambling at both, as well as making wagers on horse races and taking chances in lotteries and raffles. Nor was he a stranger to the pleasures of drinking wine. He was solicitous in laying down pipes of madeira; drank a half pint or pint of it daily when it was available, and he partook freely of champagne, claret, rum punches, beer, whiskey and other spirituous concoctions. He served out grog to his soldiers, Negroes and employees. There exists a singular contract between him and his gardener, permitting the latter, as part of his compensation, to have four dollars at Christmas, with which he might become drunk for four days and four nights; and two dollars at Easter and Whitsuntide for the same purpose.

He was tolerant of the opinions of others in all things. His friendships were numerous; he set much store by the letters and company of his friends. There are few more touching instances of affection than the reciprocal love between Lafayette and himself, or of mutual admiration than his relationship with Benjamin Franklin. Franklin termed him "my friend and the friend of mankind."

Washington was meticulous about his personal finances. His concern in this regard was that of an honorable man who had a horror of debt. Although a great landowner, he was almost always poor in cash resources, even having to borrow money to attend his first inauguration as President. Nevertheless, there is instance after instance of his generosity in making loans and contributions to friends and acquaintances. His charitable largesses were innumerable, as befitted one of the most liberal men of his generation. His attitude toward payment for his public services was disinterested; he refused to take any salary as Commander-in-Chief of the Revolutionary forces, and his allowances as President never equaled his expenditures. During the Revolution he pledged, on several occasions, his personal fortune to borrow gold to pay his troops, and neglected his own estate while engaged in the public service.

He was an inveterate speculator in real estate. His eagerness to buy Western lands, at bargain prices, from fellow officers of his early campaigns savors of hard acquisitiveness. Tenacious of his legal rights and a prudent manager of his properties, he seems to have had a pronounced liking for business affairs; even during the Revolution he sought a share in a privateer, a form of speculation that sometimes returned large profits. His passion for financial order is interestingly displayed in his will, by which, without the assistance of a lawyer, he disposed of over sixty thousand acres of land and an abundance of other possessions, constituting one of the largest American fortunes, in a fashion testifying alike to the clarity of his mind, to his public spirit and to his affection for his relatives and connections.

In person Washington was of commanding stature, straight as an Indian, standing six feet three and one half inches in his stocking feet. He had large bones and joints. His hands and feet were literally enormous and his physical strength uncommonly great. His voice was agreeable, his walk graceful, his countenance benevolent and dignified. He had blue-gray eyes, set wide apart, dark brown hair, a straight nose and a firm mouth. His teeth gave him constant trouble, until his natural ones were at last replaced by a set of substitutes manufactured out of hippopotamus ivory. His pale complexion had been somewhat marred by smallpox contracted at the age of nineteen during his sole foreign excursion, when he accompanied his brother Lawrence to Barbados. With age, he became somewhat deaf. His general appearance was imposing and attractive; Lafayette, after frequenting for many years the best society on two continents, said of him that he had never beheld so superb a man.

His health was often troublesome; he was a frequent sufferer from dysentery, and at various times had other annoying ailments. Medical knowledge in his day was decidedly limited, the ordinary country practitioner being prone to treat any disease, as would a barber-surgeon of Spain, by bleeding. At the age of sixty-seven, he contracted a severe chill, following exposure to rain and snow during a tour of his farms. He was first cupped by his overseer; later in the day he was bled three times more, by as many doctors, dosed with calomel and tartar emetic and scarified with blisters and poultices. In spite of these heroic remedies, strangulation persisted. He sank rapidly but retained his understanding to the end.

He was buried at home. The obsequies were simple. They were attended, in accord with Mrs. Washington's wishes, only by some neighbors and friends, local officials, Free Masons from Alexandria, and a small company of militia. Troops formed the escort, then came four of the clergy; after them, the General's horse, with his saddle, holsters and pistols, led by two grooms in black, preceded the coffin. Out on the broad bosom of the Potomac a schooner fired a salute of minute guns, the cannon on the shore boomed a reply, the illustrious body was deposited in the family vault, and Mount Vernon, which he so greatly loved, became his permanent resting place.

In youth he was ambitious of fame, but as he grew older, he preferred the diversions of life as a country gentleman to any others, and only the imperious march of great events sufficed to draw him from his retirement. When, as a young man, he courted glory on dangerous expeditions, he felt himself equal to any martial station. Jealous of his rank, he was uncommonly free in the tone in which he lectured his superior, the Royal Governor of Virginia; but his humility increased with age, and he came to mistrust his capacity for positions of highest responsibility. He affirmed with deep sincerity that he did not deem himself properly qualified to command the Revolutionary army; later he questioned his fitness to act as President. Moderate in ambition, he disdained the thought of personal aggrandizement at the expense of the general good. To the suggestion he be made King, he returned an indignant reply, for he always opposed the institution of a monarchy in the United States.

There never was a military leader loved by his soldiers in whose hands civil liberties were so safe; he abhorred the idea of a dictatorship supported by a praetorian guard. Indeed, his deference to the Continental Congress was a decided handicap to his military operations. His refusal to be a candidate for a third term as President set a precedent that until recently was never successfully violated.

Although he enjoyed his fame, he never truckled to the mob, nor did he advocate measures because he thought they might prove popular. When ten thousand people, massed day after day in the streets of Philadelphia, threatened to drag him from his house and effect a revolution in the government or compel it to declare in favor of the French Revolution and against England, he stood firm for neutrality. In the case of the Jay treaty he disregarded the clamor of the populace and of the politicians, forcing its ratification, amid threats of violence and scenes of personal execration, because of his conviction that it would afford the best settlement of the discord between the United States and Great Britain. This action required rare courage, for popular feeling against the treaty was bitterly unfavorable.

His temper was tempestuous, but usually he kept it under control. His wrath, when he thought Charles Lee had failed him at Monmouth, was overpowering, as was his reaction, many years later, to the news that St. Clair had been ambushed by Indians; but in both cases his anger passed away like a thundershower. When a poacher, who had been warned off the Mount Vernon property, threatened Washington with his gun, he was dragged out of his boat by the scruff of his neck and given a severe beating by the unarmed planter. During the encampment before Boston, upon being apprised of disorder in a company of Virginia riflemen Washington leaped, on horseback, over a fence, into the middle of the combatants, seized two of them and banged their heads together as if they had been ninepins.

He was always gallant to women. While in his teens he lost his heart not once but often. He was unfortunate in his love affairs, cherishing a schoolboy longing for a "Lowland Beauty." Before he came of age, he wished to marry Miss Betsy Fauntleroy, who rejected him. He seems to have had other amatory mischances, but the great love of his life was Sally Cary Fairfax. She was one of the most captivating of Virginia belles, the daughter of a great landowner and scholar, and married a man who would, it was expected, inherit the title and the vast estates of Thomas, Lord Fairfax. It was a hopeless passion; she flirted with him, but how seriously she regarded his love will never be known. Many years after her death in England, faded letters from Washington to her were found among her effects. Written by him when he was on the frontier and while he was engaged to Martha Custis, they leave no doubt of his love for Mrs. Fairfax. After his marriage, she and her husband were frequently at Mount Vernon, and the Washingtons often visited them at their plantation, Belvoir. It is possible that, except for the two letters treasured by her, no word of love ever passed from one to the other. The impression, however, that she left upon him was ineffaceable; when he was an old man and she a Loyalist exile in England, he wrote to her a last time, saying nothing had been able to eradicate from his mind "the recollection of those happy moments, the happiest in my life, which I have enjoyed in your company."

Disappointed in love, Washington did not abandon the idea of marriage, which, he once declared, he considered "the most interesting event of one's life, the foundation of happiness or misery." At the age of twenty-six he wed Mrs. Martha Custis.

For forty years they were a devoted couple. During the war Mrs. Washington, or as she was called by her husband's legions, "Lady Washington," used to visit the camp every winter, spending almost half the period of hostilities with the General. The records of that time present a pleasant picture of postprandial domesticity—the Commander in Chief sitting at his field desk after dinner, writing, by the light of guttering candles, letters east, west, north, and south, beseeching additional levies of troops and supplies, and his wife knitting socks for soldiers. They had no children, but he treated her two children by her first marriage as if they had been his own, and eventually brought two of her grandchildren to live with them, regarding them in every respect as if they were his own descendants. She survived her husband, whom she idolized, twenty-nine months.

Washington's first essay into politics, as a candidate for the Virginia House of Burgesses, was unsuccessful. Once again he was defeated for the same office, but the third time he had learned the technique of electioneering, and by a vote of 310 votes to his opponent's 45 was swept into office on a flood of liquor. Incredible as the quantities appear, the electors received on this last occasion, at Washington's expense, persuasive draughts amounting, approximately, to forty gallons of rum punch, twenty-eight gallons of wine, twenty-six gallons of rum, forty-six gallons of beer, six gallons of madeira, three and half pints of brandy, and other miscellaneous potations, all in direct violation of a Virginia statute declaring treating of voters illegal. Having entered upon his new duties, his first legislative effort was, with Mr. Pendleton, to prepare and bring in a bill "to preserve the Water for the use of the Inhabitants of the Town of Winchester, and the limits thereof, by preventing Hogs from running at large therein." From this time until he became head of the army Washington was regularly elected to the House of Burgesses, and the voters continued to slake their thirst at his charge.

He took a prominent part in the events leading up to a declaration of war against England, serving in both the first and the second Continental Congresses. His extensive interests in the West, to which he felt British policy, especially as expressed in the Quebec Act, was inimical; his personal experience of the impositions to which tobacco growers were subjected by the Acts of Navigation and the Acts of Trade; his own resentment against overbearing colonial Governors; his observations during the Braddock expedition; his sensitiveness to the callous treatment of colonials and of colonial pretensions by officers and ministers of the Crown; and his realization of the intense selfishness of the imperial colonial policy caused him, in advance of the promulgation of the Stamp Act, to view jealously any encroachments by the mother country upon the rights of Virginians to legislate for themselves in representative assemblies. Before a definite break occurred between the Colonies and England, he was attending indignation meetings, subscribing to nonimportation agreements, and writing and talking against taxation without representation.

Like Chatham, Burke, and Fox he asserted the rights of Englishmen on every continent to the privileges of liberty. He was reluctant to sever his ties with a kindred people, with whom in blood and sentiment Virginians especially had so much in common. For a while it seemed to him impossible that George III would sanction the antagonistic measures advocated by his ministers against their American possessions, peopled by Englishmen, which absorbed anually one third of the entire export trade of Great Britain. But the restrictions adopted by Parliament after the Boston tea party, annulling the charter of Massachusetts, quartering troops in the Colonies and otherwise chastising the rebellious colonists, left no doubt in the mind even of a loyal Virginian that the Americans must, in the words of their King, "either triumph or submit."

The choice for Washington was clear; he waited until "time, the never-failing expositor of all things" had clearly demonstrated that the Hanoverian King was as mad a ruler as ever tossed away an empire, and that his satellites and sycophants, who had debauched the British electorate, were determined to abet their King's vindictive and oppressive schemes, before he pledged his life and fortune to resist their arrogance.

After the war was over, Washington's services to his country were again to be enlisted. Peace with England found the new nation bankrupt, with a Congress powerless to maintain the credit of the country by taxes, or its existence by arms. The gradual dissolution of such ties as had bound the Colonies together during their war effort filled Washington with alarm. He believed there must be an indissoluble union of the states under one federal head, a federal judiciary, a proper military establishment and "the prevalence of that pacific and friendly disposition among the people of the United States, which will induce them to forget their local prejudices and policies; to make those mutual concessions, which are requisite to the general prosperity; and, in some instances, to sacrifice their individual advantages to the interest of the community."

After a convention had embodied these new ideas in a new Constitution, and that Constitution had been ratified, and after he had reluctantly accepted the responsibility of becoming, by unanimous choice of the electoral college, the first President of the United States, he entered upon a task which for political complexity has rarely been surpassed.

Washington chose as members of his Cabinet men with whom he had enjoyed long personal association, naming Thomas Jefferson as Secretary of State, Edmund Randolph as Attorney General, Alexander Hamilton as Secretary of the Treasury, and Henry Knox as Secretary of War. To the office of Chief Justice of the United States he appointed John Jay, a man of great ability and unblemished reputation.

Washington's political system was a simple one. In domestic matters he sought to contemplate the United States as one great whole; to consult only the substantial and permanent interests of the country, and to overlook all personal, local and partisan considerations. Wishing to destroy party spirit, not to create it, he did his utmost to reconcile the flaming and divergent party fidelities of Jefferson and Hamilton. Although a farmer, he felt deeply the importance of manufactures and commerce, and labored unsparingly to promote them. With the modern theory of democratic government he would have had little sympathy. Like John Randolph, he might have said, "I am an aristocrat, I love liberty, I hate equality." He believed in a governing class composed of men who had proved their fitness to govern. In his day, in Virginia, universal suffrage was unknown; offices were held by landowners and merchants who legislated according to their own settled convictions and not in obedience to pressures. Perhaps no other man of his time had as wide and as sympathetic an acquaintance with the real needs of the American people as did the first President, but he was a leader, not a demagogue, and was willing to oppose popular tendencies when he considered them harmful to the real interests of the nation.

During his administration he established an adequate army; put down the Whiskey Rebellion; made a treaty with England for the surrender of her Western trading posts, which had been a most vexatious and dangerous source of contention between the two nations; negotiated, through Thomas Pinckney, a treaty with Spain, settling the Florida boundary and securing to our country the navigation of the Mississippi; pacified the Indians; fathered the development of the West; and stood firm for the daring financial measures, advocated by Hamilton. He was free from pomposity, manifesting no concern over political contentions as to whether his title should be "His Highness," "His Highness the President of the United States and Protector of Their Liberties," or "His Highness the President-General"; nor did he care whether, as Jefferson desired, the terms "Excellency," "Honor," "Worship," and "Mister" should disappear from usage.

His foreign policy was founded upon a belief that altruistic conduct to other nations might be dangerous to an infant republic. To use his own words: "My policy has been, and will continue to be while I have the honor to remain in the administration, to maintain friendly terms with, but to be independent of, all the nations of the earth; to share in the broils of none; to fulfill our own engagements; to supply the wants and be carriers for them all; being thoroughly convinced that it is our policy and interest to do so."

In his Farewell Address he further expressed his thoughts in this regard, saying, "Permanent, inveterate antipathies against particular nations, and passionate attachments for others should be excluded . . . there can be no greater error than to expect or calculate upon real favors from nation to nation."

One of his chief aspirations was to open the Western country by inland navigation and to connect it with the Eastern seaboard by canalized waterways. He was a leading exponent of Western settlement, his utterances concerning the future development of the frontier were almost as prophetic as was his insistence upon plans for a federal city, designed for the needs of eight hundred thousand inhabitants, to arise upon the waste area of land now known as the District of Columbia.

He was for many years an Episcopalian vestryman, an office which in colonial Virginia was rather secular than ecclesiastical. He attended church frequently, but also transacted business on Sunday. He disliked denominational disputes, saying: "Being no bigot myself, I am disposed to indulge the professors of Christianity in the church with that road to Heaven, which to them shall seem the most direct, plainest, easiest, and least liable to exception."

He favored emancipation of Negroes, and manumitted his own slaves by his testament. He was familiar with the degrading triangular traffic that brought Negroes from Africa to be sold for molasses in the East Indies, converted the molasses into rum in New England, and shipped the rum in New England bottoms to Africa for more slaves. He was familiar, also, with the shameful brutalities of the Middle Passage, where Negroes were often shipped in such large numbers that they were obliged to lie one upon another, like sardines in a tin, the healthy, sick and dying being chained together, and women giving birth while chained to corpses. Nor was he unmindful of the miseries suffered by slaves at the hands of cruel or negligent masters, or of the moral obloquy attendant upon their ownership. From his own experience he realized the inefficiency of slave labor and the baneful effect of the institution upon the South. There is no evidence, however, that he was ever sufficiently aroused by its iniquities to make a determined effort to bring about its general abolition; in political discussions, his silence on the subject was influenced by his conviction that an attack on the institution would be disruptive of the Union. At the proper time he hoped emancipation would be brought about. "Not only do I pray for it on the score of human dignity," he said, "but I can clearly foresee that nothing but the rooting out of slavery can perpetuate the existence of our union by consolidating it in a common bond of principle."

His attitude toward the Indians was a callously practical one, apparently tinged with no sympathy for their rights as a dispossesed people. He knew how to deal with them. He often sat in their councils during frontier operations and gained the respect of many of their leaders. He distributed rum amongst them to win their support against the French, and took pleasure in their savage dances. He adopted their methods of forest warfare, and a modified form of their dress for some of his soldiers. As President he treated them with severe justice, pacifying many unruly tribes. His record in regard to them was free from the blots that so signally disgraced many later pages of American history.

The real lodestone of Washington's existence was Mount Vernon. Even in the midst of the busiest scenes a nostalgia for country life pervaded his thoughts. This instinct was hereditary. Although one enterprising genealogist has attempted to derive his ancestry from Odin, the supposed founder of Scandinavia, we know he was descended from good English country stock, with an admixture of Huguenot blood. Some of his ancestors had been knighted for gallantry in battle, others had led bucolic lives, but all had clung to ownership of the soil. In the year 1657, during the rule of Oliver Cromwell, John and Lawrence Washington, brothers, had emigrated from the north of England and settled at Bridges Creek on the Potomac River, in Westmoreland County, Virginia.

The former of these brothers was the great-grandfather of George Washington. John Washington's departure from England, like that of many loyalists during the Cromwellian period, was probably due to the attractions of Virginia where sympathy with the Roundheads was notoriously slight. This movement, beginning with King Charles's execution in 1649, contributed largely to the growth of the white population in Virginia from fifteen thousand persons, in 1649, to thirty-eight thousand in 1670.

It was an interesting land to which the brothers had come. Already its short history was tinctured with romance. Sir Walter Raleigh, "admiral and shepherd of the ocean," one of the most extraordinary and winning of the superb group of gentlemen adventurers who adorned Elizabeth's court, was beheaded by King James before his prophecy was completely realized that he would live to see Virginia an English nation. But he lived long enough, after the first settlers at Roanoke had been swallowed up by the wilderness as mysteriously as if they had been engulfed in a huge volcanic fissure, to be satisfied of the permanence of English plantations in the New World, and to have popularized the use of tobacco and potatoes in the Old World.

The first settlement at Jamestown, in 1607, was menaced, three years later, by the afflictions of the Starving Time. During that dread period the number of settlers was reduced from five hundred to sixty. After this disaster, the discovery of the adaptability of the soil to tobacco culture, "the most momentous fact in Seventeenth Century Virginia history," assured the economic success of the colony.

When John Washington arrived in Virginia, he found the cultivation of tobacco soundly established there. The search for Eldorado no longer intrigued the colonists. They had grown skeptical of finding the Pacific Ocean a few nights' sleep beyond the Blue Ridge Mountains. The first Negro slaves had been imported in 1619, and a considerable number of white indented servants were on the plantations. There was little danger to be apprehended in settled localities from the Indians, although they were still a menace upon the frontiers.

John Washington was not long in fitting himself into the life of the community. About twenty years after he landed, he was made commander of the forces of Virginia with the title of Colonel. He had for some time been a member of the House of Burgesses. When he died, he owned more than twelve square miles of land. During his campaigns against the Indians he was given by them the title of Conotocarious, "Destroyer of Villages," a cognomen by which his most illustrious descendant was also, almost a century later, to be known by the Indians.

The grandfather and father of the first President were prominent Virginians. George's father, Augustine, married twice, and had two sets of children. Augustine's second wife, the mother of George, was Mary Ball, of Virginia, a strong-minded woman who loved a good pipe of tobacco. There is little evidence that she possessed many social graces; her disposition appears to have been somewhat querulous and exacting. She named her eldest son after her guardian, Major George Eskridge, a native of Wales, who was said to have been captured near his Welsh home by a press gang and sold into slavery in Virginia.

Washington's conduct to his mother was always marked by a high degree of filial rectitude, but she was somewhat of a trial to him. She prevented him, as a lad, from going to sea, and always discouraged his military ambitions. Indeed, she had little conception of the conditions of a martial life; in the midst of the Braddock campaign she wrote to her son requesting that he send her a Dutch servant and some good butter. When he was nine years old his father died; and he removed as soon as he could from his mother's house to that of his elder half-brother Lawrence.

He found a wise friend and adviser in Lawrence, who had been educated in England and whose early death from tuberculosis was a great loss and sorrow to his brother and protégé. As a result of this death George Washington, after the termination of certain life estates, became, in his early twenties, the owner of Mount Vernon, which had been so named in honor of Admiral Vernon, under whom

Lawrence had served at Cartagena, in the war carried on to avenge
the loss of "Captain Jenkins' ears." One of these famous ears had
been sliced off, under circumstances of unusual brutality, by the
cutlass of a Spanish lieutenant, and, when produced by Captain
Jenkins out of a box, in which it had been carefully preserved, before
the British House of Commons, had aroused that body to a warlike
pitch.

Supervising the plantation at Mount Vernon was an exacting occupation. George Washington owned, together with his wife, about
two hundred and seventy slaves, as well as some white indented
servants. When these latter had worked out their terms of service,
including repaying the cost of their passage from England, they
became free. Many of them were poor farmers or workingmen, who
had come to the New World to better their lot.

The dependence of such a number of men upon a plantation owner
bred in him a habit of command and an acute sense of responsibility.
Nor were their activities confined to farming. Among the slaves and
servants at Mount Vernon were sawyers, coopers, brickmakers,
masons, weavers, blacksmiths, tanners, shoemakers, carpenters, and
a distiller. The woods furnished charcoal to the blacksmith and to
the mansion, and staves to the cooper, who fabricated hogsheads for
tobacco, flour and whisky. Spinners, weavers and knitters made
coarse cloths and stockings. A fishery did a thriving business in
herring, shad and sturgeon. A schooner carried flour, manufactured
at the plantation water mill, to markets as distant as the West Indies.
Tobacco, grown on the place, was loaded at Washington's wharf and
carried directly to England.

Washington had little love for tobacco; he did not smoke it, and
he disliked its culture. Indeed the system of tobacco cultivation
practiced in Virginia was not only wasteful but unsightly, since its
rapid exhaustion of the soil obliged the deforestation of large tracts
of land. He finally abandoned the growing of tobacco in favor of
wheat and Indian corn. These he raised in quantity, milling the
wheat into high-grade flour and using the corn as a staple of diet
for men and horses on the plantation. Later he planted much grass,
grazing hundreds of sheep and cattle upon his fields. His woods
were filled with droves of hogs. He was a scientific farmer delighting
in experimental work, planning elaborate crop rotations and himself
inventing a plow and a barrow for sowing wheat.

After his retirement from the presidency he spent a great deal of time embellishing his estate, planting Maryland apple trees, New York limes, New England evergreens, Canadian firs, English holly, Spanish chestnuts, and other trees and shrubs in great numbers. Presents flowed in from Europe and America; partridges from France, swans, wild geese, Chinese pigs and pheasants, white-tailed deer and various birds and animals. He never tired of his agricultural pursuits, enthusiastically cherishing the belief that "the life of a husbandman is the most delectable. It is honourable, it is amusing, and with judicious management, it is profitable. To see plants rising from the earth and flourish by the superior skill and bounty of the labourer fills a contemplative mind with ideas which are more easily to be conceived than expressed."

Much of his time was spent in sport. Quail, ruffed grouse, wild turkey and deer were found at Mount Vernon throughout the year, while in autumn and spring vast flocks of swans, geese and ducks ferried up and down the Potomac. Sometimes wild pigeons appeared in numbers sufficient to obscure the sun. Besides shooting, Washington enjoyed fishing, and dredged for sturgeon, or caught bass in the river.

But Washington's greatest sporting interest was in horses and hounds. It was a saying that a Virginian would walk two miles to catch a horse on which to ride one mile. His stables always held a fine string of thoroughbreds. He visited and inspected them each morning about sunrise. Mounted on Chinklin, Ajax, Blueskin, Valiant or another mettlesome hunter, dressed in blue coat, scarlet waistcoat, buckskin breeches and velvet cap, he hunted the fox with his own jack of hounds until within five years of his death.

The daily routine at Mount Vernon was simple. The master rose before daybreak and worked in the library or made a round of the house and stables. At seven he breakfasted on Indian cakes, honey and tea. Until afternoon he rode about the plantation, comprising nine thousand acres, superintending the manifold activities of his men. Sometimes he dismounted and assisted them at their labors. Dinner was served at three o'clock, and the rest of the afternoon and evening was passed at cards, tea, reading, writing or conversation until nine o'clock, when General and Mrs. Washington ordinarily retired. The house was seldom free of guests. He was an indefatigable dancer, and during the Revolution amazed onlookers at a party by dancing for three hours, without pausing, with General Greene's wife. While he was a member of the Virginia House of Burgesses, he passed the season at Williamsburg, where he was an assiduous attendant at the theater, and patronized horse races and cockfights.

It is pleasant to imagine him, in his last days, not as the father of a nation, not as a celebrated general and statesman, but as a Virginia country gentleman, riding over his broad acres, pausing to hear the mellow voices of the Negroes singing their harvest song, "Cool Water," admiring the admirable displays of bountiful nature, and ready, when the call came, to cross that bourne over which few men as great as he had preceded him.

John Adams

Born: October 30, 1735.

Married: 1764.

Member of Continental Congress: 1774-78.

First voyage to France: 1778.

Minister Plenipotentiary to negotiate peace with
Great Britain: 1780-82.

Secured recognition of American independence
from Holland: 1782.

Minister to Great Britain: 1785.

Vice President: 1789-97.

President: 1797-1801.

Died: July 4, 1826.

JOHN ADAMS

As JOHN ADAMS, ex-President of the United States, awaited death on his farm at Quincy, Massachusetts, in his ninety-first year, he must often have reviewed the stirring events in which he had played a major part. In the early stages of the Revolution, as the foremost champion of separation from the mother country, he had won the sobriquet "the Atlas of Independence." During the first few years of war he had been a member of some ninety Congressional Committees, and Chairman of twenty-five, including the most important, the Board of War and Ordnance.

Sent to Europe as Commissioner to France, in 1778, he had revisited the Continent again as Minister Plenipotentiary to conclude peace and make a commercial treaty between the former colonies and Great Britain. He had been Minister to Holland; later he was the first Minister from the United States to the Court of Saint James.

Upon his return from an exacting and successful diplomatic career abroad, Adams had served for eight years as the first Vice-President of his country; for the succeeding four years he was its President. Even the Constitution of the new nation was in debt to him for so many of its theories that he was termed "the Great Constitutionalist."

The old man must have recalled with satisfaction his founding of the American navy, as well as of the military academy at West Point. By courageous decisions he had avoided what would undoubtedly have been a ruinous war with France. His ambition, extinguishable only by death, was vicariously gratified by his son's occupancy of the White House. Could he have foreseen the future, he would have had the further gratification of knowing that his

35

lineal descendants would by their public services make the name
of Adams the most illustrious family name in American political
annals.

But dissatisfaction gnawed at his heart. Despite his honors he
was unhappy. He felt that his contemporaries had proved ungrate-
ful to him, and that posterity would not accord him a deserved
esteem. Nor was he mistaken. Even during his lifetime his greatest
rival, Jefferson, had said: "No history has done him (John Adams)
justice. . . . To him more than any other man is the country indebted
for its independence." Later historians have done little to remedy
this early neglect. The downfall of the Federalist party, coinciding
with Adams' failure of re-election as President, by involving him
hopelessly in its ruin, obscured the brilliance of his past career. No
devoted personal or political following remained to shield the unsuccessful candidate from the bitter charges of his party managers and
opponents.

The fame of this truly great man has since declined to a degree
otherwise almost unknown in our political history. He had, to his
cost, neglected his own cynical maxim: "A man must be selfish, ever
to acquire great popularity. He must grasp for himself, under specious pretences for the public good, and he must attach himself to
his relations, connexions, and friends, by becoming a champion for
their interests, in order to form a phalanx about him for his own
defence, to make them trumpeters of his praise, and sticklers for his
fame, fortune and honor."

The diminution of Adams' popularity during his lifetime is not
however ascribable alone to his conduct as a public man. His character was a combination of the sublime and the ridiculous. Vain as
a peacock, he was jealous, pompous, irascible, opinionated and
tactless; added to these defects what would now be termed a persecution complex rendered his behavior at times so erratic as to justify
Benjamin Franklin's judgment of him: "John Adams is always an
honest man, often a wise one, but sometimes and in some things
absolutely out of his senses."

Yet he possessed many estimable qualities. Thomas Jefferson said
of him: "He is as disinterested as the being who made him: he is
profound in his views, and accurate in his judgment, except where
knowledge of the world is necessary to form a judgment." Like
Washington, standing aloof from strict party ties, he did not set his
sails to catch the prevailing political wind. In 1811, upon being

accused of a change of party ideals, he retorted in typical fashion: "The Hyperfederalists are become Jacobins, and the Hyperrepublicans are become Federalists. John Adams remains Semper Idem, both Federalist and Republican in every rational and intelligible sense of both those words."

Unlike Washington, he had no strong personal magnetism and consequently did not attract adherents whose reputation and honor were inseparable from his own. The Hamiltonians, having succeeded in betraying him, made him the scapegoat for their mistakes, and pilloried him for having rescued the country from the implications of their foreign policy. Hamilton himself pursued Adams, while the latter was President, with an ill-concealed animosity which reflects the gravest discredit upon that accomplished financier, even if allowance is made for Adams' ungenerous remark that the famous Secretary of the Treasury was the "bastard brat of a Scotch pedlar."

Adams' great-great-grandfather had emigrated to Massachusetts from England about 1636, and had bequeathed a small patrimony to his offspring. The later Adamses slowly bettered their material condition. The father of John Adams combined the occupation of farmer with the trade of shoemaker in the village of Braintree, Massachusetts, now called Quincy. He was sufficiently affluent to enroll his eldest son, John, in Harvard College. In this supposedly democratic institution, students were graded according to their social standing in the community. By this rule Adams was placed fourteenth in a class of twenty-four, although in scholastic grade he was third.

At the time of his entrance into Harvard the life of New England was still dominated intellectually by the Church. The life of the New England communities was to remain repressed by clerical influences long after the death of John Adams.

Members of his family expected Adams, after his graduation from Harvard at the age of nineteen, to take holy orders. But, happily for his country, he finally decided against this profession, finding many of its tenets unacceptable to his inquisitive mind. A constant champion of religious toleration, he was fond of ecclesiastical reading, both orthodox and skeptical; the arguments of Bolingbroke, Voltaire and others never shook his belief in the existence of a benevolent Deity.

Upon his graduation from Harvard, being obliged to earn his living, he accepted a post as master in a grammar school at Worcester, whither he rode on horseback, making the journey of sixty miles in a single day. There he considered his future. Having eliminated the Church, he was tempted to become a soldier, or to practice medicine, but eventually chose to study law.

The profession of law was not, at this period, held in the best of repute. Prejudice against it was strong in sparsely settled communities, where persons were impatient of circumscription by legal technicalities.

The rise of a mercantile class and the necessity of defining and protecting property rights were to diminish this prejudice, although it strongly persisted throughout the eighteenth century. Adams found his native town was to afford excellent opportunities to display his legal learning, for a saying, "as litigious as Braintree," passed current in the province. But even in 1764, when he married Miss Abigail Smith, the daughter of a Congregational minister at Weymouth, Massachusetts, Adams found himself viewed askance by certain friends of his wife's family on the grounds of his profession.

His reading was omnivorous. He devoured books, no matter how long or formidable their contents. In his old age he wrote to Jefferson that he had been a lover and a reader of romances all his life, from *Don Quixote* and *Gil Blas* to the *Scottish Chiefs*, and a hundred others. At the age of eighty he was reading weightier treatises, fifteen volumes of Grimm, seven volumes of Tucker's *Neddy Search*, twelve volumes of Dupuis, and Tracy's *Analysis*, and four volumes of Jesuitical history—"romances all" he called them.

His own writings were voluminous. In a *Defense of the Constitutions of the United States of America against the attack of M. Turgot*, he drew deeply upon the stores of modern, medieval and ancient history. At times his style was turgid and diffusive; at others, incisive and powerful.

Some of his familiar letters are very graceful. Those interchanged between Jefferson and himself, the octogenarian of Monticello and the nonagenarian of Quincy, after an alienation of many years, are charming. They discussed government, theology, antiquarianism, philosophy and literature.

When he indulged in sarcasm, his pen dripped gall. Silas Deane, whom he replaced as Commissioner to France, had written an unfortunate address to the people of America which appeared to Adams "evidence of such a complication of vile passions, of vanity, arrogance, and presumption, of malice, envy, and revenge, and at the same time of such wickedness, indiscretion and folly as ought to unite every honest and wise man against him; that there appeared to me no alternative left but the ruin of Mr. Deane or the ruin of his country; that he appeared to me in the light of a wild boar, that ought to be hunted down for the benefit of mankind."

His energy was ceaseless, and he often complained of wasting his time. In one diary entry he wrote: "Age 23. What pleasure can a young gentleman who is capable of thinking, take in playing cards? It gratifies none of the senses, neither sight, hearing, taste, smelling, nor feeling; it can entertain the mind only by hushing its clamors. Cards, backgammon, etc. are the great antidotes to reflection, to thinking, that cruel tyrant within us."

Adams, as an orator, owed little to external advantages. There was nothing in his appearance to betoken ability or to charm auditors. In stature he was beneath middle height. He was inclined to corpulency, and later was dubbed "His Rotundity" by Senators who twitted him with being overfat and overfond of titles. He had a massive forehead and a well-shaped head, which, like that of his son, John Quincy Adams, time was to render bare as a billiard ball.

His speaking manner was, from an early age, unprepossessing. But his fluency of speech, his copious vocabulary, his passionate sincerity and convictions rendered him formidable in debate. He was, in Jefferson's words, the "Colossus" of the debate upon the adoption of the Declaration of Independence, and made a speech, or series of speeches, upon that occasion, worthy of a great orator. And he found in speaking and reading aloud a form of physical exercise, for when he was a young man he wrote in his diary: "Yesterday and today I have read aloud Tully's Orations against Catiline. The sweetness and grandeur of his sounds, and the harmony of his numbers, give pleasure enough to reward the reading, if one understood none of his meaning. Besides, I find it a noble exercise; it exercises my lungs, raises my spirits, opens my pores, quickens the circulations, and so contributes much to health."

Like all the early American Presidents, Adams was a lover of country life. When he is on a trip to Connecticut, he pines for home: "Braintree pleases me more; I long to be foul of Deacon Belcher's orchard; I am impatient to begin my canal and bank, to convey the water all round by the road and the house; I must make a pool in the road by the corner of my land, at the yard in front of the house for the cool spring water to come into the road there, that the cattle and hogs and ducks may regale themselves there."

Adams had no artistic appreciation, but was gifted with qualities of imagination. In painting he preferred pictures pointing a moral or adorning a familiar tale. In 1780 he wrote from Paris:

"It is not indeed the fine arts which our country requires; the useful, the mechanic arts, are those which we have occasion for in a young country as yet simple and not far advanced in luxury, although perhaps much too far for her age and character. . . . The science of government, it is my duty to study, more than all other sciences; the arts of legislation and administration and negotiation, ought to take place of, indeed exclude, in a manner, all other arts. I must study politics and war that my sons may have liberty to study mathematics and philosophy. My sons ought to study mathematics and philosophy, geography, natural history and naval architecture, in order to give their children a right to study painting, poetry, music, architecture, statuary, tapestry and porcelain."

Adams was deeply jealous of George Washington's fame. He entertained other jealousies, for instance of Benjamin Franklin and of Thomas Pinckney, when the latter was a possible rival for the presidency, but his touchiness about the Virginian was always paramount. He regarded Washington as his own creation, which in a sense was true. While Boston was being besieged by the continental troops, and while the Continental Congress was in session, John Adams was the first person to see the necessity of the adoption of the colonial army by Congress, and the wisdom of appointing as its Commander-in-Chief a man who would irrevocably bind the Southern states to those of the North. His decision in this matter was, as events proved, of great importance to American liberty. The army was adopted, but the question of who was to be its Commander had been contested until Adams championed the name of Washington. New Englanders felt entitled to appoint one of their own experienced officers to the place; even amongst the Virginia delegation there was strong opposition to the choice of Washington. Adams' richest client, John Hancock, would have liked the honor, but, brushing aside every consideration except what he believed to be in the best interests of all the States, Adams bullied, persuaded and cajoled the members into selecting his candidate.

Adams never regretted having made Washington Commander-in-Chief of the Army. It was his most useful contribution to the cause of independence, but he shortly began to find fault with the General's popularity. However conscientiously he strove to bottle up his vanity, it escaped periodically. "Vanity, I am sensible," he had written at the age of twenty, "is my cardinal vice and cardinal folly; and I am in continual danger when in company, of being led an ignis fatuus chase by it, without the strictest caution and watchfulness over myself."

Alas for his resolves: having accompanied the newly named Washington, in June 1775, on his start to Boston, he complained to his wife of the enthusiastic farewell to the General: "Such is the pride and pomp of war. I, poor creature, worn out with scribbling for my bread and for my liberty, low in spirits and weak in health, must leave others to wear the laurels which I have sown; others to eat the bread which I have earned; a common case."

His tactlessness almost matched his jealousy, James McHenry said of him: "Whether he is sportful, playful, witty, kind, cold, drunk, sober, angry, easy, stiff, jealous, careless, cautious, confident, close, open, it is almost always in the wrong place or to the wrong person."

On October 27, 1777, he wrote, apropos of the successes to the northward and at the Delaware River, "Congress will appoint a thanksgiving; and one cause of it ought to be, that the glory of turning the tide of arms is not immediately due to the Commander-in-Chief nor to Southern troops. If it had been, idolatry and adulation would have been unbounded; so excessive as to endanger our liberties, for what I know. Now, we can allow a certain citizen to be wise, virtuous and good, without thinking him a deity or a saviour."

Yet he was always on excellent terms with Washington and appreciated his great qualities. It was Adams who moved a unanimous vote of thanks to him by Congress, and the striking of a gold medal, commemorating the evacuation of Boston and bearing the effigy of the Commander-in-Chief as its deliverer.

After the war his jealousy of Washington somewhat diminished, but it flared up again when he himself became President and was compelled to recognize how secondary a part he played in his own inauguration as compared with that accorded to the retiring statesman.

He was also subject to sectional jealousy. He believed that a New Englander was superior in every respect to the inhabitant of another colony. He was envious of the prominence achieved by the Southern states. Nor was he better disposed to admit superiority in the middle provinces. During his first visit to New York he observed: "With all the opulence and splendor of this city, there is very little good breeding to be found. We have been treated with an assiduous respect; but I have not seen one real gentleman, one well-bred man, since I came to town."

However, even New Englanders, when he was discussing them with another New Englander, were far from perfect. In 1776 he wrote to his wife: "Our New England people are awkward and bashful, yet they are pert, ostentatious and vain; a mixture which excites ridicule and gives disgust. They have not the faculty of showing themselves to the best advantage, nor the art of concealing this faculty; an art and faculty which some people possess in the highest degree. Our deficiencies in these respects are owing wholly to the little intercourse we have with strangers, and to our inexperience in the world. These imperfections must be remedied, for New England must provide the heroes, the statesmen, the philosophers, or America will make no great figure for some time."

But, if his local prejudices were strong, his national patriotism knew no bounds; as compared with anything foreign, every part of the United States could, according to his views, boast something superior. When the population of the new country was about four million, he claimed for it in his state papers an equal place with the greatest empires, demanding that its representatives be treated as emissaries of a "great, free, powerful, and independent nation." No reverses, no tribulations, ever shook his belief in the future greatness of his country. In spite of a protracted residence abroad he formed no desire to stay there longer than was necessary to transact his official business.

His uncertain temper was likely to explode with the suddenness of a thunderclap. "I have heard," wrote Jefferson, "that my predecessor (Adams) sometimes decided things against his Council by dashing and trampling his wig on the floor." Impatient of cant and of opposition to his personal opinions, he was never loath to express his views on any subject, to any audience.

Adams' first experience as a diplomat was unrewarding. Sent to Paris in 1778 to help bring about an alliance with France, he found upon arrival that this object had already been accomplished. Only a sense of public duty had prompted him to accept the employment, for his health had already been impaired by his arduous labors in Congress. However, he attempted to bring order into the rather confused account and minute books of Franklin and the other commissioners, and unselfishly advised Congress to leave Franklin in Paris as its sole representative.

His suggestion to Congress regarding Franklin was accepted, but he was not himself recalled. Indignant at Franklin's invitation to remain in Paris and amuse himself at the public's expense, he burst out: "But I cannot eat pensions and sinecures, they would stick in my throat," and returned home as quickly as possible. However, his reunion with his family was brief; for after a few months he was again sent to France, this time to conclude a treaty of peace with Great Britain, if and when the time should prove opportune.

In these days of easy ocean transportation it is difficult to conceive of the discomforts of Adams' voyages to Europe. His first trip had occupied over six weeks, in the course of which the ship was struck by lightning and almost overwhelmed by storms. They had narrowly escaped capture by a British warship, and had themselves captured a prize and taken it triumphantly into France. Moreover, had Adams been captured, he could have expected no mercy from the British, who regarded him as an arch rebel and had expressly exempted him, at one time, from pardon.

He was always interested in everything pertaining to ships and shipping. In 1779 he met in France the famous John Paul Jones. Of him Adams formed a vivid impression. "This is the most ambitious and intriguing officer in the American Navy. Jones has art and secrecy, and aspires very high. . . . Eccentricities and irregularities are to be expected from him. They are in his character, they are visible in his eyes. His voice is soft and still and small; his eye has keenness and wildness and softness in it."

When Adams arrived in Paris for the second time, in 1780, after a rough overland journey from a Spanish port, he found the time premature for any understanding with Great Britain. The foreign office of France was under the direction of the Count de Vergennes, whose policy was to undermine the national enemy, England, in every way possible, and whose assistance to the American colonies had been finally determined by that motive. Adams quickly realized the situation, namely that although a large number of Frenchmen enthusiastically favored the American cause the court policy was devoted purely to national interests; except for using the colonies as an instrument to weaken British power, the American revolutionaries could not, once peace became imminent, count on De Vergennes to secure or protect them in the rights for which they were struggling. "It was intended," said Adams, "to keep us embroiled with England as much, and as long as possible, even after a peace." Unfortunately Adams proceeded within a short time, by an avalanche of tactless letters, to embroil himself with the Foreign Minister. De Vergennes had secured from the American Congress pusillanimous instructions to its peace representatives in France that they were to proceed to an understanding only by the advice and with the approval of the French foreign office. Jay and Adams disregarded these instructions. Prevailing upon Franklin to follow suit, they arrived at a peace treaty, and later a commercial treaty, with England, so satisfactory in all respects as to constitute a great triumph for American diplomacy. Although Adams, modestly for once, stated that praise for this signal success belonged to Jay, he was himself, to his unfeigned delight, called by the French "Le Washington de la négociation." Indeed, in this matter he appeared at his best; by his dignity, resourcefulness, and even suavity, he wrung from the English concessions a weaker man would never have extorted.

But meanwhile, between the time of his arrival in France and the signature of the definitive treaty with Great Britain, he had achieved a very remarkable diplomatic success in Holland. There he had caused the American colonies to be acknowledged as a nation and himself as its minister. He had also negotiated a treaty of alliance, and the first of a series of loans from Dutch bankers that were to save the credit of the United States. So important were these transactions, only brought to fruition by the patient skill of Adams in educating the Dutch people to appreciate the future prospects of America as a source of profit to themselves, and so adroitly had he arrived at the desired end, that this achievement, in the words of his grandson and biographer, "well merits to be ranked as the greatest triumph of his life."

In 1785, Adams, having arrived in England to take up his duties, was presented to George III. That monarch insinuated that he had learned something of Mr. Adams' lack of good will to the French court. The new minister replied firmly: "I must avow to Your Majesty, I have no attachment but to my own country." George III, liking his candor, answered, "An honest man will never have any other."

However, George III did not again bother to be courteous to Adams. With few exceptions the American Minister met with little except insolence, neglect and contempt from the English ruling class. Nor was his situation otherwise satisfactory. His pay was inadequate to support his position with dignity, and his usefulness hampered by the weak condition of the American government, sunk into a supine and discreditable inertia from which it was to be aroused only by the adoption of the federal Constitution.

Adams was intensely happy when his wife joined him in England. Upon his first trip to Europe he had been obliged to leave her at home, being accompanied only by his boy John Quincy. The second trip he had also made without her, but as the separation grew from months into years she decided to brave the perils of the seas.

Abigail Adams was an altogether exceptional woman. "I am a mortal enemy," she once wrote to her husband, "to any thing but a cheerful countenance and a merry heart, which, Solomon tells us, does good like a medicine." Always delicate, she was often ill for extended periods. She managed to run her house on somewhat meager resources, for Adams was never a man of large fortune, and there was, in view of the heavy expenses necessitated by his various public positions, constant need for economy at home. She brought up a family of a daughter and three sons, one of whom was to be President, and at the same time preserved in her social relations an equanimity and gaiety which made her everywhere admired, loved and respected. Her delightful letters have highly recommended her to posterity.

One of Mrs. Adams' greatest trials as a housekeeper occurred when, during her husband's presidency, they became the first inhabitants of the then uncompleted White House, in the equally uncompleted city of Washington. The house required about thirty servants, and she observed: "To assist us in this great castle, and render less attendance necessary, bells are wholly wanting, not one single one being hung through the whole house. . . . We have not the least fence, yard or other convenience without, and the great unfinished audience-room I make a drying-room to hang up the clothes in. The principal stairs are not up, and will not be this winter."

As a young lawyer John Adams succeeded in building up so good a practice that at the time of his entry into politics it was said to have been the largest in the province. His cases took him far and wide, making him lead what he referred to as a "rambling, roving, vagrant, vagabond life." Finally, at the solicitation of his friends, he moved to Boston, although he never became permanently fixed in that city.

Before moving there, he was favorably known in the province for his resistance to the Stamp Act. Some time later, probably with a view to securing the silence of such a formidable opponent of parliamentary authority, the royal Governor Bernard approached him through a friend with the offer of the lucrative post of Advocate General at the Court of Admiralty. Adams refused it, with the forthright explanation that the British government was persevering in a system wholly inconsistent with his ideas of right, justice and policy, and therefore he could not place himself in a situation in which his duty and his inclination would be so much at variance.

Although Adams, just before the outbreak of the Revolution, was made Chief Justice of the General Court of the Colony of Massachusetts Bay, he never assumed the duties of that office, and later resigned it. His greatest case as a lawyer, and one reflecting honor on his moral courage, was when he defended Captain Preston and some British soldiers against charges growing out of the famous "Boston Massacre."

This disturbance was the outcome of the mistaken British policy of quartering troops in Boston, where, regarded with hatred and suspicion, they were derided as "lobsters, redcoats and bullies." On the night of March 5, 1770, a British sentry was insulted and assaulted by a group of town hoodlums, of whom a barber's boy was the ringleader. A corporal and six men of the guard, under the direction of Captain Preston, came to the relief of the sentinel. What immediately followed is somewhat obscure, but the rioters appear to have used stones, oyster shells, cinders, clubs, sticks and other weapons, and it was open to doubt whether the soldiers fired upon their assailants before it was the only recourse left to save their own lives. At any rate, seven of the soldiers, either under orders or without orders, fired into the mob killing five of its number. Captain Preston having at once withdrawn his men, the Lieutenant Governor of the province succeeded in having the townspeople disperse.

The next morning, process was issued against Preston, and he was committed to prison. More than seven months later he and his soldiers were brought to trial. Feeling ran high in Boston against the perpetrators of this so-called "Bloody Massacre." Any lawyer who would dare to represent them courted unpopularity and even bodily harm. The prisoners asked John Adams and Josiah Quincy Jr., to defend them; these two were the most prominent of the Boston lawyers in opposition to British government policy. In spite of remonstrances from friends, and in the teeth of public disapproval, they accepted.

When the trial took place, popular clamor had subsided, extenua-
ting circumstances were proved, Captain Preston and six soldiers
were discharged. The other two, against whom the evidence strongly
pointed, were found guilty of manslaughter, branded in the hand,
and released. For his services in the case Adams received a fee of
nineteen guineas. Moreover, the townspeople, whose cooler judgment now reasserted itself, admired his courage and elected him to
the Massachusetts House.

Having thus translated from law into politics, a great part of
Adams' life was thenceforth devoted to public questions. It may be
said, however, that Adams became a politician, in the first instance,
against inclination, out of a sense of civic duty. "Politics are an
ordeal path among red hot ploughshares," he wrote. "Who, then,
would be a politician, for the pleasure of running about barefoot
among them? Yet Somebody must." But his prejudice against holding public office was short-lived, and politics, for many years, was
the breath of his nostrils.

Following the rejection of tea by the colonists, the British Parliament proceeded to chastise the town of Boston, regarded as the focus
of colonial discontent; the charter of the colony was abrogated, jurisdiction over cases of tumult and riot was transferred to the English
courts, the port of Boston was closed.

Apparently Boston must submit to the Crown's demands or perish,
unless the other colonies should come to the assistance of the dis-
tressed Massachusetts. The last contingency speedily occurred. The
Atlantic seaboard was aflame with apprehension; committees from
the various provinces prepared to assemble at Philadelphia, to deliberate upon what measures "should be recommended to all the colonies for the recovery and establishment of their just rights and
liberties, civil and religious, and the restoration of union and harmony between the two countries, most ardently desired by all good
men." John Adams was named a member of the Massachusetts committee.

The only act performed by the first Continental Congress, in its
less than two months of life, was a nonexportation, nonimportation
and nonconsumption agreement. But it had been the occasion of
bringing together many of the leading men from the different American colonies, acquainting them with each other's viewpoints, removing sectional jealousies, and promoting the foundation of a national
policy of resistance to British tyranny.

Adams, however, had been impatient of its deliberate proceedings. "I am wearied to death," he wrote from Philadelphia, "of the life I lead. The business of the Congress is tedious beyond expression. This assembly is like no other that ever existed. Every man in it is a great man, an orator, a critic, a statesman; and therefore, every man upon every question, must show his oratory, his criticism, and his political abilities. The consequence of this is, that business is drawn and spun out to an immeasurable length. I believe, if it was moved and seconded, that we should come to a resolution that three and two make five, we should be entertained with logic and rhetoric, law, history, politics and mathematics, and then—we should pass the resolution, unanimously, in the affirmative."

The following May, Adams again went to Philadelphia to attend the meetings of the second Continental Congress. In spite of the battle of Lexington and the imminent outbreak of war in various quarters of the country, the majority of the members of Congress were not yet ready to take any decisive step to sever their allegiance to England. Overruling the spirited objections of Adams, they voted to send a last humble petition to George III to redress their griev-ances. But before this olive branch was actually proffered to the monarch, Adams succeeded in having the Congress adopt the irregu-lar army, which was besieging Boston, as its own.

There were other delegates to Congress as prepared as was Adams for stern measures, but he happened to be the most aggressive and forceful individual amongst them.

From then on his duties were multifarious. For a time his reputa-tion for sagacity was gravely impaired by the capture of the bearer of some of his letters to friends in Massachusetts, and by their subse-quent publication. In these letters he recklessly criticized several of his colleagues, observing of the patriotic though cautious John Dickinson: "A certain great fortune and piddling genius, whose fame has been trumpeted so loudly, has given a silly cast to our whole doings. We are between hawk and buzzard." Dickinson ceased to speak to him. Other colleagues shunned him in the streets, but he soon atoned for his indiscretion by untiring and effective services.

Having succeeded in the recognition of the army, and the selec-tion of a Commander-in-Chief, he pressed on to his other great object —the declaration of complete independence. In his management of this question he displayed uncommon political skill. Although he had probably, since the battle of Bunker Hill, made up his own mind to the inevitability of separation from the mother country, he wished to have his associates united before they took the irretrievable step. "America is a great unwieldy body," he observed in 1775. "Its progress must be slow. It is like a large fleet sailing under convoy. The fleetest sailors must wait for the dullest and slowest. Like a coach and six, the swiftest horses must be slackened, and the slowest quickened, that all may keep an even place."

Finally the time was ripe; on July 4, 1776, the independence measure, framed by Jefferson, was adopted, after Adams had spoken, as Jefferson said: "With a power of thought and expression which moved the members from their seats."

Throughout his service in Congress, Adams was undiscouraged by any victories of the British armies, since he never despaired of the ultimate success of the Americans. His firm demeanor did much to hearten more timid patriots. One of his fellow members wrote, in 1777, in these eulogistic terms: "I never can think we shall finally fail of success while Heaven continues to the Congress the life and abilities of Mr. John Adams. He is equal to the controversy in all its stages. He stood upon the shoulders of the whole Congress when reconciliation was the wish of all America. He was equally conspicuous in cutting the knot which tied the colonies to Great Britain. In a word, I deliver you the opinion of every man in the House, when I add that he possesses the clearest head and firmest heart of any man in the Congress."

Adams' diplomatic career abroad severed him from an active part in domestic politics until his election as Vice-President. However, in this interval, his theories of constitutional government had a tremendous influence on the formation of the various state Constitutions, as well as on that of the federal Constitution. His constitutional principles were comparatively simple. They had been generally expressed in a letter written in 1775 to Richard Henry Lee who was interested in the adoption by Virginia of a new state constitution. "A legislative, an executive, and a judicial power," he wrote, "comprehend the whole of what is meant and understood by government. It is by balancing each of these powers against the other two, that the efforts in human nature towards tyranny can alone be checked and restrained, and any degree of freedom preserved in the constitution."

In order to establish this balance, Adams insisted upon the necessity of a bicameral legislature, a single executive invested with broad powers, and an independent judiciary. His fundamental principle was to provide a balance between the will of the many and the wisdom of the few. He believed the constituted authorities should, during their tenure of office, oppose all measures, however aggressive the public demand for them, that were forbidden by the Constitution or proscribed by their own judgment.

Nothing contributed so much to Adams' unpopularity as his constitutional theories, avowed by him with a courageous frankness, and now firmly imbedded in the law of every state in the Union. That men were of unequal talents and that politicians must so recognize was one of his basic theories. "By the law of nature," he said, "all men are men, and not angels—men and not lions—men and not whales— men and not eagles—that is, they are of the same species and this is the most that the equality of nature amounts to. But man differs by nature from man, almost as much as man from beast. The equality of nature is moral and political only, and means that all men are independent. But a physical inequality, an intellectual inequality, of the most serious kind, is established unchangeably by the Author of nature; and society has a right to establish any other inequalities it may judge necessary for its good."

In a letter to Samuel Adams he observed: " 'The love of liberty,' you say, 'is interwoven in the soul of man.' So it is, according to La Fontaine, in that of a wolf. The numbers of men in all ages have preferred ease, slumber, and good cheer to liberty, when they have been in competition. We must not then depend alone upon the love of liberty in the soul of man for its preservation. Some political institutions must be prepared, to assist this love against its enemies."

He insisted that the poor must be protected from the tyranny of the rich, but he equally insisted that: "To place property at the mercy of a majority who have no property, is to entrust the lamb to the wolf." He added: "My fundamental maxim of government is: Never to trust the lamb to the custody of the wolf."

"Where the people have a voice, and there is no balance," wrote Adams, "there will be everlasting fluctuations, revolutions, and horrors, until a standing army, with a general at its head, commands the peace, or the necessity of an equilibrium is made to appear to all and is adopted by all."

"If the poor are to domineer over the rich, or the rich over the poor, we shall never enjoy the happiness of good government; and, without an intermediate power, sufficiently elevated and independent to control each of the contending parties, in its excesses, one or the other will forever tyrannize."

Adams was accused by the followers of Jefferson of being a monarchist, a lover of titles and overfond of ceremonies. That he would have reconciled himself to the establishment of a limited monarchy in America, if it had been founded on his theory of constitutional government, is probable from some of his utterances. Actually no executive ever did more to give stability to republican government or was a stancher republican. However, he was deeply antagonistic to the idea of political democracy in the sense that the word "democracy" was used in his generation.

He felt the necessity of constitutional checks and balances to restrain minorities from exploiting majorities, and also to restrain majorities from the exploitation of minorities. He was firmly convinced that men were guided only by self-interest. Fourteen years after his retirement he wrote to John Taylor: "Democracy has never been and never can be so desirable as aristocracy or monarchy, but while it lasts, is more bloody than either. Remember, democracy never lasts long. It soon wastes, exhausts, and murders itself. There never was a democracy that did not commit suicide."

On another occasion he described democracy as "the most ignoble, unjust and detestable form of government." He did not hesitate to avow that, in Europe, titles and ceremonies had contributed to the cause of good government.

"The Duke of Braintree" was accused of being a pompous popinjay, a "perfect tailor in his ability to adjust the etiquette of loops and buttons." This may have been true, but, on the other hand, egocentric as Adams was, it was respect for the office and not for the man that he advocated.

In answer to the charge that he was overfond of titles, he replied: "For my own part, I freely own that I think decent and moderate titles, as distinctions of offices, are not only harmless, but useful in society, and that in this country, where I know them to be prized by the people as well as their magistrates, as highly as by any people or any magistrates in the world, I should think some distinction between the magistrates of the national government and those of the state governments proper. There is not, however, in the United States, personally a citizen more indifferent upon the subject, or more willing to conform to the public will or wish concerning it."

The excitement aroused by the question of a proper title for the

President was intense. Some were for "Majesty," some for "Highness," some for "Excellency," and some for no title. The Senate finally decided to call Washington "His Highness the President of the United States and Protector of the Rights of the Same," but before he was officially proclaimed as such, it was discovered that the Constitution had already designated him "President of the United States."

Adams was not deterred by criticism or ridicule from suggestions regarding dignities. He is said to have proposed that the Sergeant at Arms of the Senate be called the "Usher of the Black Rod," and he referred to Washington's inaugural address as "His Most Gracious Speech." In writing to Washington, in 1789, regarding the President's civil list, he said: "In all events, the provision for the President and his household ought to be large and ample. The office by its legal authority, defined in the constitution, has no equal in the world, excepting those only which are held by crowned heads; nor is the royal authority in all cases to be compared to it. The Royal office in Poland is a mere shadow in comparison with it. The Dogeship in Venice, and the Stadtholdership in Holland are not so much. Neither dignity nor authority can be supported in human minds, collected into nations or any great numbers, without a splendor and majesty in some degree proportioned to them."

While Adams, as Vice-President, was being accused of love of grandeur, he was living in a boarding house in Philadelphia and taking his meals with the other boarders, the only concession to his position being that he occupied the head of the table. He was without question vain but he did not have so great an itch for the trappings of office as the Jeffersonian press alleged. The same press, which had taxed Washington with being a "crocodile" and a "hyena," was wont to see nothing but blemishes in every Federalist. Meanwhile, in the Philadelphia streets, people wearing liberty caps, calling each other "Citizen," dancing the carmagnole, singing "Ça Ira," wondered whether a little such bloodletting as was characterizing their beloved French Revolution would not be healthy in America.

As Vice-President, Adams presided over the Senate, and many times, especially during his first term, cast his deciding vote on the Federalist side when the division was equal. Since his Federalist principles were firm, it was natural that upon Washington's retirement he should be selected as that party's candidate for President. Duplicity on Alexander Hamilton's part cost him some votes, but he was elected, while Jefferson, the leader of the opposition party, was chosen as Vice-President, an anomaly made possible by the existing electoral system. "He was then," Adams wrote of himself in 1813, "President for four years. A tale told by an Idiot, full of sound and fury, signifying Nothing."

Had Adams never been elected President, his popular reputation would perhaps today be greater than it is: had he never been elected President, however, our country might not today exist in its present constitutional form. For during his tenure of office he took the resolute decision which staved off war with Napoleon.

This, the chief event of his magistracy, is too well known for detailed repetition. The French, like the English, were preying upon our merchant vessels, and both nations were treating our remonstrances with contempt. Adams sent a mission to Paris; its members were received by Talleyrand's representatives who demanded a bribe for the foreign minister. The Commissioners returned home; when this insult was divulged in Congress, a warlike spirit swept the country. The "War Hawks," headed by Hamilton, wished to cut off all relations with France. "Millions for defense but not one cent for tribute" was the cry. Three cabinet members, Timothy Pickering, Secretary of State, Oliver Wolcott, Secretary of the Treasury, and James McHenry, Secretary of War, were hostile to the President who had continued them in office as appointees of Washington, and were subservient to Hamilton. Some of their state opinions on important questions submitted to them by the President were even dictated by Hamilton.

Adams prepared to arm the country. Washington, appointed Lieutenant-General, in command of all the armies of the United States, selected Hamilton as his next in command, against Adams' wishes. The Jeffersonians, who had favored amicable relations with France, were in eclipse. Party feeling ran high. When Congress met in November 1798, Griswold, a Federalist leader, made an invidious remark to Lyon, a Democrat from Vermont, who spat in Griswold's face. A few days later, while Lyon was seated at his desk in the House, Griswold struck him from behind with a hickory stick. When Lyon retaliated with coal tongs, they clinched and rolled on the floor.

Adams donned a uniform, wore a sword and rode on the crest of a wave of popularity, although the Republicans hung him in effigy, singing:

"See Johnny at the helm of State,
Head itching for a crowny;
He longs to be, like George, great,
And pull Tom Jeffer downy."

Rumors were broadcast that the French were sending a squadron to attack our seaports. Hamilton conceived a grandiose scheme by which he would, at the head of an American army, in concert with the British invade Louisiana, Florida and Mexico, and conquer an empire there, of which he would presumably become the head, leaving England to compensate herself out of the Spanish possessions to the southward. Jefferson discouragedly hoped for a happy issue out of these afflictions. The whole country seemed to have gone mad. A conflict, for which the United States was militarily unprepared, appeared inevitable.

Without warning to his Cabinet, Adams took upon himself the responsibility for actions which eventually led to a peaceful solution of the difficulties with France. That nation received our new commission with proper respect.

Hamilton never forgave him for this course, since it was in direct defiance of his own advice and wishes. Adams widened the breach by discharging the treacherous Pickering and McHenry, who, though admirable men in many respects, had placed themselves in the position of being as cabinet officers disloyal to their President at the bidding of a private citizen. Wolcott, adding to disloyalty the unenviable quality of hypocrisy, continued to supply Hamilton with confidential memoranda for use against the President. Wolcott's infamy was never discovered by the President, who, before leaving office, appointed him a Federal Judge for life.

Having avoided war with France (an act which Adams wished to have inscribed on his tombstone in these words: "Here lies John Adams who took upon himself the responsibility of the peace with France in the year 1800") the President felt entitled to a second term. He was the undoubted choice of the rank and file of the Federalist party and was its only really promising candidate, since neither Hamilton nor Jay, its other most distinguished members, had widespread appeal. He won the nomination, but was defeated for election by Jefferson, owing chiefly to two circumstances.

The first was the unpopularity of Adams' party caused by the Alien and Sedition Laws. Passed at a time of popular hysteria by a narrow margin in both houses of Congress, these laws gave the Jeffersonians a campaign issue they were quick to turn to their advantage.

The alien law empowered the President: "To order all such aliens as he should judge dangerous to the peace and safety of the United States, or should have reasonable grounds to suspect were concerned in any treasonable or secret machinations against the government thereof, to depart out of the territory of the United States within such a time as should be expressed in such order."

The sedition act, strikingly similar to that passed by Congress during the First World War, was by far the more unpopular of the two measures. It imposed a fine and imprisonment for unlawfully combining or conspiring, with intent to oppose the measures of the government, when directed by the proper authority; for impeding the operation of any law of the United States; and for intimidating an officer from the performance of his duty, or counseling or advising, with similar intent, insurrections, riots or unlawful combinations. It also imposed similar but lighter penalties for the publication of false, scandalous and malicious writings against the government of the United States, either house of Congress, or the President, with intent to bring them into contempt, to stir up sedition, or to aid or abet a foreign nation in hostile designs against the United States. The right of the accused to give the truth in evidence, and of the jury to judge both of law and fact, were secured by the act, and its duration was limited to two years.

The sedition law was only enforced against a few persons, the most noted of whom was Callender, an alien and a fugitive from justice, whose fine was later remitted by Thomas Jefferson.

Matthew Lyon, to whom reference has previously been made, was fined one thousand dollars and sent to prison for four months for publishing a letter stating that: "With Adams every consideration of the public welfare was swallowed up in a continual grasp for power, and unbounded thirst for ridiculous pomp, foolish adulation and selfish avarice." A Mr. Baldwin of New Jersey was indicted, tried, convicted and fined because when Adams passed through Newark and some cannon were fired in compliment to the President he had expressed the wish that the wadding from the discharge might lodge in Mr. Adams' backsides. One editor was fined and imprisoned for writing that President Adams was "hardly in the infancy of political mistake."

The second factor militating against Adams' re-election was the

extraordinary conduct of Alexander Hamilton. Hamilton while os-
tensibly supporting Adams at the time of his first election had
attempted, by a specious trick, to elect Thomas Pinckney in his
stead. Four years later, Hamilton's dislike of Adams had turned to
bitter and contemptuous hatred, largely due to the latter's independence of character and to the manner in which he had disregarded
Hamilton's pressure for war with France. Hamilton wrote a pamphlet, entitled *The Public Conduct and Character of John Adams
Esq.*, originally intended for limited circulation. It was a bitter denunciation of Adams' private character and public principles, but
closed with the strange request that he be supported for the presidency.

Aaron Burr, having obtained a copy of the pamphlet, distributed
it widely. It was instrumental in defeating Adams. In this attack,
Hamilton condemned Adams' official acts, referring to "the disgusting egotism, the distempered jealousy, and the ungovernable indiscretion of Mr. Adams' temper."

Adams did not forgive Hamilton, even after the latter's unhappy
death at the hand of Burr. Years later, in private letters, he referred
to Hamilton as "an insolent coxcomb, who rarely dined in good
company where there was good wine without getting silly and vapor-
ing about his administration. . . . This creature was in the delirium
of ambition . . . and he hated every man . . . who stood in his way,
or could in any manner eclipse his laurels or rival his pretensions.

"He took advantage of a moment of fermentation wickedly excited
by himself and his fellow conspirators to come out with the most
false, malicious and revengeful libel that was ever written. To this
he had no provocation but because I would make peace with France
and could not in conscience make him commander-in-chief of an
army of fifty thousand men. But this caitiff too came to a bad end.
Fifteen years of slanders against Burr, great numbers of which I
heard myself, provoked a call to the Field of Honor, as they call it,
and sent him—to his long home by a Pistol Bullet through his spine."

Hamilton was a financial genius and by his abilities earned the
gratitude of his countrymen, but he also exhibited distinctly unat-
tractive traits. His egotism almost rivaled that of Adams. Washington had treated him with almost paternal affection, but when he died
Hamilton's reaction was that "an aegis very essential to me" had been
removed. Of McHenry, the Secretary of War, who had served him

with unswerving fidelity, Hamilton remarked: "My friend McHenry is wholly insufficient for his place, with the additional misfortune of not having himself the least suspicion of the fact."

Toward the end of his administration Adams performed an act that was to perpetuate the influence of the Federalist party indefinitely—the naming of John Marshall to be Chief Justice of the Supreme Court of the United States. His last official deed was to sign the papers appointing the "midnight judges," another Federalist attempt to obtain the remaining rich spoils of office.

On the very morning of Jefferson's inauguration Adams was guilty of the most ungracious action of his life; he drove away from Washington before dawn thus refusing to see his successor installed in his place.

The remainder of his days was spent at Quincy, clouded by the apprehension that his deserts had been unjustly appraised, but illuminated by the brilliant career of his son, John Quincy. His strong persecution complex did not forsake him in old age. He wrote bitterly to Cunningham: "You speak of the fortunate issue of my negotiations with France to my fame!!! I cannot express my astonishment. No thanks for that action, the most disinterested, the most determined and the most successful of my whole life. No acknowledgment of it ever appeared among the Republicans, and the Federalists have pursued me with the most unrelenting hatred, and my children too, from that time to this; covered, however, with the thickest veil of hypocrisy because there was some danger in being too open. My fame!!! It has been the systematical policy of both parties, from that period especially, and indeed for twelve years before, to conceal from the people all the services of my life. And they have succeeded to a degree that I should hardly have believed it possible for a union of both parties to effect."

Age did not dim the fires of his ardent patriotism and love of freedom. The slave problem was not an issue during his administration, but he heartily disliked the institution. Shortly before his death he wrote: "I have, through my whole life, held the practice of slavery in such abhorrence, though I have lived for many years in towns where the practice was not disgraceful; when the best men in my vicinity thought it not inconsistent with their character; and when it cost me thousands of dollars for the labor and subsistence of free men, which I might have saved by the purchase of negroes at times when they were very cheap."

A few days before he died, when asked to suggest a toast for a public occasion, the old man offered "Liberty forever."

His correspondence with Thomas Jefferson had been one of the great solaces and amusements of his declining years. As he lay dying on the fourth of July, fifty years after Jefferson and himself had given the Declaration of Independence to the nation, he murmured, "Jefferson still survives." But he was mistaken—by an extraordinary coincidence, on this significant date, the philosopher of Monticello had a few hours earlier preceded his New England friend to the only state in the universe with whose Constitution they were entirely unfamiliar.

Thomas Jefferson

Born: April 13, 1743.
Married: January 1772.
Elected to Continental Congress: 1775.
Elected Governor of Virginia: June 1, 1779.
Re-elected Governor of Virginia: June 1, 1780.
Mrs. Jefferson died: September 1782.
Minister to France: May 1784.
Appointed Secretary of State: September 1789.
Resigned as Secretary of State: December 1793.
Elected Vice-President: November 1796.
Inaugurated as President: March 4, 1801.
Louisiana Treaty signed: May 2, 1803.
Re-elected President, November 1804.
University of Virginia established: 1818.
Died: July 4, 1826.

THOMAS JEFFERSON

"**I** HAVE sworn upon the altar of God," Thomas Jefferson wrote to a friend in 1800, "eternal hositility against every form of tyranny over the mind of man." This passion of the third President of the United States for freedom, in the largest sense of the word, was life-long. He desired to be remembered after his death not as President, Vice-President or Secretary of State, not as Governor of Virginia or Minister to France, not as a supreme party leader, but as the author of the Declaration of Independence and of the Virginia Statute for Religious Freedom, as well as the Father of the University of Virginia: in these capacities he had been instrumental in liberating the human intellect from the bonds of autocracy, superstition and ignorance. Although the most intensely American of individuals, his indignation was awakened by intolerance no matter where it occurred. *Écrasez l'infâme* was as much his watchword as it was Voltaire's. His soul responded with generous enthusiasm to any struggle against bigotry or oppression.

Today Jefferson is chiefly remembered as the great exemplar of those democratic principles of government that animate our political institutions. But the man himself, with his complex character, intelligent curiosity, thirst for knowledge, gentleness, charm, serenity of temper, sweetness of affection and catholicity of interests was in personality more fascinating than in his achievements, significant though they were.

Jefferson's father, Peter, of Welsh descent, was a Virginia planter and surveyor, a member of the House of Burgesses, a Colonel of militia, who lived near the edge of the wilderness on a tract of virgin land, from which by cultivation he drew his livelihood. A very

Porthos in stature and strength, he possessed no advantages of higher education, though his reading included the Bible, Shakespeare, Addison and Swift. But for his eldest son Thomas he desired a classical training. Before he died, when the boy was fourteen, he had so impressed this idea on his child that his wishes were fulfilled, and his son became sufficiently familiar with Greek and Latin to make them his favorite reading.

Of Jefferson's mother we know little, except that she was of the aristocratic Randolph family, and consequently in her veins flowed the blood of the romantic Indian Princess, Pocahontas. From her the future President inherited the Randolph love of horses, a source of perennial pleasure to him until the day, a few weeks before his death, when he could mount a thoroughbred no longer. One of his ancestors had such a fondness for a favorite horse, Shakespeare, that he kept him in a stall, paneled like a drawing room, with an alcove for his groom's sleeping quarters.

No other American statesman, with the exception of Franklin, possessed a mind so acute yet so flexible, so inquisitive yet so temperate, as did Jefferson. That Nature was lavish in her gifts to him we can well believe, but to what was intuitive he added by ceaseless industry.

To such good use had he applied his early schooling under country masters that, when he entered the College of William and Mary, the highest center of education in Virginia, his attainments caused him to be immediately welcomed to the intimacy of the three most stimulating personages in Williamsburg—Francis Fauquier, the gay Lieutenant Governor of the colony; George Wythe, lawyer and legislator, who was to become the legal preceptor of Jefferson, John Marshall and Henry Clay, as well as Chancellor of Virginia and a signer of the Declaration of Independence; and, third, Dr. William Small, a professor of mathematics who had taken all profane knowledge as his province and who upon his eventual return to England achieved eminence as a scholar and as the devoted friend of Darwin.

Related by birth to many of the great Virginia families, he took part in the country-house entertainments so frequent in colonial life. He was an accomplished violinist, and delighted in music which he called "the favorite passion of my soul." Among his friends at this period was Patrick Henry, afterwards one of the most brilliant orators known to history, who once won from Jefferson the admiring tribute: "He appeared to me to speak as Homer wrote."

Thomas inherited a fine landed estate from his father. The elder Jefferson had, by patent and purchase, accumulated a considerable property, four hundred acres of which represented a sale to him by his friend William Randolph, in consideration of "Henry Weatherbourne's biggest bowl of arrack punch." These tracts of land are near the present city of Charlottesville, Virginia, but when patented were on the western frontier of colonial civilization.

To the man who carved out of the forest a clearing on which he grew tobacco, and whose house was a log cabin or a frame dwelling built perhaps by his own hands, allegiance to the decrees of the British Parliament across the seas seemed a matter of sentiment only, and not of obligation. This spirit of the frontier left an indelible stamp on the mind of the young Jefferson; it was perhaps the main cause of his lifelong reluctance to relinquish any rights of man to government, except those obviously necessary to the common requirements of society.

Upon his graduation from William and Mary, Jefferson applied himself to the study of law. He soon became one of the undisputed leaders of the Virginia Bar. Before he retired from active practice because of political duties imposed upon him by the Revolution, his earnings averaged over two thousand dollars a year; with the addition of a similar amount accruing from his farming operations this income in those days constituted a handsome competence.

In 1772 he doubled the ease of his circumstances by marriage with Martha Skelton, a twenty-three-year-old widow, daughter of a prominent Virginia lawyer. He took her home to Albemarle County where he had already commenced, after his own plans, the erection of his house Monticello, one of the most beautiful of American homes, which drew from the Marquis de Chastellux the comment: "Mr. Jefferson is the first American who has consulted the fine arts to know how he should shelter himself from the weather." The situation chosen by Jefferson for this building is so magnificent that one is inclined to agree with de Chastellux that "it seemed as if from his youth he had placed his mind, as he had done his house, on an elevated situation, from which he might contemplate the universe."

Of his union with Mrs. Skelton, Jefferson had five daughters and one son, only two of whom (and those both daughters) survived the infant mortality so deadly in colonial days. We know little of Jefferson's wife except that she was an accomplished musician, but his devotion to her was immeasurable, and when she died ten years after their marriage, he fell down in a faint and was for a long time as if bereft of his senses. Thereafter he assumed the entire care of his children. His affectionate relations with them drew from them and their descendants such expressions of love as have honored few men.

Jefferson wished his children to be such paragons of learning and accomplishment as would scarcely have been possible for human beings. Incapable of idleness himself, he prescribed for his ten-year-old daughter Martha the following regimen:

From 8 to 10, practice music.

From 10 to 1, dance one day and draw another.

From 1 to 2, draw on the day you dance, and write a letter the next day.

From 3 to 4, read French.

From 4 to 5, exercise yourself in music.

From 5 till bed-time, read English, write, etc.

During his residence in France he had first one and then both of his children with him, himself attending to all the minutiae of selecting their clothes and diet, and superintending their activities. When separated from them, he wrote frequently and most affectionately to them as well as to their husbands, one of whom, Thomas Mann Randolph, became Governor of Virginia, and the other, John Wayles Eppes, after serving five terms in the national House of Representatives became a United States Senator.

His daughters regarded him with a love and gratitude bordering on worship. In fact, his temper was so equable that it would have been difficult not to have enjoyed familiarity with him. He is said never to have spoken a harsh word to children. His treatment of his slaves was so just that, upon his return from France, they took the horses from his carriage and themselves drew him to Monticello, where with tears and laughter they pressed about him kissing his hands and feet. The death of his younger daughter, Polly, in 1804 elicited from him a letter to his close friend, Governor Page, in which he displayed his dependence upon his children: "The part you take in my loss marks an affectionate concern for the greatness of it. It is great indeed. Others may lose of their abundance, but I, of my want, have lost even the half of all I had. My evening prospects now hang on the slender thread of a single life."

Jefferson detested the idea of women intermeddling in politics; during the last year of his presidency he informed Gallatin: "The appointment of a woman to office is an innovation for which the public is not prepared, nor am I." He believed that women should be taught French, music and dancing, with the qualification that, as in France, women should not dance after marriage but should confine themselves to domestic duties.

Although he seldom craved female society outside his family circle, it was not for want of attractive qualities in himself. Six feet two and a half inches in height, with almost as much muscular strength as his herculean father, he was a fine figure of a man. His hair was sandy, his eyes hazel, and in his countenance there was a blend of strength and good nature. The high cheekbones may have been an inheritance from the Indian strain in the Randolph blood. His complexion was ruddy and slightly freckled. On horseback he was almost as superb as Washington, but afoot there was something loose-jointed and almost gangling in his movements. A hoarseness of voice, when speaking, kept him from being an orator, but in conversation he was easy, affable and discursive. He was especially winning in his manners. There was said to have been a shiftiness in his glance; this his enemies ascribed to insincerity, his friends to shyness. His enemies were probably correct in ascribing a measure of insincerity to him, an excessive pliability and desire to please, which made him, on occasions, double-faced in his political dealings, and inclined him to duplicity and dissimulation.

There was a great contrast between the democratic political principles professed by him and his mode of life. He lived lavishly, although he died insolvent, extending at Monticello an openhanded hospitality. As many as fifty guests, on one occasion, slept in his house. One foreign friend, with six relations, spent ten months in residence there. His appointments were of the finest. Owning ten thousand acres of land and two hundred slaves, the "Mammoth of Democracy" was extravagant. He was meticulous about his table. Although he was almost a vegetarian, his dinners consisted of the finest varieties of food, prepared by a French chef. He did not care for ardent spirits but was a lover of wines, which he drank not during meals but at their conclusion. For some years at the White House his expenditure for liquors amounted to more than ten per cent of his salary, provoking from one of the opposition the wish that the President's politics might be as sound as his French wines. He wished Americans to become users of light wines. If cheap, he considered that they would discourage drunken habits and offer a happy substitute for the evils of whiskey.

In only one respect was Jefferson negligent in his personal habits, and that was in the article of dress. When he returned home from his foreign sojourn he wore, as Secretary of State, the red waistcoat and breeches that had been his usual attire in Paris, and which were not of the mode in New York and Philadelphia. The British Minister, Mr. Merry, complained bitterly to his Foreign Office that, when he was first presented to Jefferson, during the latter's presidency, the head of the American Government was garbed in slippers, run down at the heel, and in a slovenly and stained undress.

The same British Minister, Merry, protested against Jefferson's rule of pêle-mêle; this, in effect during part of his tenure of the White House, abolished precedence at dinner parties. To the horror of Merry, the President allowed his guests to enter the dining room in whatever order they pleased, the ladies in mass preceding the gentlemen, and to seat themselves at will at his table. Such informality resulted in complications, but it must be remembered that in Jefferson's time there had been a fierce outcry against the President assuming the habits and state, in his social intercourse, of a European monarch, and that not assigning seats at table was a common custom at some of the most exclusive houses of pre-revolutionary Paris.

The President himself had deprecated the formality insisted upon by Washington and Adams in connection with White House functions. He issued invitations to that mansion in the name of Mr. Jefferson. Between himself and state Governors he drew no distinction of rank. He abandoned the weekly levees, and decreed with the consent of the Cabinet that, "when brought together in society, all are perfectly equal, whether foreign or domestic, titled or untitled, in or out of office." Merry's complaint against having been asked to dine at the same table with the French chargé d'affaires, at a time when their respective nations were at war, was quite justifiable, for it was highly indecorous of Jefferson to have placed a diplomat in such a false position, but the other grievances of the British Minister were exaggerated.

But if Jefferson did not endear himself to all foreign emissaries, his own politeness was beyond cavil. Once when driving with his young grandson near Monticello a stranger slave bowed and took off his hat to them. Jefferson returned the bow, tipping his hat, but noticing that his grandson had made no acknowledgment of the greeting he remonstrated: "Thomas, do you permit a slave to be more of a gentleman than yourself?" His engaging personality, which elicited even from stern Abigail Adams the judgment that he was "the chosen of the earth," was in no small measure due to his sweet disposition and to a resourceful mind that never knew boredom. The encyclopedic nature of his learning made his talk interesting in any company, nor did his distinctly literary, musical and scientific tastes prevent him from captivating ill-educated people, who seemed instinctively to trust and admire him.

One of the secrets of his mildness of disposition was, no doubt, his perfect health. His teeth always remained perfect. His eyesight was almost unimpaired until death, although he used glasses for reading small print. He attributed his freedom from catarrhs to the habit of immersing his feet in cold water each morning upon arising from bed. He never smoked or played cards. Although he shot and was fond of horses, he was not a fox hunter and had an inexplicable dislike for dogs, regarding them as useless animals.

Martha Jefferson often said: "My father never gave up a friend or an opinion." He attracted to himself a host of friends, among them two later Presidents of the United States, Madison and Monroe, whom he affectionately termed "pillars" of his happiness. Even toward his enemies he found it difficult to preserve harsh feelings, save concerning their political principles—a bust by Ceracchi of his most notable opponent, Hamilton, occupied a place of honor in the hall at Monticello. His admiration of Washington was somewhat blinded, toward the close of the latter's career, by the undue influence which he believed Hamilton exercised over the General's decisions. He spoke of Washington as having, from the moment of his own retirement as Secretary of State, been in the hold of the Federalists.

Jefferson's reading was multifarious. In 1815, after the national library at Washington had been burned by the British, he offered Congress at its own price his collection of about ten thousand books, constituting the finest private library on the American continent. It was particularly full in rare Americana. Congress accepted the offer, paying him $23,950, a sum representing about half the cost of their acquisition by him. He had certain strong literary prejudices, especially against Scott's novels, disliking their glorification of feudal institutions, and against Hume's *History of England* and Blackstone's *Commentaries*, considering them to be permeated by pernicious Tory doctrines. He cared little for fiction; it is said that *Don Quixote* was the only work in that department of literature which he ever read twice. Homer, Virgil, Dante, Corneille, Molière, Racine, Cervantes, Pope, Shakespeare, Milton, Aeschylus, Sophocles and Euripides were along his favorite authors. He was not partial to the romantic school of British poetry, and did not like the verses of Byron and Coleridge. He was a lover of Burns's poems, and in his old age was fond of the lyrics of Thomas Moore, laughing at the venomous lines in which the ill-tempered Irishman, who dearly loved a Lord, had apostrophized him as a democrat:

> That inglorious soul,
> Which creeps and winds beneath a mob's control,
> Which courts the rabble's smile, the rabble's nod,
> And makes, like Egypt, every beast its God.

Besides perusing Greek and Latin with almost the same facility as he did English, he was widely versed in French, Spanish and Italian literature, reading them in the originals. Of Anglo-Saxon he became sufficiently a master to write a monograph upon it. He was always keenly interested in American Indian dialects. With infinite trouble he collected some forty distinct Indian vocabularies with a view to comparative philological studies concerning them, but they were lost in the James River during their transit from Washington to Monticello, after his retirement as President.

Aside from his other reading, Jefferson had been a most diligent student of law. Because of his diffidence and distaste for public speaking, he was, during the few years of his active practice, what would now be termed an office lawyer, being retained in a single year as attorney in four hundred and thirty cases. Jefferson had a real love and admiration for his profession, although in later years he was disgusted by the argumentative tendencies displayed by lawyers in legislative bodies. It was Jefferson, incidentally, who was responsible for the Justices of the Supreme Court of the United States abandoning the use of the monstrous wigs which, he said, make "the English judges look like rats peeping through bunches of oakum."

His greatest work as a lawyer was done in connection with the codification of the laws of Virginia; this he accomplished in conjunction with Wythe and Pendleton. He was successful in forcing through the Virginia Legislature bills to abolish entails and to sweep away the privileges of primogeniture, measures which earned him the enmity of many of his own social class and sounded the death knell of the Virginia landed gentry. When, in connection with the second proposition, one of his collaborators sought to modify it by giving a double portion to the eldest son, Jefferson answered him with the observation that he would agree to such a proposal when the eldest son could eat twice as much or do twice as much work as his brothers. His educational bills for the more general diffusion of knowledge, for establishing a public library and for amending the constitution of the College of William and Mary were never acted upon, but were far in advance of any other schemes for popular education advanced by his contemporaries.

Jefferson considered popular education an essential safeguard to liberty. "No other sure foundation," he wrote to George Wythe, "can be devised for the preservation of freedom and happiness. . . ."

His bill for establishing religious freedom in Virginia was more fortunate, although not finally passed until 1786. He considered it one of his real claims upon the gratitude of posterity. It provided: "Be it therefore enacted by the General Assembly, that no man shall be compelled to frequent or support any religious worship, place, or ministry whatsoever, nor shall be enforced, restrained, molested, or burthened in his body or goods, nor shall otherwise suffer, on account of his religious opinions or belief; but that all men shall be free to profess, and by argument to maintain, their opinions in matters of religion, and that the same shall in no wise diminish, enlarge, or affect their civil capacities."

The notion that Jefferson was an atheist and wished to destroy church establishments was nourished for many years by his opponents. Actually he attended church frequently, although he did not partake of communion. His children were baptized into the Episcopal Church as he had been, were married, as he had been, and buried, according to its ritual. He never used profanity or words of impiety, and contributed to the erection of churches, to Bible societies and to other religious objects, including the giving of pecuniary assistance to distressed clergymen.

During his presidency Jefferson compiled for his own use, by cutting from the texts of the Evangelists such passages as he believed were those spoken by Christ and uncorrupted, a book which he labeled the *Morals of Jesus*. To the English he added the French, Greek and Latin renderings, side by side, and read daily from these extracts. He resented the imputation that he was an anti-Christian, and told Dr. Benjamin Rush: "To the corruptions of Christianity I am, indeed, opposed; but not to the genuine precepts of Jesus himself. I am a Christian, in the only sense in which He wished any one to be; sincerely attached to His doctrines in preference to all others; ascribing to Him every *human* excellence; and believing He never claimed any other."

Jefferson loved birds, flowers and trees. He was more moved by the notes of the mockingbird than by the grandest European art. He held the same opinion as John Adams of the necessity for Americans of his generation to devote their attention to utilitarian subjects in order that their descendants might cultivate artistic ones. His mind turned with ease from a discussion of Greek vowels to the invention of the swivel chair or the leather buggy top. He settled the basis of the present coinage system of the United States. A plow invented by him won a prize from the French National Institute of Agriculture; the principle of its moldboard is in common use today. He never patented his own inventions, wishing the people to have free use of them. Grieved by the dreadful mortality amongst laborers in the Southern wet rice fields, whose working life is supposed to have averaged only eight years, he strove to introduce the cultivation of Egyptian, Algerian and Italian rice, and attempted to import some as well from Cochin China. He sent over olive trees from France for experimental planting in South Carolina and Georgia, but their culture never succeeded. He also promoted the cultivation, in the South, of figs, mulberry trees and sugar maples. Farming in the United States was, in his day, negligently conducted—in 1815 he complained of obtaining only six to eighteen bushels of wheat from an acre, while the best farmers got only ten to twenty bushels. It was his constant aim to improve agricultural yields; he was the first American importer of a threshing machine, which he lent to his neighbors, as well as of broadtail sheep from Barbary, Calcutta hogs, and a superior kind of guinea pigs.

During his eight years in the White House he kept a record of the first and last appearance each season in the Washington market of thirty-seven varieties of vegetables, such as carrots, turnips, broccoli and asparagus.

During his long residence in France he was in frequent correspondence on such varied subjects as innovations in wagonmaking, designs for cabriolets and balloon ascensions, properties of minerals, new mechanical processes, astronomical phenomena, literature and philology. He recommended improved watches and pedometers, argued concerning the relative humidity of the American and French climates, and emerged triumphant from a controversy with the celebrated Buffon on points of natural history, in the course of which, to prove a contention, he had sent to Paris the horns, bones and skin of a moose. He proposed to compare the vocabulary of the African Berbers with that of the Creek Indians to see whether there could be any foundation for the suggestion that the Creeks were descendants of the Carthaginians. His mind roved from speculations on the practicability of a canal through the Isthmus of Panama to the arrangements of a private aviary and the best manner of packing china cups and saucers.

Architecture, one of his favorite subjects, received much of his attention. "Here I am," he wrote from Nîmes, "gazing whole hours at the Maison Carrée, like a lover at his mistress." Later he said of his passion for an example of architecture: "While in Paris I was violently smitten with the Hotel de Salm."

He discussed central heating systems and paleontology, described cheese and winemaking, recorded the dates of the budding of flowers, the croaking of frogs and the singing of nightingales. A stream of statistical, political and ethnological reports flowed from his pen across the Atlantic. Although his express duties in Paris were confined to a few objects, such as the receipt of American whale oils, salted fish, salted meats and rice and tobacco on favorable terms, he spent considerable time in traveling about France and examining the condition of its people. He advised Lafayette that, in order to understand the needs of his countrymen, he must "ferret the people out of their hovels as I have done, look into their kettles, eat their bread, loll on their beds under pretense of resting yourself, but in fact to find if they are soft." He wrote rather wistfully: "Travelling makes men wiser, but less happy. . . . They learn habits which cannot be gratified when they return home." His pleasant intercourse with the French governing class did not blind him to the evils inherent in their system, which, Voltaire said, made every Frenchman either the hammer or the anvil. After one year in France he wrote: "Of twenty millions of people supposed to be in France, I am of the opinion there are nineteen millions more wretched, more accursed in every circumstance of human existence than the most conspicuously wretched individual of the whole United States."

In preparing traveling notes, in 1778, for the use of friends visiting Europe, he displayed his confirmed detestation of monarchies by

advising that, as objects of attention for Americans, courts should
be seen "as you would the Tower of London or menagerie of Ver-
sailles with their lions, tigers, hyaenas, and other beasts of prey,
standing in the same relation to their fellows. A slight acquaintance
with them will suffice to show you that under the most imposing
exterior, they are the weakest and worst part of mankind."

Jefferson was a patron of exploration tours. He was especially
interested in the contributions they might make to the advancement
of science, for whose tranquil pursuits he thought Nature must have
intended him, since she had rendered them his supreme delight.
He started the traveler Ledyard on a wild expedition across Russia,
whence it was hoped he would make his way, via Nootka Sound, to
the west coast of the American continent, and thence back to civilization. The Empress Catherine, however, probably saved the intrepid
Ledyard's life from Siberian cold, or American savages, by arresting
him about two hundred miles from Kamchatka and sending him to
Poland, where he was dismissed.

During his presidency Jefferson patronized the successful expeditions, in the Southwest, of Zebulon Pike, the first American to explore
the valley of the Arkansas, as well as the Upper Mississippi beyond
the falls of St. Anthony. He also sponsored and directed the organization of the still more important twenty-eight-month tour of Lewis
and Clark, in the Northwest, the story of whose wanderings, through
thousands of miles of territory between Missouri and the Pacific
Ocean never before trodden by the foot of a white man, can still be
read with fascination in the journals that record one of the most
romantic adventures in American history. In compliment to Jefferson, Madison and Gallatin the explorers named three branches of
the Missouri River after them; three affluents of the Jefferson were
called by the explorers Philosophy, Wisdom and Philanthropy, the
last of which is now known as Stinking Water.

Jefferson, always intensely interested in the Northwest, had been
one of the Virginia delegates who executed a deed in 1784, trans-
ferring from Virginia to the nation her holdings in that direction.
In drafting an ordinance for the temporary government of the
Northwestern Territory, he had suggested as names for the new
states, Sylvania, Michigania, Cherronesus, Metropotamia, Asseni-
sipia, Illinoia, Polypotamia, Saratoga, Washington and Pelisipia—
luckily the map of the United States is still innocent of most of this
nomenclature. In his original draft of this most important ordinance

he had embodied an antislavery clause, the elimination of which by Congress was most unfortunate, as its retention might have avoided the conflicts that later precipitated the Civil War.

In no part of Jefferson's life was his humane character more marked than in his personal treatment of Indians and Negroes. Indeed, he deceived himself by thinking that the Indians were superior in intellect to what has since proved to be the case. Although by purchase of "treaties," during his administration, the government wrested from them tens of millions of acres of land, he was alert to spare them, where possible, from oppression. In his boyhood he had met many of them at or near his father's house, and this early contact had left a lasting imprint upon his mind. He believed that their welfare could best be achieved by diverting them from warfare and hunting to agricultural work and domestic manufactures, but in this respect he reckoned without their own roving instincts. He had no objection to their intermarrying with whites.

As for the Negroes, he was a lifelong opponent of slavery, although he thought its entire elimination would be in his own time impossible. He feared, however, any emancipation which would leave the former slaves in America, and wished them when freed to be colonized in Africa or the West Indies, where he hoped they might eventually civilize their neighbors. "Nothing is more certainly written in the book of fate," he said, "than that these people are to be free." He was unalterably opposed to their miscegenation with white people, but was always the kindest and most considerate of masters. In 1785 he wrote: "I believe the Indian to be in body and mind equal to the white man. I have supposed the black man, in his present state, might not be so; but it would be hazardous to affirm, that, equally cultivated for a few generations, he would become so." When revising the laws of Virginia, he recommended that all slaves born after a certain date should be set free on reaching a designated age, and, after being given a mechanical education should be deported to Africa. He abandoned this provision only upon being convinced that public opinion was not ripe for it. Later the value of slaves in the cultivation of rice, and especially of cotton, was so great that a balance of power between slave and free states became an economic fetish in the Southern states, and Jefferson was too fond of his popularity to make a determined and useless stand for abolition.

As a diplomatist Jefferson commenced his career with a graceful

tribute to Benjamin Franklin. Upon the depature of Franklin from
Paris in 1785, the Count de Vergennes, French Minister for Foreign
Affairs, said to Jefferson, "You replace M. Franklin, I hear." "I succeed, no one can replace him," replied the new Minister. Although
it was not to be expected that any American diplomat would enjoy
the same astonishing popularity in Paris as had the aged Philadel-
phian, whose appearance was almost as well known in the capital as
that of the King, and was better welcomed, Jefferson made a distinguished place for himself there. In Paris at the time of the fall of the
Bastille, the author of the American Declaration of Independence
was regarded as a mentor by the enthusiastic sponsors of a new order
in France. In 1789 he received the truly extraordinary honor of
being asked to assist in the deliberations of the committee appointed
by the National Assembly to draft a Constitution. Because of his
official position he was, of course, constrained to decline this invitation, but he conferred frequently with Lafayette and other leaders of
the popular cause, giving them wise and temperate advice. He
relinquished his post before the horrors of the Terror were even
anticipated, but upon his return to America regarded sympathetically
the efforts of the French to form a republican government.

Precedents established by Jefferson as Secretary of State for dealing with foreign affairs are still considered models for our present
guidance in these matters. His firm handling of the Gênet case, and
his dignified dismissal of that impertinent Minister, evoked even the
congratulations of the Federalists, who had, like Hamilton, considered him "electrified plus with attachment for France," and influenced by a "womanish resentment against Great Britain." But
probably his most important despatch was regarding the recognition
by the United States of a foreign government, in which he laid down
what he termed "the Catholic principle of republicanism" as follows:

"We certainly cannot deny to other nations that principle whereon
our government is founded, that every nation has a right to govern
itself internally under what forms it pleases, and to change these
forms at its own will; and externally to transact business with other
nations through whatever organ it chooses, whether that be a King,
Convention, Assembly, Committee, President, or whatever it be.
The only thing essential is the will of the nation."

As President, Jefferson's conduct of diplomatic negotiations was
often tortuous and secretive. There was no inclination on his part
to favor "open covenants openly arrived at." One sometimes won-

ders whether his negotiations, distinguished by the most unquench-
able optimism, were inspired by vacillation of purpose or whether
they were the product of intelligent though dark design. At any
rate, he cajoled, threatened and bluffed to good effect, and if results
are any criterion the Louisiana Purchase, which was more peculiarly
his work than that of Madison, Livingston or Monroe, entitles him
to high rank as a successful diplomat. His attempt to buy or seize one
or both of the Floridas was less praiseworthy, although the task in
the then temper of Spain was from the outset impossible.

Jefferson is of course best remembered as the author of the Declaration of Independence. This production is chiefly responsible for
the title sometimes bestowed upon him of being the greatest political
philosopher of the eighteenth century. Before imperishably setting
his mark upon it he had served a long political apprenticeship. At
the age of twenty-six he had been elected to the Virginia House of
Burgesses, and also became Chief Commander in Albemarle County
of the King's militia, as well as Surveyor of the county. His first
important state paper was drafted for the Virginia Convention which
met in Williamsburg, in August 1773, to consider the grievances of
the colonies against the British government. Although this production, known as a *Summary View of the Rights of British America*,
was rejected by the convention as being too extreme in tone, it was
widely read and was republished in London, where it was sufficiently
disliked to cause the author's name to be included in a bill of at-
tainder. In this disquisition Jefferson advanced the then novel doctrine that the Americans had formed a new society, subject to no
laws except those to which they had assented or which they had
themselves adopted, and that as pioneers they were completely
exempt from the operation of the British Constitution; that by natural
right the colonists had acquired title to the territories they had
settled, the Crown having no authority to grant any colonial lands;
and that, by "the common right of mankind," they were entitled to
be governed by the laws of their own assemblies independently of
all charters.

In June 1775, Jefferson set out for his first trip North, and made
the trip in ten days from Williamsburg, Virginia, to Philadelphia. In
the first Continental Congress he won golden opinions from his colleagues, who admired the felicity of his writings and the modesty
of his demeanor. John Adams said of him: "Though a silent
member in Congress, he was so prompt, frank, explicit and decisive

upon committees and in conversation—not even Samuel Adams was more so—that he soon seized upon my heart." When the Declaration of Independence was to be drafted, the following year, the other members of the committee, John Adams, Benjamin Franklin, Roger Sherman and R.-R. Livingston, unanimously delegated the preparation of the instrument to Jefferson. The document was, with the exception of two or three verbal changes suggested by Franklin and Adams to whom he had separately submitted it for their corrections, entirely his own work. For the thoughts it expressed, and for portions of the phraseology, he was in some measure indebted to Locke, Kames and George Mason's Virginia "Bill of Rights," but after ascribing full credit to others it remains a production of original majesty.

Jefferson's doctrine of natural rights was dear to him. He conceived that the individual had certain rights of personal competency, such as thinking, speaking and writing, which required no external power for their maintenance, but that other rights, such as a modification of his control over property, might by compact be transferred to society in return for its protection. To these principles he was, in theory, always faithful, but, when he became President was not indisposed in times of crisis to have the national government encroach upon the reserved rights of individuals and of states, in order to achieve results promising lasting benefits to the people.

During the Revolutionary War, Jefferson was first an active and exceedingly useful member of Congress, and afterward for two terms Governor of his native state. During his last term Virginia was overrun by British troops and the Governor narrowly escaped being captured in his own home. Indeed, one of his plantations was thoroughly plundered, his slaves were carried off, most of his livestock was confiscated and, what seemed to him especially brutal, the throats of some of his thoroughbred horses were cut.

He has been accused of slackness in not having put Virginia in condition to resist a British invasion. However, impartial students of the period are convinced that the state could not have been defended without causing a serious derangement of Washington's plans. Washington drew from it all its available militia, equipment and supplies for use in portions of the colonies where he thought them to be more sorely needed.

After having twice previously declined the appointment, Jefferson went, in 1784, as Minister to France, and was abroad at the time of the adoption of the Constitution of the United States. He approved heartily, however, of that instrument with two exceptions: first, he disliked the re-eligibility of the President for the chief magistracy, and, second, he desired a Bill of Rights, which was later adopted in the form of amendments to the Constitution.

For a short time, upon his return from France, Jefferson seems to have been inclined to prefer one chamber of Congress to two. He took Washington to task for having counter-balanced the House of Representatives with a Senate. They were seated at breakfast together, and Washington responded by asking: "Why did you pour that coffee into a saucer?" Jefferson said it was too hot to drink. "Even so," observed Washington, "we pour legislation into the senatorial saucer to cool it."

Returning home in 1789 to repatriate his young daughters, he intended to return to Paris and resume his duties there, but, at the earnest solicitation of Washington, consented to become Secretary of State. His occupancy of the office led him into constant conflict with Alexander Hamilton, against whom he said that he was, in cabinet meetings, pitted as if they were two fighting cocks.

In truth, between Hamilton and Jefferson there was no possibility of permanent peace, for their political principles were in fundamental antagonism. The brilliant native of the West Indies, with his handsome face, gay personality, sparkling intellect and tireless industry, offspring of a French mother by a Scotch father, with a bar sinister upon his legitimacy, and owing his rise in the world to the force of his own talents, was by temperament an autocrat, distrustful of the people, believing in their venality and considering that they should be dominated by an oligarchy founded on wealth and abilities. "Your people, sir," he once said at a New York dinner, "your people is a great beast." Jefferson, on the other hand, by birth, habits and manners an aristocrat, possessed an abiding faith in the innate honesty and good sense of the common people, insofar as they were literate and were agricultural in their tastes and occupations. He resented Hamilton's efforts to strengthen the powers of the central government at the expense of the reserved rights of the states, and, even more, Hamilton's belief in the corruptibility of the electorate. He thought Hamilton "a man of acute understanding, disinterested, honest, honorable in all private transactions, yet so bewitched and perverted by the British example as to be under the thorough conviction that corruption is essential to the government of a nation."

Jefferson's philosophy was physiocratic and decidedly limited by his view that American society was likely to remain largely agricultural. He was suspicious of the artisan class and of urban populations. Later in life he modified these views, in part, and concluded that "an equilibrium of agriculture, manufactures and commerce, is certainly become essential to our independence, manufactures sufficient for our consumption, of what we raise the raw material (and no more), commerce sufficient to carry the surplus produce of agriculture beyond our own consumption, to a market for exchanging it for articles we cannot raise (and no more). These are the true limits of manufactures and commerce. To go beyond them is to increase our dependence on foreign nations and our liability to war."

The real secret of his power lay in the lifelong appeal that he made to the hopeful idealism of the American people to preserve a nation which should be simple, virtuous and intelligent, where opportunity to excel should not be stifled by accidents of birth and fortune, and where emphasis should be placed on the spiritual aspects of civilization rather than on its material and practical ones.

The responsibilities of the highest executive office apparently altered his views on revolution, for in 1786 he had been almost lyrical in his approbation of an occasional fraternal affray. Apropos of Shay's Rebellion in Massachusetts and New Hampshire, he had then written to Mrs. Adams: "I like a little rebellion now and then. . . . The spirit of resistance to government is so valuable on certain occasions that I wish it to be always kept alive. It will often be exercised, when wrong, but better so than not to be exercised at all."

His views on secession also were scarcely orthodox. At the end of his first term as President he informed Dr. Priestley that he thought it not very important to the happiness of either part of the country whether it remained in one confederacy or separated into Atlantic and Mississippi confederations. At another time, speaking of a possible separation he saw no reason to take sides with the Atlantic states against the Western ones, but wished that "God bless them both, and keep them in unison if it be for their own good, but separate them, if it be better."

The decision of Chief Justice Marshall in *Madison vs. Marbury*, in which Marshall established the right of the Supreme Court of the United States to pass upon the validity of every act of Congress and to pronounce any law a nullity if it should be repugnant to the terms of the federal Constitution, was gall and wormwood to Jefferson. He blandly ignored the import of the Chief Justice's decision except to score the great jurist as a bigoted Federalist.

Although his nullification resolutions, written on the occasion of the protest by Kentucky against the Alien and Sedition Laws, pronounced that each state had an equal right to decide for itself as well of infractions as of the mode and measure of redress, whenever Congress palpably exceeds its powers, he did not adhere to such a proposition in his later life.

But if the tenacity of his opinions was liable to change, his belief in republicanism, as opposed to monarchy, was immovable. The most that can be said of republicanism, he maintained, is that "the republican is the only form of government which is not eternally at open or secret war with the rights of mankind."

After they entered Washington's Cabinet, a quarrel between Jefferson and Hamilton was inevitable. Before Jefferson realized it, the Secretary of the Treasury had succeeded in his program to fund the entire national debt, domestic and foreign, principal and interest, at par value, representing a total of about fifty million dollars, a part to bear interest at six per cent and a part at three per cent, while interest on the remainder was to be deferred for ten years. In vain did Madison and others protest against the payment at par of the domestic debt, which had fallen to a small fraction of parity. Hamilton carried the day. Long before the decision of Congress was known, speculators, including many legislators, aware of the projected operation, sent agents by swift-sailing ships and on horseback to remote districts where they bought up the depreciated debts by payment of specie at a fraction of the prices for which they were shortly funded. As a result most of the old bonds became concentrated in the hands of Boston, New York and Philadelphia owners.

The second point of Hamilton's program was the assumption by the federal government at face value of the revolutionary obligations of the states, amounting to some twenty million dollars. This measure was bitterly contested. Certain states, such as Virginia, had already cared for their own debts and had little to gain by assumption, although it would greatly benefit Massachusetts and other states. At last Jefferson, to his undying regret, was persuaded to win the necessary votes to carry the bill, on the ground that the creditor states might secede from the Union if it were not adopted and on the understanding that, in return for the support of himself and his friends, the capital of the country would after an interim of ten years' location at Philadelphia be established on the Potomac River.

Hamilton's next move was to charter a Bank of the United States, empowered to engage in a general banking business and to issue notes, under certain restrictions, redeemable in coin, which would be legal tender for all payments due to the United States. It was fiercely opposed by Jefferson, who denied that the implied powers of the Constitution conferred any sanction on such a step. "Banking establishments," he thought, "are more dangerous than standing armies," and he said, "I have never observed men's honesty to increase with their riches." Again Jefferson lost.

By these measures Hamilton built up a powerful moneyed interest to support a strong central government. The conditions bred by the charter of the Bank of the United States alarmed James Madison to the last degree. "Stock and scrip," he wrote in 1791, "the sole domestic subjects of conversation—speculations—carried on with money borrowed at from 2½ per cent a month to 1 per cent a week." Although speculation enriched a favored class, and the success of Hamilton's program allowed the Treasury Department to exercise excessive authority over legislative deliberations, it is now apparent that these bold and to some degree tainted measures were on the whole beneficial to the country, for they in a short time substituted for its ruined credit an unchallenged fiscal stability.

But Hamilton's success was bitter to Jefferson, who believed that the Federalists, whom he called Anglomen and Monocrats, intended to aim at more despotic objects, even the institution of a monarchy. Of this suspicion the anti-Federalist or Republican, eventually to become the Democratic, party was born. It represented roughly the antagonism of agriculture to banking and business enterprise. From the State Department, administered by the Secretary with the assistance of two clerks, one of whom was a foreign language translator, Jefferson watched with increasing alarm the expanding patronage and influence wielded by the Treasury.

Nor was Hamilton serene. Anonymously he attacked his colleague's principles in the newspapers, meeting in return the diatribes of the Republican press, whose foremost journal was edited by Jefferson's foreign language clerk, Philip Freneau, a college classmate and friend of Madison. The startling spectacle of two cabinet officers in epistolary conflict, albeit one wrote anonymously and the other neither wrote nor directed but merely approved his subordinate's expressions, worried President Washington, who vainly besought them to moderate their opposition and to reconcile their views. He respected both men, and nowhere does he appear to better advantage than in his efforts to mollify them.

This impossible situation continued until the definite retirement of Jefferson from the Cabinet on December 31, 1793; an example which his rival, for pecuniary reasons, was later forced to follow.

Upon his retirement from office Jefferson went to Monticello, whence through correspondence he fostered the growth of the Republican party. It was his belief that duty required one at times to sacrifice individual views to party unity, but as he was the founder of a party and its undisputed head even during the presidential administrations following his own, he was seldom called upon for his own part to put this precept into practice. As a party leader Jefferson was unique. He held his adherents in rigid discipline, at the same time retaining their devotion and respect. No one since, in American history, has probably ever been so successful a factional chief. When he was defied, as he occasionally was, notably by John Randolph, he let the erring go their way, but such desertions of his policies were uncommon.

The rapid growth of Jefferson's party was displayed in the election following the retirement of Washington. Washington had been twice unanimously elected, but his successor, John Adams, received but 71 votes to Jefferson's 68. Under the law, as it then existed, they became President and Vice-President respectively. In 1797 Jefferson therefore returned to public life and presided over the Senate, for whose guidance he drew up a manual of parliamentary procedure that is a standard work today. This is the only literary production, if it can be so called, not including state papers, that Jefferson published, with the exception of his *Notes on Virginia*.

By 1800, Jefferson had perfected his organization. The caucuses that nominated Presidents for many years and became an accepted institution in 1804, were in 1800 held in secret by both the Federalists and the Republicans. Although a spirited campaign ensued, in the course of which the voters of Middletown, Connecticut, drank to the toast, "Thomas Jefferson, may he receive from his fellow citizens the reward of his merit—a halter," at the election Jefferson and Burr received 73 votes, John Adams 65, Pinckney, of South Carolina, 64, and John Jay one vote. Despite the manifest intention of the Republican voters to select Jefferson as President and Aaron Burr as Vice-President, under the constitutional provision then operative the election was because of the tie vote thrown into the House of Representatives where, after long intrigue, effect was given to the will of the people, and Jefferson was chosen President, with Burr as Vice-President.

His inaugural address breathed moderation. In it he said that a good government was one which, while it shall "restrain men from injuring one another, shall leave them otherwise free to regulate their own pursuits of industry and improvement, and shall not take from the mouth of labor the bread it has earned. This is the sum of good government, and this is necessary to close the circle of our felicities."

Jefferson's Cabinet consisted of James Madison, of Virginia, Secretary of State; Albert Gallatin, of Pennsylvania, Secretary of the Treasury (a post which he continued to occupy longer than has any other incumbent in our history); General Dearborn, of Massachusetts, Attorney General; Gideon Granger, of Connecticut, Postmaster General; and Robert Smith, of Maryland, Secretary of the Navy.

The responsibilities of the individuals in Jefferson's Cabinet were great, for in his cabinet practice he made it a rule to submit all matters of importance or difficulty to the Heads of Departments. Experience was to demonstrate Jefferson's good fortune in having included in his Cabinet such a faithful coadjutor as his devoted friend Madison, and such a brilliant financier and administrator as the Swiss-born Gallatin, one of the ablest men who ever participated in the public life of the United States.

Much pressure was brought upon the President to replace Federalists in office by deserving Republicans, but he made less than twenty removals for political reasons—the rest of the removals in his time being for misconduct in office.

Jefferson promptly reduced the army from four thousand to twenty-five hundred men. He abolished excise taxes, lopped off numerous federal employees, freed all prisoners under the Sedition Act, reduced the diplomatic establishments and the naval program, and cut the expenses of government, in his first year of office, from $7,500,000 to $5,000,000 per annum.

Although Jefferson believed the election of 1800 constituted a revolution as real as that of 1776, the change was one of men and not radically one of principles, except for rigid economy in government. The contests between the Republicans and Federalists were, in Jefferson's opinion, "contests of principle, between the advocates of republican and those of kingly government." However, the changes brought about by the new President wrought no great upheaval in the habits of the people.

It was difficult, indeed, for any radical change to be made in the government itself. The Constitution is supreme over the people who give voice only through their representatives. "My construction of the Constitution . . . is that each department is truly independent of the others, and has an equal right to decide for itself what is the meaning of the Constitution in the cases submitted to its action," said Jefferson, but this contention was promptly denied by Marshall. His predilection for Indian government, with its loose tribal organization, was not applicable to a great nation, and as President he found that pure democracy, or a reasonable simulacrum of it, must remain an ideal untranslatable into fact. As the constitutional power of a popular majority ended with the adoption of the Constitution, which requires a change to be proposed by a two-thirds majority, and ratified by three-fourths, of the states, he contented himself by carrying out within constitutional limits what he thought were the genuine wishes of a majority of the people. But to speak of his election as having marked a revolution in the principles of government is absurd. The initiative, referendum and recall were not even contemplated in his day, and the veto of the Supreme Court was as threatening to innovations in our fundamental principles of government in his time as it now is.

One of his first desires was to repeal the Judiciary Act, passed for partisan motives at the end of the preceding administration. In this he succeeded. Jefferson seems to have been always suspicious of the judiciary, and jealous of the influence which it exerted by its construction of constitutional law. "The great object of my fear," he once said, "is the Federal Judiciary. That body, like gravity, ever acting with noiseless foot and unalarming advance, gaining ground step by step, and holding what it gains, is engulfing insidiously the special governments into the jaws of that which feeds them." The stalwart Federalist, John Marshall, appointed Chief Justice of the Supreme Court by Adams, was regarded by him with a mixture of personal dislike and hearty disapproval. But Marshall's sturdy expositions of the authority of his court, and his advocacy of a strong centralized government were never influenced by Jefferson's hostility. Marshall did much to perpetuate forever in our institutions Federalist policies abhorred by Jefferson.

Marshall had a contempt for Jefferson's leveling doctrines, and seems to have regarded him as little better than an irresolute demagogue. The ill-feeling between them reached its height during the

Burr trial, at which time, although Jefferson refused to obey a subpoena to appear before the court, Marshall in turn by his decisions
and actions rebuked the Chief Executive's attempt to convict the
accused. No accommodation between the two men was ever sought
for or arrived at, and the Chief Justice's strictures on his fellow Virginian are the most severe ever visited upon Jefferson by a man of
undoubted integrity of character and constructive brilliance of
intellect.

Marshall could scarcely have been expected to view with tolerance Jefferson's attacks upon the judiciary. Had the President been
suffered to do so, he probably would have reduced the federal courts
to a state of dependence upon the whims of the executive, the legislature and the electorate. In Congress, and in various states, there
was a strong attempt made to have the tenure of federal Judges
limited to a term of years, and to make them removable by the
President on motion by two thirds of both houses.

The successful impeachment of Judge Pickering, who was proved
to be not only a habitual drunkard but insane, was followed by an
attack upon Judge Chase of the Supreme Court, a signer of the
Declaration of Independence who had so far forgotten his judicial
dignity at the behest of his violent Federalist prejudices as to deliver
intemperate political harangues from the bench.

Although the impeachment proceedings against Chase fell flat,
they left Marshall aware that during the Jeffersonian Administration
he could look for no quarter from his enemies. Had he capitulated
to the Democrats and acknowledged Jefferson's claim that the interpretation of the Constitution and of acts of Congress, by each department was valid, the revolution which the President asserted he had
effected in the fundamental principles of American government
might indeed have taken place.

Except for being worsted in some of his attempts upon the judiciary, Jefferson's first term was one of which any President might
well have been proud. His original and much ridiculed design to
reduce the navy to complete impotence by laying up the seven larger
men-of-war in the eastern branch of the Potomac, where they would
be under the immediate jurisdiction of the Navy Department, and
would require but "one set of plunderers to take care of them," was
followed by the suggestion, in his second annual message to Congress, that the entire navy be stored in a large dry dock, to be built
at Washington. Another use, however, was found for the warships.

In ten years the United States had paid to the infamous Barbary pirates almost two million dollars in tributes and ransom money. Collections were taken up in churches for the release of Americans who sweated in chains at the oars of pirate galleys, or languished in fetid dungeons. Jefferson resolved to make an end to this disgraceful subservience. His fleets harried the Bashaw of Tripoli to such good effect that, in 1805, a peace was signed terminating the annual toll of $83,000 in money and presents which Tripoli had formerly received from the American government, although tributes continued to be paid until 1815 to other Barbary potentates.

The expenditure for 1802, excluding debt interest, was $3,737,000, the last time in American history the annual budget did not exceed four million dollars. Rigid economy was insisted upon by the President, who wished to extinguish the national debt as quickly as possible, believing that no generation has the right to pass on a burden of debt to another generation. The diplomatic establishment was reduced to a few representatives, and lapsed commercial treaties were not renewed. An age of laissez-faire seemed to have dawned. Although there were threats and rumblings, in 1803, that the Essex Junto of Massachussetts and the "River Gods" of Connecticut were planning a new confederacy of the New England states and New York, the great majority of the people were well satisfied with their government, which had in the same year performed one of the greatest achievements their history was ever to record, namely the annexation of Louisiana. The price stipulated for the 1,171,931 square miles that Louisiana was later found to have contained, an area greater than that of the combined thirteen original states, was fifteen million dollars, three quarters of which went to France in the form of six per cent bonds, and the remaining one quarter was obligated to citizens of the United States holding certain claims against France.

This extraordinary transaction gave to the United States all the territory now within the borders of Arkansas, Mississippi, Iowa, Oklahoma, Kansas, Nebraska and South Dakota, besides large portions of the present states of Louisiana, Minnesota, North Dakota, Colorado, Montana and Wyoming, comprising the entire continent from the Rocky Mountains to the east bank of the Mississippi River, and from the Canadian border to northern Texas.

For its consummation Jefferson was himself more responsible than any other individual except Napoleon. This territory, taken possession of by France through the great explorer La Salle in 1682, had, in 1763, been handed over by France to Spain, and retroceded by the latter to France in 1800 by the secret treaty of San Ildefonso, according to the terms of which the recipient was expressly forbidden to alienate Louisiana to any foreign power.

When news of the Spanish cession to France was known, there was an outcry of lamentation, fear and indignation in America, and Jefferson resolved that Napoleon's possible ambition to erect a new empire in the New World must be thwarted. "There is," said he, "on the globe, one single spot, the possessor of which is our natural and habitual enemy. It is New Orleans, through which the produce of three-eighths of our territory must pass to market. . . . France, placing herself in that door, assumes to us the attitude of defiance. . . . The day that France takes possession of New Orleans, fixes the sentence which is to restrain her forever within her low-water mark. It seals the union of two nations, who, in conjunction, can maintain exclusive possession of the ocean. From that moment we must marry ourselves to the British fleet and nation."

Jefferson having instructed his Minister in Paris, Livingston, to buy New Orleans and, if possible, adjacent territory, sent Monroe to assist in the negotiations. Hardly had the latter envoy arrived when Napoleon, discouraged by the death of his brother-in-law, Leclerc, by the decimation of his army in San Domingo (which island had been the center of his colonial schemes, and compared to which Louisiana was of subordinate importance), and being desirous of obtaining money to support his designs of further conquest on the European continent, abandoned entirely his American dream and offered the whole of Louisiana to the astonished Livingston. Livingston and Monroe were staggered at the proffer of an extent of territory which they had no authority to buy, but accepted the bargain. In vain Spain protested against this flagrant violation of the treaty of San Ildefonso, for Napoleon held her by the throat. Nor was he more mindful of the provision of the French Constitution requiring the consent of the Chamber of Deputies to such a cession. The First Consul did not consult the Chamber regarding the matter, and rated his brothers soundly for their opposition to his plans.

The happy news was slow in arriving from France, although not so tardy as it might have been in 1793, when for three months a series of westerly gales had prevented any vessel leaving a European port from reaching America. At first Jefferson had doubts about the constitutionality of the purchase and wished an amendment for its ratification. But, being advised that the mind of Napoleon was liable to sudden changes, he resigned himself to a loose construction of the Constitution and approved the purchase. A few scattered voices were raised against the annexation of Louisiana, but the mass of the people, fired by the prospect of a great addition of free land, rejoiced in its acquisition.

Jefferson's first term ended in a blaze of glory. He was triumphantly re-elected by 162 votes against 14 for C. C. Pinckney. For the first time candidates for the office of Vice-President were separately selected; George Clinton, of New York, a Republican, received 162 votes to Rufus King's 14. At home, peace and prosperity reigned, but ominous clouds were gathering on the foreign horizon.

The four fat kine of Jefferson's first administration were fated, in John Randolph's words, to be eaten up by the four lean kine of his second term.

Of all important events in American history, the Burr conspiracy was the most mysterious; as might well be expected in view of the habitual mysteriousness of Burr's own conduct, which led John Randolph to say at the time of his trial that "should he be hanged for treason, I dare say he will contrive to make posterity doubt whether he was actually executed."

Burr's career is an interesting and tantalizing one. An intrepid officer in the Revolution, a wily, resourceful lawyer, a master of political management, winning to men, irresistible to women, captivating in his manners, stoical in his disposition, profligate, generous and spendthrift in his habits, he almost became President of the United States. While Vice-President, unable to enter certain states because there were warrants out for his arrest over the killing of Alexander Hamilton in a duel, he was regarded by many as a murderer and was distrusted by his own political associates. Yet, when he delivered his farewell address to the Senate, in which were seated some of his inveterate enemies, the dignity of his presence and the melodious pathos of his language reduced so many Senators to tears, that, when the voice of the orator ceased there was scarcely a dry eye in the chamber. Only one human being seems to have shared his whole love and confidence—his ill-starred, beautiful and brilliant daughter Theodosia, whose own end, during a sea voyage, caused by the fury of the elements or the brutality of pirates, broke her father's heart and severed his last tie, to borrow his own language, with the human race.

That Burr desired to lead an expedition into Mexico, conquer it and become its emperor, he himself admitted. Such a project was not, however, a new thing. Alexander Hamilton had once formed and attempted to carry out a somewhat similar plan, expecting to invade, with the co-operation of the British, Louisiana and the Floridas, and after marching into Mexico, to disrupt the Spanish empire in America, and distribute portions of it as spoils to England, the United States and to the Venezuelan adventurer, Miranda, who was the father of the project.

Moreover, at the time of Burr's conspiracy, many soldiers of fortune in the West, and even conservative businessmen in New Orleans, looked with favor on the conquest of Mexico. Jefferson himself is not above suspicion of having been privy to this portion of the plot. At that period war with Spain over the Floridas seemed highly possible. No valid evidence was adduced at his trial that Burr planned to invade Mexico unless war should first have broken out between the United States and Spain. But whether Burr seriously intended as well to separate by force the Western settlers from the Union, thinking that New England would also secede, is open to doubt; three months before his death, when discussing the matter he stated: "I would as soon thought of taking possession of the moon, and informing my friends that I intended to divide it between them." However he never denied there might have been a proposal to establish a Western empire by consent, though his reputation as a trifler with the truth impairs the creditibility of statements in his own defense.

Then, too, the whole scheme may have been merely a great land-speculating proposition, involving an attack on Mexico only if the United States should speedily become involved in war with Spain. At any rate, Burr attempted to enlist the aid of Great Britain in his undisclosed project. With consummate impudence he even received some money from the Spanish Minister in furtherance of his designs. Rumors were abroad that he intended to fill Washington with men in disguise, seize the President, Vice-President and other high officers, the public money and the arsenal. In spite of frequent and urgent warnings, Jefferson refused for a long time to notice Burr's movements and machinations, but finally ordered him to be arrested for being in process of conducting an expedition against Spain, and to be tried for treason against the United States. Burr, learning of the President's proclamation, became a fugitive. Exchanging clothes with a boatman, he attempted to escape through the wilderness to the coast, where he hoped to take ship for England. Apprehended in northern Alabama he was taken to Richmond for trial.

Few political trials have ever equaled that of Burr. The President of the United States, who had in the past often expressed in private his dislike and distrust of Burr, while receiving him affably and frequently at the White House (and even pressing attentions on him), now pursued the prisoner with malignant rage, announcing to Congress, before the jury trial, that his "guilt is placed beyond question." In the courtroom Chief Justice Marshall presided. The grand jury, of which John Randolph was named foreman, included a future Secretary of War, several Senators and three future Governors of Virginia. One of the defendant's lawyers was Edmund Randolph, Attorney General under Washington and a former Governor of Virginia. One of the lawyers for the prosecution was the silver-tongued William Wirt. The chief witness for the prosecution was General James Wilkinson, Commander-in-Chief of the military forces of the United States, who had long been in correspondence with Burr, but who was now denouncing him. Of all unmitigated scoundrels in American history Wilkinson is the most contemptible, for he did not possess even the physical courage for which the traitor Arnold was conspicuous. The subject of several courts-martial, from each of which he emerged with a dubious acquittal, his rise in the army had been continuous, owing to the small size of the military establishment and the dearth of general officers. This man, who alleged that Burr had meditated treason against his country, had, since 1787, been secret agent number 13 on the records of the Spanish Foreign Office. "Wilkinson is entirely devoted to us," the Spanish Minister advised Madrid at this period; "he enjoys a considerable pension from the king."

Jefferson hounded on the prosecution and let it be generally known that he would try to remove Marshall from the Bench if Burr were acquitted. Burr was acquitted, on technical grounds, but Marshall continued to occupy his place as Chief Justice of the Supreme Court, even though he had further antagonized Jefferson by issuing a subpoena for the President's personal appearance at the trial, an appearance which Jefferson properly refused to make.

Burr's acquittal did not cause any popular indignation, although the general impression of his probable, even if unproved, guilt effectively blasted his future career. The conquest of Mexico was favorably viewed by most of the people of the South and Southwest, who cared little about the rights of Spain when set against their thirst for expansion. But Jefferson's conduct of the case, prejudging the guilt of the accused and making use of such a tool as Wilkinson, whom the President continued to cherish, constitutes a blemish upon his reputation. Nor was Marshall's attitude as presiding justice one for which his admirers could enthusiastically commend him. He attended a private dinner given in Burr's honor before the latter's acquittal, and he permitted his dislike of the administration to be patent in his demeanor on the bench.

During the Burr trial, and only three months before his acquittal in September 1807, an event occurred which displaced it as an item of supreme interest in the popular imagination. The American frigate *Chesapeake*, having refused to surrender some sailors alleged to be deserters from the English navy, was fired upon by the British warship *Leopard*, and three of its crew were killed and eighteen wounded. The commander of the *Leopard* seized four seamen and carried them off, one of them being later hanged as a deserter at Halifax. A national outburst of indignation followed the outrage. Jefferson issued a proclamation, ordering all armed vessels of Great Britain out of American waters and denying the sale of supplies to them. That war did not follow is a subject for wonder, since the unprovoked attack was only one of a long series of somewhat similar instances, in which, by impressment, by search, by blockade and by other impositions, the British violated almost every maritime right of a free people. Congress, however, which Jefferson felt the Executive should not commit to any course of action except one inspired by it, supinely accepted all insults; the British people, who seemed almost as a unit at this period to hate and despise the Americans, believing that the Americans were too cowardly to resent any depredations, encouraged their government to continue in its course.

The crisis brought about by British raids on American commerce, which was at the same time being preyed upon by Napoleon in an equally severe fashion, gave Jefferson an opportunity to test his favorite policy, that of peace. At a period when the continent of Europe was drenched with blood he held to the idea that the United States should keep itself free, in spite of almost any provocations, from war with a foreign power. "Peace is our passion," he wrote, "and wrongs might drive us from it. We prefer trying *every* other just principle, right and safety, before we would recur to war."

Later in the year 1807 the continual and flagrant disregard of American rights by both Great Britain and France, enforced by the former's Orders in Council and by the latter's Decrees, apparently designed to drive the shipping of the United States from the ocean, seemed to leave no alternative but to declare either an embargo or war against one or both of the offending nations. On December 22, 1807, an embargo was laid by Congress, prohibiting American vessels from sailing for foreign ports, and restricting foreign vessels from taking out cargoes from American ports.

This measure was one of the most drastic ever taken in our history, and that Jefferson was able to secure the passage of an act so arbitrary and confiscatory demonstrates what a firm dominance he exercised over congressional deliberations. At the same time the Non-importation Law went into force. The result was to tie up American shipping, shut off the produce of farmers from their foreign markets, throw thousands of sailors out of employment and cripple the prosperity of New England. Wholesale deflation set in. Efforts to evade the law by smuggling brought the imposition of severe enforcement acts that, culminating in the "Force Bill," bade fair to effect a separation of the New England states from the Union. The only good arising out of the embargo was the growth of industries fostered in the United States to supply the manufactured necessities, formerly imported, from the purchase of which our people were wholly cut off. Suffering resulted in England and France from their loss of the American market, but not sufficient to cause those Governments to withdraw their obnoxious Orders and Decrees. In spite of widespread protests and ruin Jefferson persisted in this most tyrannical of measures, in the belief that if his countrymen would strictly obey its provisions both foreign nations might alter the conduct which had cost the United States the loss of thousands of tons of shipping, the impressment of hundreds of American citizens, the blockade of New York City by a British squadron, and the confiscation of goods consigned even for a purely neutral trade.

Whether, if persevered in and faithfully obeyed by American merchants, the embargo might have ultimately accomplished its objects will always remain a moot question. Though now regarded as a dark, costly and humiliating phase of our history, it is difficult to believe that we would have been more prosperous or less insulted if we had, with our inadequate resources, declared war against both the Mistress of the Seas and the greatest military genius of modern times. Jefferson was, however, mistaken in his hope that foreign nations wanted our trade so much that they would live at peace with us from self-interest. Also he made no allowance for the sentiments of many Englishmen who considered resistance to these measures a desertion by one branch of the English-speaking people of another branch which was fighting not only its own battle but that of civilization against a megalomaniac.

In justice to Jefferson, it must be observed that some influential Englishmen, in addition to their legitimate fears of Napoleon, were disturbed by the rapid growth of American trade and seized upon their struggle with Napoleon as a pretext for repressing its activities. Also, their conduct toward us at this period was marked by even more stubbornness and tactlessness than had customarily characterized their diplomatic relations with us.

A few days before the expiration of his second term Jefferson signed the repeal of the embargo, leaving upon his friend and successor James Madison the onus of evolving a new orientation of foreign policy.

In spite of the vicissitudes of his last four years of office, and the national humiliations entailed by his management, the retiring President, secure in popularity with the masses of the American people, had been able to dictate the nomination and election of Madison. It was even generally supposed that had his principles permitted he would have been certain of re-election for a third term. Although discontent with him had been sufficiently prevalent in New England, prior to the repeal of the embargo, to have constituted a real threat to the integrity of the Union, the address presented to him on February 6, 1809, by the legislature of his native state shows in what esteem he was held in Virginia.

It was not in Jefferson's nature to be idle. Although he was glad to be released from his long spell of public duty, and to return to Monticello, which he loved with the same passion as Washington had Mount Vernon, he continued in communication with his friends and was frequently consulted by Presidents Madison and Monroe. His letters bearing upon the possible interference by European nations in the affairs of North and South America, are of particular interest. On August 4, 1820, he wrote to William Short: "The day is not distant, when we may formally require a meridian of partition throughout the ocean which separates the two hemispheres, on the hither side of which no European gun shall ever be heard, nor an

American on the other; and when, during the rage of the eternal wars of Europe, the lion and the lamb, within our regions, shall lie down together in peace. . . . The principles of society there and here, then, are radically different, and I hope no American patriot will ever lose sight of the essential policy of interdicting in the seas and territories of both Americas, the ferocious and sanguinary contests of Europe."

When, in 1823, it was rumored that the Holy Alliance proposed to interfere between Spain and her revolted colonies, in an attempt to re-establish the sway of Castile over South America, and England, in alarm, requested the interference of the United States in the matter, President Monroe wrote to Jefferson for his advice. The reply of Jefferson (who had told Monroe on another occasion, "I have ever deemed it fundamental for the United States never to take active part in the quarrels of Europe,") proposed to Monroe, on October 14, 1823, essentially the same doctrine which, on December 2, 1823, the President officially promulgated in his famous message to Congress. Jefferson's reply reads:

"The question presented by the letters you have sent me, is the most momentous which has ever been offered to my contemplation since that of Independence. That made us a nation, this sets our compass and points the course which we are to steer through the ocean of time opening on us. And never could we embark on it under circumstances more auspicious. Our first and fundamental maxim should be, never to entangle ourselves in the broils of Europe. Our second—never to suffer Europe to meddle with cis-Atlantic affairs. America, North and South, has a set of interests distinct from those of Europe, and peculiarly her own. She should therefore have a system of her own, separate and apart from that of Europe."

The greatest interest of Jefferson's declining years was the establishment of the University of Virginia. He founded it, and raised the $162,000 required for its erection; he was its architect; he supervised its building, selected its professors, laid down rules for its administration and was its first rector. "This institution of my native State," he said proudly, "the hobby of my old age, will be based on the illimitable freedom of the human mind to explore and expose every subject susceptible of its contemplation." It was to be the first college or university established in the United States in which the teaching of religion was to be no part of the curriculum, although Jefferson expressly proposed to allow any sectarian school of divinity to establish itself on the outskirts of the university, so that its students might have access to the lectures of such a school. Moreover, all enrolled students were to be allowed an uncontrolled choice in the lectures they should choose to attend, although diplomas were not to be awarded to anyone who "has not passed such an examination of the Latin language as shall have proved him able to read the highest classics in that language with ease, thorough understanding, and just quantity; and if he be also a proficient in the Greek let that too be stated in his diploma."

Even today on the campus, flanked by neoclassic brick colonnades and buildings composing one of the finest architectural groups in the world, students refer to "Mr. Jefferson" in the affectionate and natural tone which the Greeks used toward the tutelary genius of a place whose bright spirit, they believed, haunted benevolently the dwellings loved by it in life.

The last years of Jefferson's existence were clouded by pecuniary distress. Within six months of his death most of his personal property was sold for debt, and all of it within a year. Later the lands and mansion house were sold, and Monticello passed away from the possession of his kindred.

Except for his financial troubles and the burden of his correspondence, his old age was happy and serene. His wonderful health did not fail him until he was in his eighty-fourth year. The last letter he wrote was in response to an invitation to take part in a celebration of the fiftieth anniversary of the signing of the Declaration of Independence.

Fifty years, to a day, after the date on which he had signed the Declaration of Independence, the soul of Thomas Jefferson peacefully quitted his weary body to join, it is trusted, the spirits of the small and privileged company of other great apostles of human freedom and enlightenment.

James Madison

Born: March 16, 1751.

Graduated from Princeton: October 7, 1771.

Took his seat in the Virginia House of Delegates: October 6, 1776.

Took his seat in the Continental Congress: March 20, 1780.

Named as a delegate to the federal Constitutional Convention: December 5, 1786.

Signed Constitution: September 17, 1787.

Elected to national House of Representatives: February 2, 1787.

Married: 1794.

Assumed office as Secretary of State: May 2, 1801.

Inaugurated as President: March 4, 1809.

Issued proclamation taking possession of West Florida: October 27, 1810.

Issued proclamation of war: June 19, 1812.

Inaugurated as President for second term: March 4, 1813.

Sent treaty of peace to Congress: February 18, 1815.

Retired from presidency: March 4, 1817.

In Virginia Convention: 1829.

Died: June 28, 1836.

JAMES MADISON

IT WAS during the first half of James Madison's almost uninterrupted public career of forty years that he established his real title to fame. The great causes championed by him: religious freedom, the unimpeded navigation of the Mississippi and the adoption of a national Constitution, were won before he was elected to the presidency as successor to Jefferson. His term of office as Chief Executive, although marked by some useful accomplishments, was an unhappy interlude in a life which otherwise paralleled the course of American history for eighty-five years in a comparatively tranquil manner. His talents, as a legislator and as a student, were peculiarly fitted to the cabinet and most unsuited to the field. When he was thrust by the importunity of the reckless War Hawks into war with Great Britain, he proved to be as ill equipped for its martial exigencies as were the inadequate military and naval forces under his command.

Fortunately for him, the Peace of Ghent closed the last contest in which the two great English-speaking nations have found themselves in opposition, and left the respective belligerents in almost precisely the same position, territorially and otherwise, occupied by them before their fruitless resort to arms. It is true that American national pride was chagrined over the failure to capture Canada. The optimisitic Western Lochinvars had prophesied that this operation would be merely a matter of a few weeks marching and countermarching, but there were compensations in the patriotic reflection that American privateersmen had more than held their own when pitted against the frigates of the Mistress of the Seas, and that American backwoodsmen, under Andrew Jackson, had inflicted fearful slaughter on Pakenham's red-coated regulars at New Orleans. The coming of peace opened up a bright vista of commercial and agricultural prosperity. The sectional bitterness engendered by "Mr. Madison's War," together with the threatened secession of certain New England states and the near-bankruptcy of the federal government, were quickly forgotten, so that the popularity of the President, no longer in eclipse, lighted his last years in office with a golden glow.

James Madison was born in Virginia in 1751, of good native stock long established there. His father, a planter, was County Lieutenant of Orange, a responsible post. From him the son inherited the estate of Montpelier where in rare intervals of leisure he attended to the farming of his twenty-five hundred acres and led the life of a typical Virginia country gentleman. He loved Montpelier with a passionate devotion; in the latter part of his life the extravagant hospitality he extended to visitors almost ruined him.

His early schooling was under a Scotch master. Then followed private instruction by the clergyman of his parish, until his entrance at the age of seventeen into the College of New Jersey, now Princeton University, which had less than one hundred students on its rolls.

After his graduation from Princeton he continued to reside at the college for another year, studying Hebrew and following an ecclesiastical course, with the apparent intention of becoming a minister. At this period his health was poor. Soon after reaching his majority he wrote to a friend: "I am too dull and infirm now to look out for any extraordinary things in this world, for I think my sensations for many months past have intimated to me not to expect a long or healthy life." His presentiments of ill-health and of an early dissolution were happily so erroneous that he seems to have remained hearty until he was crippled at an advanced age by rheumatism.

When he graduated from college, his temperament was moody and serious, and his gravity unusual in one of his years. Perhaps it was the influence of the stern Old Testament writers which caused him, at this period, to advise his friend William Bradford against an addiction to the reading of belles lettres, with the observation: "I myself used to have too great a hankering after the amusing studies. Poetry, wit, and criticism, romances, plays, etc., captivated me much; but I began to discover that they deserve but a small portion of a mortal's time, and that something more substantial, more durable, and more profitable, befits a riper age. It would be exceedingly improper for a laboring man to have nothing but flowers in his garden, or to determine to eat nothing but sweet meats and confections. Equally absurd would it be for a scholar and a man of business to make up his whole library with books of fancy, and feed his mind with nothing but such luscious performances."

Soon after his return to Virginia he appears to have abandoned any thought of devoting himself to the ministry, although he continued to study the Scriptures assiduously. At the age of twenty-three he was already contemptuous of ecclesiastical bigotry. "Religious bondage," he said, "shackles and debilitates the mind, and unfits it for every noble enterprise, every expanded project."

Having been rejected for the army in 1775, because of physical shortcomings, he acted as Chairman of the Committee of Public Safety for Orange County. The following year he was elected to the Virginia House of Delegates. He failed of re-election, chiefly owing, it is said, to his refusal to treat the voters with rum, a gratuity to which they considered themselves as entitled as did sailors to a double allotment of grog before engaging in battle. The same year, however, he was chosen a member of the Council of State, an advisory cabinet for the Governor, and in 1779 was elected a delegate to the Continental Congress.

While in this Congress, he suggested a scheme to care for the interest on the public debt by apportioning that part not met by import duties among states on the basis of population, but counting a slave as being only three-fifths of a white man in such an enumeration. This principle was adopted, and reaffirmed four years later in the provisions of the federal Constitution. In the course of debates on the subject, savage attacks were made on behalf of and against Madison's proposal, some delegates wishing to disregard slaves entirely in any calculation of population, on the ground they were chattels personal or real estate and were no more to be considered than if they were cattle or horses, while certain Northern Congressmen contended they were producers of wealth and should be rated for taxation the same as white men.

After the expiration of his term in Congress in 1783 he returned to Virginia and pursued the study of law. Upon being elected the next year to the House of Delegates, he repaired to Richmond, where in 1785 he introduced Thomas Jefferson's famous bill for establishing religious freedom in Virginia, and was largely instrumental in bringing about its passage. Madison was a churchman, although not a communicant. He was never accused, as was Jefferson, of infidel tendencies, but like his friend was unalterably opposed to any alliance between church and state, or to any sectarian discriminations.

Madison was from early manhood an earnest advocate of the free navigation of the Mississippi River and he drew, in 1780, the paper of instructions to John Jay on that subject.

While a member of his state legislature, Madison, as Chairman of its Judiciary Committee, performed an essential labor in transmuting the old colonial statutes into a body of modern law, but his chief usefulness was in preparing the way for the meeting of the Annapolis Convention, the forerunner of the great Constitutional Convention at Philadelphia. To the latter Convention he was sent by Virginia as a delegate, together with George Washington, Edmund Randolph, John Blair, George Mason, George Wythe and James McClury. The object of its deliberations, namely the replacement of the weak Articles of Confederation, under which Robert Morris said the authority of Congress was almost "reduced to a metaphysical idea," by a strong federal compact, was ardently advocated by him. Perhaps more than any contemporary statesman except George Washington and Alexander Hamilton he realized its necessity. Before the convocation of the Convention he had written and submitted to his Virginia colleagues a paper, *The Vices of the Political System of the United States,* calling attention to the weakness of a confederacy acting upon states only and not directly upon individuals.

His labors in the Philadelphia Convention made him "The Father of the Constitution." His sincerity in debate, and his stores of apposite learning regarding the charters of other countries, both ancient and modern, in which branch of study no other American except John Adams was his equal, were powerful factors in framing the Constitution as finally adopted.

In conjunction with other Virginia delegates he had prepared the "Virginia Plan," the basis of the Convention's deliberations. It is interesting to note how far from the present conception of the democratic ideal in politics were some of the proposals supported by Madison. He advocated a property qualification for electors of Senators, but opposed an equality of votes by states in the Senate, suggesting proportional representation in both houses of Congress; he believed in a strong central government with a veto upon state legislation, with control of the state militias and with power even to coerce a state; and he adverted to the dangers of republican government, opposing the proposition to restrict the right of originating money bills to the popular branch.

His views on suffrage would now be considered wholly reactionary. "The Freeholders of the country," he said, "would be the safest depositories of Republican liberty. In future times, a great majority of the people will not only be without land, but any other sort of property. These will either combine under the influence of their common situation; in which case, the rights of property and the public liberty will not be secure in their hands, or, which is more probable, they will become the tools of opulence and ambition; in which case there will be equal danger on another side."

Always an opponent of slavery, he disapproved, like many other Southerners, the compromise allowing the unlimited importation of Negroes for twenty years, and the right to recover slaves, no matter where they took refuge.

Madison's careful and copious notes on the proceedings of the Convention are an invaluable record. After its adjournment he wrote, in conjunction with Hamilton and Jay, the *Federalist*, without whose influence it is probable the Constitution would never have been ratified: of the eighty-five papers, certainly twenty, and perhaps nine others, were written by Madison. But the greatest struggle of his life was his championship of the new compact in the Constitutional Convention of Virginia. If it had been defeated there, its adoption by sufficient other states to have made it operative would have failed. In opposition to him was Patrick Henry, the greatest natural orator ever produced in the United States, the idol of the Virginia populace, and such prominent Virginians as James Monroe, John Tyler, Benjamin Harrison and William Grayson, as well as George Mason, a statesman who stood second in his native state to Washington.

Henry opposed the fundamental principle of the new Constitution changing a confederation of independent states into a mixed federal government, while Mason deplored the absence of a Bill of Rights, the great powers granted to the President and to Congress, the sanction of the slave trade, the authority embodied in the Senate and the insufficient representation in the House, all of which he felt would lead to an aristocratic rather than a republican system of government. The Convention was in sesssion for nearly a month, and the issue was always doubtful until Madison carried the day by a vote of 89 to 79. At no other time in his life did he so admirably exhibit his powers of persuasion, eliciting from John Marshall, who attended the sessions of the Convention, the statement: "If convincing is eloquence, he was the most eloquent man I ever heard."

His opposition to Henry cost him the hostility of the latter; he was defeated by Richard Henry Lee and Grayson in his attempt to be elected one of the first Senators from Virginia, although shortly afterwards he was elected to the House of Representatives over James Monroe, who had been nominated as a moderate anti-Federalist.

Madison became the leader of the new House of Representatives. Washington, during his first term as President, frequently called upon him for counsel, once saying to him: "I am troublesome, but you must excuse me; ascribe it to friendship and confidence." When Washington did not expect to be a candidate for a second term, he asked Madison to draft him a farewell address, extracts from which he used five years later in his famous last message. At one time he wished to have Madison in the Cabinet, but later withdrew his confidence in him, as a result of their differences of political opinion and of Madison's hostility to important administration measures.

Madison approved the payment in full of the foreign debts but advocated a discrimination between original and actual holders of the domestic debt. This antagonized Hamilton, and while it did credit to Madison's desire for equitable treatment of the debt holders, was so impracticable as to reflect on his good judgment. He was the strongest opponent in Congress of the assumption of the state debts, by which Virginia would not benefit, and which would be of utility to no Southern state except South Carolina. He also opposed the Bank Bill and wrote for the President a veto message regarding it. This was never used, since Washington finally decided to sign the act.

From having been in favor of a strong central government, Madison became head of the congressional opposition to the Hamiltonian system, and, probably due in large measure to Jefferson's influence, embraced a policy of strict constitutional construction. Although for many years he was a party man, it may be doubted that he was ever as partisan in his political principles as Jefferson.

After the close of the War of 1812 he abandoned several favorite Republican tenets. When the struggle for nullification by South Carolina was a burning issue, he came out as an ardent Unionist. His last counsel to his country was: "The advice nearest to my heart and deepest in my convictions is, that the union of the States be cherished and perpetuated."

Like Jefferson, under the impact of great events Madison ceased to be a strict constructionist and favored both the Louisiana Purchase and the embargo. But these were later developments. While he was in congressional opposition, he discovered an "Anglified complexion" in Washington's neutrality proclamation of 1793, and denounced the Jay treaty. He was above all a Virginian and an agrarian aristocrat, with a dislike for the keenly developed commercial instincts of the New Englanders and a distrust for Hamilton's program of building up a class of moneyed magnates who would in return for favors received be expected to support a centralized authority.

In Congress, Madison proposed nine amendments to the Constitution; their principles were adopted by the states in the form of the first ten amendments of that instrument. Largely at his prompting, Freneau's famous anti-Federalist paper, the *National Gazette*, was established. Madison wrote for it, but never indulged, as did Hamilton in the Federalist journals, in personal animadversions upon political opponents.

On the day that Jefferson became Vice-President in 1797 Madison retired from Congress, but continued to be an acute observer of passing events. The following year, in connection with the Virginia Resolutions, he expressed his opposition to the Alien and Sedition Laws, declaring that the legislature viewed "the powers of the Federal Government as resulting from the compact to which the States are parties, as limited by the plain sense and intention of the instrument constituting that compact; as no further valid than they are authorized by the grants enumerated in that compact." He further declared: "In case of a deliberate, palpable, and dangerous exercise of other powers, not granted by the said compact, the States, who are parties thereto, have the right and are in duty bound to interpose for arresting the progress of the evil, and for maintaining within their respective limits, the authorities, rights and liberties appertaining to them."

This language, which was of course written before John Marshall in no uncertain terms let it be known that the Supreme Court would be the final judge of infractions of the Constitution, was not nearly as extreme as the terms used by Jefferson in his resolutions for the Kentucky legislature, which asserted that acts in palpable infraction of the Constitution are null and void, that state legislatures are competent not only to declare them but to make them so, and that states could secede from the Union rather than submit to such acts, if they should be forcibly carried into execution.

On several occasions Madison explicitly disclaimed his adherence to the doctrine enunciated by Jefferson in the Kentucky Resolutions, and also, at a late period of his life, stated that the Virginia Resolutions were not meant to assert a right in any one state to arrest or annul an act of the general government, as that is a right that can only belong to the states collectively. Nullification and secession he characterized as "twin heresies that ought to be buried in the same grave."

When Jefferson became President in 1801 Madison, his closest friend and disciple, inevitably became Secretary of State. This office he continued to occupy until his own election as President. His part in the conduct of foreign affairs was, in effect, a subordinate one, since Jefferson himself dictated the policies of the State Department. In 1806 Madison published *An Examination of the British Doctrine which Subjects to Capture a Neutral Trade not open in Time of Peace,* an argument against the highly contentious subject of Great Britain's Rule of War of 1756. He handled the negotiations attending the Louisiana Purchase with requisite skill, and directed the diplomatic business of the country with satisfactory diligence, but was not, as his presidential career was conclusively to prove, endowed with real executive ability.

In dealing with foreign Ambassadors and Ministers, his communications were temperate, well phrased and dignified, but betrayed a trait deemed by Henry Adams to be characteristic of him: "A willingness to irritate and a reluctance to strike." Temporizing opportunism in foreign affairs would, in any case have been imposed on him by Jefferson's predilection for such action, but when Madison himself became President, and, because of Smith's incapacity was virtually his own Secretary of State, he continued the same ineffective line of policy.

Upon Jefferson's refusal, in 1808, to be a candidate for a third term, he favored Madison as his successor. Although Madison was bitterly opposed by George Clinton and by John Randolph of Roanoke, he was elected President, defeating C. C. Pinckney of South Carolina, the Federalist candidate, by 122 votes to 47. George Clinton, who had been Vice-President during Jefferson's second term, was again elected to that office.

Madison desired to make Albert Gallatin, possibly the ablest man in the Republican party, Secretary of State, but a powerful senatorial faction forced him to name Robert Smith of Maryland to the place, leaving Gallatin at the Treasury. With the exception of the latter, the Cabinet was composed of mediocrities; William Eustis of Boston was Secretary of War; Paul Hamilton of South Carolina, Secretary of the Navy; and Caesar Rodney of Delaware, Attorney General.

The cabal of Robert Smith's friends in the Senate, known as the "Invincibles," in spite of Smith's preferment over Gallatin continued its hostility to Gallatin. They opposed his financial policies, and even rejected some of Madison's nominations, leaving him during much of his first term in such a doubtful position of authority that John Randolph asserted he was "President *de jure* only."

However, in foreign affairs it seemed that the new President would achieve a signal success. He had inherited from Jefferson the commercial policy that had subjected the United States to countless outrages by both France and Great Britain. But within six weeks of his inauguration it appeared as if Madison had reached a settlement with Erskine, the British Minister. Erskine, disregarding certain conditions that his government had commissioned him to insist upon, agreed that Great Britain would exempt American vessels from the obnoxious Orders in Council, if the United States would annul all commercial interdicts against England and maintain the Nonintercourse Acts against France, so long as the Milan or Berlin decrees remained in force.

This supposed agreement was hailed with joy by the Americans, their ships hastened to clear for foreign ports, and they at once prepared for a great maritime trade revival. Madison's popularity became commanding. The former antagonism to England was diverted against Napoleon. Unfortunately, as soon as Erskine's action was reported to Westminster, Canning repudiated the agreement. Erskine was replaced by Jackson, a diplomat whose behavior exceeded in tactlessness almost anything recorded in American diplomatic annals. This gentleman arrived in Washington in September 1809, accompanied by his fashionable Prussian wife. His complaint that Washington "resembles more nearly Hampstead Heath than any other place I ever saw" was too true not to be galling.

Unfortunately for his career, Jackson did not confine his criticism to the physical appearance of his post. He first insinuated, then repeated the charge that the President must have known the precise terms on which Erskine had been authorized to deal with the American government. This was too much for the usually patient Madison, who terminated Jackson's American mission on November 8, 1809.

The position of the United States in 1810 as respects France and Great Britain was as unsatisfactory and humiliating as it had been for some years past. The ambitious British Secretary for Foreign Affairs, Canning, persisted in the course instituted by his predecessors of sanctioning wholesale impressment from the crews of American merchant vessels, and of confiscating the property of American citizens. Prior to the War of 1812 it is estimated that about six thousand American sailors, who claimed to be citizens of the United States, were impressed by the British without being given an opportunity to prove their citizenship.

Nor were the French backward in aggression. By Napoleon's edicts and decrees, neutral ships became lawful prizes and were everywhere seized, so that it was as unsafe for them to sight the French as the British flag.

Madison, however, continued to hope that by commercial restrictions he could bring France and Great Britain to reason. For a year and a half the United States acted on the assumption that France had recalled her decrees, but actually they were not repealed until May 1812 when war between the United States and England was inevitable. Then Napoleon, delighted with the prospect of Britain's embarrassment, revoked them retroactively, in a document "purported to be dated April 1811."

Despite the disturbing events of his first term Madison made little or no effort to prepare the country, either morally or materially, for the belligerent crisis which was to mark its close. The most significant achievement of these four years, with the exception of the declaration of war in 1812, was his proclamation of October 27, 1810, announcing that Governor Claiborne would take possession of West Florida, to the river Perdido, in the name of the United States, and reasserting the claim that West Florida had been included in the Louisiana Purchase. Early in 1811, Congress, not to be outdone, authorized the President to take possession of East Florida and to hold it pending negotiations. In the same year the first Bank of the United States came to an end, and Madison, despite the pleas of Gallatin, refused to force the renewal of its charter, thereby making almost impossible the proper financing of the war which was shortly to ensue.

In spite of the real aggravations to which our trade and commerce had been subjected, the desire of the agrarian pioneers and frontiersmen for expansion was the determining factor in bringing on hostilities against England. Since France had no territories on the North American continent, they were willing to neglect her affronts. The Southern planters wanted the Floridas, which, regardless of presidential and congressional proclamations, they feared might still be considered appendages of the Crown of Castile, while the Northern agriculturists wanted Canada. The Western planters wanted not only a goodly slice of Canada but the right to occupy, free of possible British interference, the remaining Indian hunting grounds of the Northwest. In the Eastern states opposition to war was virulent, in the Middle and Southern states there was division of sentiment, but in the West the desire for battle seemed unanimous. Essentially it was an agriculturists' war that finally resulted.

A powerful group of young men in Congress, known to history as the War Hawks, ardently demanded war. Their leader was thirty-four-year-old Henry Clay, "Harry of the West," who though born in Virginia was a Westerner by choice and domicile, and typified the pioneer spirit of expansion. Besides great natural eloquence, Clay possessed an ingratiating and lovable disposition and a magnetism which made him an extraordinary leader of public opinion. Elected Speaker the first day he entered the House, he continued to hold the position as long as he was a member of that body. His capacity for inspiring affection was quite extraordinary. "I don't like Clay," Calhoun once said; "he is a bad man, an impostor, a creature of wicked schemes. I won't speak to him, but, by God, I love him." His supporters confidently boasted that Canada could be conquered in six weeks.

In the midst of the agitation for war in 1812, the question of Madison's nomination for a second term was decided. He had two serious rivals in Dewitt Clinton, Mayor of New York, and James Monroe, long his friend, who had replaced the incompetent Mr. Smith as Secretary of State. Both of these rival candidates were in favor of an immediate declaration of war. So also, it now appeared, was Madison. In April 1812 he announced a general embargo as a preliminary step; on June 1 he sent a war message to Congress. The die was cast. Madison was nominated by a congressional caucus. In November he was re-elected by 128 votes to DeWitt Clinton's 89, Elbridge Gerry, of Gerrymandering fame, being elected Vice-President.

Madison's recommendation of war with England was based on four grounds: Orders in Council, paper blockades, violation of the three-mile limit, and impressment, of which the last was the most important, being considered the great object to be settled by a peace treaty. On June 18, 1812, war was declared by a vote of 79 to 49 in the House, and 19 to 13 in the Senate.

Five days later, as yet knowing nothing of this declaration of hostilities, the British Parliament, always obtuse in its dealings with American affairs, belatedly repealed the Orders in Council. A conflict was therefore joined which speedier action by Britain would easily have averted.

The people of the United States had little reason to feel sanguine over the outcome of these hostilities. Disaffection immediately raised its head. In New England church bells were tolled and flags hung at half mast when the news of war was published. Even the Northern shipowners, who had scornfully said that Madison could not be "kicked into war," now opposed it. We had made no preparations to deal with the emergency confronting us. John Randolph had ridiculed the idea of Congress carrying on a war. He was evidently correct in his estimate of his colleagues, for on July 16, 1812, Congress adjourned without voting war taxes or providing for any increase in the navy, jubilant over the delusion that a peace treaty would shortly be carried into Quebec for signature on the bright points of American bayonets.

Most of our eight thousand troops were located at Indian posts in the West. Our naval force scarcely deserved the name. In an army never exceeding thirty thousand effectives, the scourge of sickness was to be more deadly than the bullets of the enemy. Of all the troops, regular and militia, engaged in action in the course of the war, not many more than fifteen hundred were killed, and about thirty-five hundred were wounded.

In the beginning, the War Department, in addition to the Secretary, consisted of about a dozen clerks. It is estimated by one historian that during the conflict the United States called out approximately fifty thousand regulars, ten thousand volunteers and four hundred and fifty thousand militiamen to compete with a British force which at the time of its greatest strength did not exceed seventeen thousand disciplined soldiers. In respect of marksmanship, however, our soldiers displayed an indubitable superiority over the British, and the same proved true of our seamen whose efficiency in gunfire was about twice that of their enemies.

With internal disaffection openly brewing, with a President temperamentally unsuited to ride a whirlwind or direct a storm, with a supine Congress and a skeleton army and navy, American hopes could be realized only through a high quality of generalship.

As senior Major General, the President unfortunately appointed Henry Dearborn, Secretary of War in the Jefferson Administration, who had latterly served in the customhouse at Boston. A subordinate officer in the Revolution, he was afterwards a Colonel in a New Hampshire regiment. Under him, as ranking generals, were the detestable James Wilkinson, Wade Hampton and Thomas Pinckney of South Carolina, and William Hull, Governor of Michigan Territory. All of them were well advanced in years and more or less inept at commanding men in battle.

In December 1812, Secretary Eustis, who had been a surgeon in the Revolutionary War, resigned his position. Monroe was made Secretary of War pro tempore, in addition to carrying on his regular duties as Secretary of State. Before he could reorganize the department, political jealousies caused his retirement from his temporary position, and General John Armstrong of New York formerly Minister to France, took his place.

At the opening of the war our naval forces, consisting of six first-class frigates and twice as many smaller vessels as opposed to Britain's force of almost a thousand warships, were even less adequate to the emergency than our land forces.

Although there were in the beginning only about five thousand British regulars in Canada, which had a total population of five hundred thousand, our troops made little headway against them. Less than two months after war was declared General Hull surrendered Detroit to the British, causing the greatest loss of territory ever suffered by the United States. He was promptly convicted by court-martial for cowardice. Two separate forces of American militia on critical occasions refused to leave their native soil and fight in Canada, contending that they had enlisted to defend their homes, and not to invade a neighboring country. The conquest of Canada, as a consequence, became almost immediately a lost hope.

The greatest disaster of the war was of course the occupation of Washington by the British. Although an attack upon the capital had long been a possibility, the Executive and Congress had provided only a negligible body of regulars, some inexperienced militiamen and several gunboats as a defense force. General William H. Winder of Maryland was in command of our troops, and after the British

General Ross had landed about forty miles southeast of Washington, on the Patuxent River, Winder prepared to head him off. On August 14, 1814, the two armies met at Bladensburg in Winder's own state. The President and several of his Cabinet had ridden out from Washington to witness the encounter.

The President carried a pair of pistols in his holsters but had no occasion to use them, for the firing soon became so fierce that the Commander-in-Chief observed to his Secretary of State and to his Secretary of War: "It would now be proper for us to retire to the rear, leaving the military movements to military men."

Starting for Washington he was soon overtaken by some of the militia who, like Japanese soldiers whom tradition does not allow to retreat, were "advancing backward." At three in the afternoon he reached the White House but did not rest there. Several hours later he fled across the Potomac. Meanwhile the British had dispersed the American troops; arrived in Washington, a town of eight thousand inhabitants, they set fire to the Capitol, the White House and other public buildings.

Mrs. Madison, having lingered at the White House to take away the original draft of the Declaration of Independence and the canvas of Gilbert Stuart's portrait of Washington, as well as to confide her macaw to the French porter, was almost captured. The British feared to encamp at the scene of their wanton conflagration, and three days later the President returned to view the ruined executive mansion.

At sea, in satisfactory contrast to the major disasters on land, the Americans gained some notable victories. The battle of Lake Erie, best known now through Perry's famous despatch, of September 10, 1813: "We have met the enemy and they are ours," gave the British a deadly sample of American naval gunnery.

Our privateers were ubiquitous, preying upon the enemy even in Far Eastern waters. It is estimated that sixteen hundred British merchantmen fell victims to them and to our warships. The *Trueblooded Yankee*, for example, took a town on the coast of Scotland, burned seven vessels in the harbor and captured twenty-seven vessels in thirty-seven days. The moral value of the American naval victories, such as the battering given by the frigate *Constitution* to the *Guerrière* and the *Java,* and the successes of our privateersmen were of great service in bringing about a demand by British traders and shipowners for peace.

It is true that before the end of the war the British at last brought their immense naval strength to bear so efficiently that only the *Constitution* and four smaller vessels of the United States Navy were at sea. We had lost some of our bravest commanders, such as Lawrence, whose dying words were: "Don't give up the ship!" Our coast was finally blockaded completely, the exports from New York dropping from $12,000,000, in 1811, to $200,000 in 1814, those of Virginia from $4,800,000 to $17,500. But our preceding naval exploits had instilled in the British a wholesome and new respect for American fighting methods not quickly to be forgotten.

The greatest victory on land or sea gained by either force was that won by the Americans at the battle of New Orleans on January 18, 1815, after the treaty of peace had been signed at Ghent but before the news of it had reached the South. There Andrew Jackson, commanding a body of frontiersmen, inflicted one of the most crushing defeats ever suffered by British regulars, when he repulsed with heavy slaughter an assault by Sir Edward Pakenham's army, which attacked, in close column formation by a frontal movement, earthworks protected by artillery and riflemen.

In retrospect, the most painful aspect of the War of 1812 was the conduct of some of our own citizens, especially in New England, who openly opposed the belligerent operations of our government. Henry Adams states that the intercourse between the Eastern states and the enemy was notorious, that many persons in New England actually lent money to the enemy by purchasing British bills of credit, and also sold supplies to the British and Canadians.

No financial support of any consequence was forthcoming from New England; the Governor and Legislature of Connecticut refused to supply their quota of militiamen, advising the President that "the State of Connecticut is a free, sovereign, and independent State; that the United States are a confederacy of States." There was a movement in some of the Northern states to make a separate peace with Great Britain; prominent men advocated secession from the Union. The seditious proceedings of the Hartford Convention were only harmless because of the conclusion of peace discredited its sponsors. Party spirit, during the war, between Federalists and Republicans ran high.

War had scarcely commenced before both governments gave consideration to proposals for an immediate peace. Even though the Emperor of Russia had offered to act as a mediator, nothing was accomplished until, in January 1814, Madison received a direct tender from London to discuss peace terms, with Ghent as the place of negotiation.

The American Commissioners charged with the negotiation were John Quincy Adams, Albert Gallatin, Henry Clay, James A. Bayard and Jonathan Russell. Despite internal dissensions, they were eminently successful in their deliberations, although they had to abandon their demand for a cessation of impressment as a sine qua non of peace. This subject was omitted from the treaty with the understanding that as the European wars were apparently over England would not need to continue the practice. The treaty, signed the day before Christmas 1814, decided none of the grievances that had caused the hostilities, leaving all claims on both sides open for future settlement.

The termination of the war found the finances of the United States government in a sad condition. The total amount of war debt was about $80,500,000, which increased the total national indebtedness at the end of 1815 to $126,000,000. After the capture of Washington the specie of the country had become concentrated in the New England banks; every bank in the Middle and Southern states suspended specie payments, and state banks and various corporations floated quantities of local paper, leaving the country at large without any stable currency.

In January 1814 the interest upon the public debt remained unpaid; the government was in arrears to the army and navy to the extent of about thirteen million dollars. A year later the treasury was unable to meet the drafts drawn by General Jackson, or the demands of the paymaster at New Orleans. The complete failure of the government's credit seemed to presage national bankruptcy. For its bonds floated between 1812 and 1816, totaling over eighty million dollars, the treasury received only about thirty-four million dollars, computed in specie. Prosperity was not long however in following the return of peace.

In 1816 the President signed a bill re-establishing the Bank of the United States, and another enacting a tariff on imports of about twenty per cent. Under the stress of circumstances the Republicans had adopted many Federalist doctrines. The purchase of Louisiana and the laying of the embargo had undermined their policy of strict construction; the declaration of war had forced their abandonment of a position of unalterable opposition to military and naval expenditures; the financial consequences of the war had induced them to re-establish the national bank and to impose direct taxes and a protective tariff.

On March 14, 1817, Madison retired from the presidency, turning the office over to James Monroe, who had after the retirement of Gallatin been the most conspicuous member of the Cabinet.

At the close of Madison's term the population of the country probably numbered about 8,750,000 persons. The Southern states were very prosperous, the Middle states were affluent. Business in New England was extremely depressed but was soon to recuperate. The unity of the nation seemed to have been achieved; thenceforth its interests were to diverge further and further from those of European countries. The chastisement of the Algerian pirates by a naval force under Commodore Decatur, in 1815, had freed us from our only outstanding quarrel abroad.

As he jolted over the roads from Washington to Montpelier, the retiring President had reason to be pleased with the condition of the charge just entrusted to Monroe.

Madison's life at Montpelier was like that of other prominent Virginia planters. He was the President of the local Agricultural Society, experimented with crops, raised mules, kept a stallion, stocked his woods with English pheasants, indulged his taste for gardening, sold hams, bacon, tongues and barrels of beef and pork, and gave himself up to the unceasing occupations of country life. His visitors came in swarms; on one occasion Mrs. Madison and he entertained ninety persons for dinner on the lawn.

His chief recreation continued, as always, to be in reading. He had a fine library, which he bequeathed to the University of Virginia, where it was unfortunately burned in 1895. He had always read largely in books treating of the science of government, and was much interested in natural history as well as in new inventions. When Jefferson was Minister to France, Madison requested of him the occasional purchase of "rare and valuable books," saying, "I will only particularize my wish of whatever may throw light on the general constitution and *droit public* of the several confederacies which have existed." On April 27, 1785, he wrote to Jefferson: "I received the two pamphlets on animal magnetism and the last aeronautic expedition, together with the phosphoretic matches. These articles were a great treat to my curiosity."

A year later he told Jefferson that he had "a little itch to gain a smattering in chymistry. Will you be kind eno' to pick up some good elementary treatise for me, with a good dictionary of moderate size, unless the chymical volume in the encyclopedie should be judged a competent provision." In 1787 he sent to George Washington, to be forwarded to the inquisitive Catherine the Great of Russia, incomplete vocabularies of the Cherokee and Choctaw dialects, in response to an inquiry made by that Empress for "a comparative view of the aborigines of the New Continent and of the N.E. parts of the old, through the medium of their respective tongues." He read Buffon with great pleasure, and corresponded with Jefferson on outdoor subjects, writing from New York to the latter in 1787: "I doubt whether the Virginia Red Birds are found in this part of America. Opossums are not rare in the milder parts of New Jersey, but are very rare this far Northward."

He was always interested in problems of education, and directed that of Jefferson's nephews while his friend was absent in France. He proposed to Congress, as had Washington, the formation of a national university, with equal lack of success. Associated with Jefferson in the founding of the University of Virginia, he became its Rector at Jefferson's death.

Madison and Monroe at one time became speculators in land together, and bought some wild lands in the Mohawk region, near the headwaters of the Hudson River, but the enterprise apparently did not result in any great profit. At a period when many public officials speculated in public funds Madison steadfastly refused to do so. His last days would have been passed in comparative penury had Congress not, at the suggestion of President Jackson, bought for thirty thousand dollars his manuscript of the debates in Congress and the Convention. In 1846 Congress bought the remaining letters and private correspondence of Madison, as they also did of Jefferson and Hamilton, paying in each case twenty-five thousand dollars.

On the subject of slavery Madison held liberal views. That he was consistently kind to his own one hundred odd slaves was public knowledge; to one of them, his valet Paul Jennings, he was a hero; "Mr. Madison, I think," said Jennings, "was one of the best men that ever lived." He disliked his dependence on the labor of slaves, and, when it was proposed in the Constitutional Convention to lay a tax on their importation, he expressed his distaste for admitting "in the Constitution the idea that there could be property in men."

In the same convention he worked vigorously, though unsuccessfully, with George Mason in opposition to the proslavery policies of South Carolina and other Southern states. In 1819 he advocated a gradual emancipation of bondmen, thinking the government should, by the sale of vacant territory, raise a sum requisite to recompense their owners and colonize the freed slaves in a suitable part of Africa. He considered that continent "the appropriate destination for the unhappy race among us," although, earlier, he had recommended their settlement in the Western territories.

Madison was a man of insignificant presence, which was not relieved by any elegance of dress; he habitually wore sober clothes, usually a plain black cloth coat and knee breeches with buckles, his light hair being combed back, powdered and worn in a queue behind, until with advanced years he became bald and covered his head with a gray-and-white cap. He was five feet six and a quarter inches in height, with irregular features and hazel eyes set in a pale face. His body was thin and delicate—Washington Irving said he was a "withered little Apple-John,"—but in spite of his youthful ill-health it did him good service for eighty-five years. He suffered occasionally from digestive troubles and in the last few years of his life was so disabled by rheumatism that he lived in one room.

From the record of his forebears he had every reason to expect a long life; his father had died at the age of seventy-seven and his mother at ninety-seven.

Madison's demeanor was invariably modest and diffident. Probably because of his small stature he affected when walking a springing step. His usual gravity relaxed when he was with friends, and he was a delightful and witty conversationalist. By some of his contemporaries he was considered argumentative to satiety, but if such was the case, he made no public display of this failing. Although a good debater, he shrank from addressing a large assemblage and read his first inaugural speech in a voice so low that few could hear him.

Madison was in no other respect so fortunate as he proved to be in the choice of his wife, Mrs. Dorothy Payne Todd, a widow. In the course of American history it may be doubted whether any mistress of the White House ever possessed the quality of social charm in such a supreme degree as did Dolly Madison. She was born in 1772, of excellent Virginia parentage. Both her father and mother were members of the Society of Friends, and her father, having decided to free his slaves, sold his plantation in Virginia and removed to Philadelphia. There Miss Payne married John Todd, a lawyer, whose demise of yellow fever three years later, shortly followed by that of her younger child, left her with a single boy to care for, who, in spite of the lifelong devotion of his mother and his stepfather, was to prove a worthless, shiftless fellow. Aaron Burr had made the acquaintance of the widow and introduced "the great little Madison" to her. Seven years after their marriage, when Madison was named Secretary of State, his wife, owing to President Jefferson being a widower, became the first lady in Washington society and continued to occupy that position for the following sixteen years.

After the death of Madison his widow, who had no children by him, quitted Montpelier to reside in Washington, where she died in her eighty-third year.

Madison's last days were made painful by disease. As he entered his eighty-sixth year he grew very weary, and in a little more than three months glided almost imperceptibly into another world.

James Monroe

Born: March 16, 1758.
Joined Continental Army: 1776.
Elected to Virginia House of Delegates: 1782.
Served in Congress of the Confederation: 1783-86.
Married: 1786.
Member of Virginia House of Delegates: 1787.
Elected to United States Senate: 1790.
Appointed Minister to France: 1794.
Recalled as Minister to France: 1796.
Governor of Virginia: 1799-1802.
Sent on special mission to France, Spain and England: 1803.
Commissioned regular Minister to England, 1803.
Returned to United States: 1807.
Elected to Virginia House of Delegates: 1810.
Governor of Virginia: 1811.
Secretary of State of United States: 1811-17.
President of the United States: 1817-25.
Member Virginia Constitutional Convention: 1829.
Died: July 4, 1831.

JAMES MONROE

JAMES MONROE, fifth President of the United States, was the fourth Virginian to hold that office. Before the events occurred which were forever to link his name with the promulgation of a great doctrine, he had served the public faithfully and long. Prior to reaching his majority he had been wounded while an officer of the Continental army, at the Battle of Trenton. Elected to the Virginia House of Delegates at the age of twenty-four he began his career in the Congress of the Confederation a year later. During the rest of his life he was almost continuously in the public service, as state legislator, United States Senator, Governor of Virginia, Minister to France and to England, Secretary of State and temporarily of War, and finally as President.

James Monroe was born on March 16, 1758, near Monroe's Creek, an affluent of the Potomac. He was of Scotch-Welsh-Virginia blood. His forbears had been long established in Virginia, where they were respectable but not conspicuous members of the landed gentry.

His career at William and Mary, the second oldest college in America, was interrupted by the outbreak of the Revolutionary War; for in company with several professors and a number of other students, among whom was John Marshall, he speedily volunteered for military service and joined our forces at New York as a Lieutenant in a Virginia regiment commanded by Colonel Hugh Mercer. At Trenton a ball passed into his shoulder, where it was to remain all his life, and for a time incapacitated him for the field, although he was thereafter, during the war, to attain the rank of Lieutenant Colonel.

His military career was valuable to him in many ways, not the least being the favorable commendation elicited by his soldierly qualities from Washington, who in 1779 wrote to an official concerning him as follows:

Dear Sir,—I very sincerely lament that the situation of our service will not permit us to do justice to the merits of Major Monroe, who will deliver you this, by placing him in the army upon some satisfactory footing. But as he is on the point of leaving us, and expresses the intention of going to the Southward, where a new scene has opened, it is with pleasure I take occasion to express to you the high opinion I have of his worth. The zeal he discovered by entering the service at an early period, the character he supported in his regiment, and the manner in which he distinguished himself at Trenton, where he received a wound, induced me to appoint him to a Captaincy in one of the additional regiments. This regiment failing from the difficulty of recruiting, he entered into Lord Stirling's family, and has served two campaigns as a volunteer aid to his Lordship. He has, in every instance, maintained the reputation of a brave, active, and sensible officer. As we cannot introduce him into the Continental line, it were to be wished that the State could do something for him, to enable him to follow the bent of his military inclination, and render service to his country. If an event of this kind could take place, it would give me particular pleasure; as the esteem I have for him, and a regard to his merit, conspire to make me earnestly wish to see him provided for in some handsome way.   I am etc.

GEO. WASHINGTON

After a term in the legislature in his native state, from the county of King George, the Virginia Assembly chose Monroe as a member of its delegation, headed by Jefferson, to the Continental Congress. His previous close contact with Jefferson, who had directed his early legal studies, was strengthened by this association and left a lasting impress on the younger man. Jefferson was, thenceforth, not only his friend but his political and philosophical preceptor; even when Monroe was President he continued to court and cherish the elder's advice. In 1789 he acquired property near Monticello in order to be near his master.

While a Congressman, Monroe unalterably opposed the plan of a treaty with Spain, by which the navigation of the Mississippi was to be surrendered for twenty-five years in return for commercial privileges. His insistence on the free navigation of the Father of Waters was to render him popular with the Western people, also to make him later a logical choice as a negotiator of the Louisiana Purchase. In Congress, fearful of the weakness of its powers under the Articles of Confederation, he introduced a resolution urging the several states to vest that body with authority to regulate commerce—a step in the sequence leading to the convocation of the Constitutional Convention.

But he was not a member of the Virginia delegation to that convention, since his state was represented by older and more prominent public men. In the Virginia convention of 1788, with Patrick Henry, William Grayson and George Mason he opposed the ratification of the federal Constitution, being apprehensive of the great authority conferred by that instrument on the central government, and anticipating conflict between the national and state governments. Like Jefferson, then in France, whose views on the subject Monroe believed to be in accord with his own, he distrusted the provision allowing the re-eligibility of the President. Fortunately, his struggle against ratification having failed he advocated the passage of the first ten amendments and became a determined defender of the charter.

By the Articles of Confederation, no delegate in Congress was allowed to serve more than three years in six. Therefore, in 1786, Monroe, ineligible for another term in Congress, returned to Virginia, where settling in Fredericksburg he commenced the practice of law.

The first United States Senators from Virginia under the federal Constitution were Richard Henry Lee and William Grayson. Monroe was defeated by Madison for a seat in the House of Representatives but after the decease of Grayson was elected by the legislature to the vacancy, and held his seat in the Senate for almost four years, relinquishing it only to accept an appointment to succeed Gouverneur Morris as Minister to France.

His selection by Washington for the French post was a surprise to the new Minister, since, during his senatorial career, being in opposition to the Federal principles of government, he had acted as an obstructionist of the Hamiltonian program of finance, as well as of Washington's general policies. Washington, however, disdaining partisan feelings, had continued to feel a respect for Monroe's abilities. It was evident that the cynical and brilliant Federalist

Morris was *persona non grata* to the French revolutionary leaders. After Livingston and Madison had refused the mission, Washington, still resolved to send a Republican to France, offered it to Monroe.

He was forty-five days between Baltimore and Paris, where he found an interesting condition of affairs. The butcher Robespierre had just suffered the penalty of that guillotine to which he had sacrificed so many innocents, and the pall cast over France by his savage rule had already commenced to pass away. No other nation then had an official representative in France, and the reception of Monroe by the Committee of Public Safety was therefore eagerly scrutinized and recorded.

His conduct of this mission, as was to prove true of another of his diplomatic ventures, was to subject him to a criticism that would have ruined the future political career of almost any other man. Even at this distance of time it is difficult to pass judgment as to how far on the occasion of his first French visit he violated the spirit of his instructions. Before leaving the United States he had been advised by the Secretary of State, Randolph, in the following terms: "To conclude. You go, sir, to France, to strengthen our friendship with that country and you are well acquainted with the line of Freedom and ease to which you may advance without betraying the dignity of the United States. You will show our confidence in the French Republic without betraying the most remote remark of undue complaisance. . . . Among the great events with which the world is now teeming, there may be an opening for *France to become instrumental in securing to us the free navigation of the Mississippi.*"

Like other Republicans, notably Jefferson, Monroe was a warm supporter of the French Revolution. He was flattered by the notice accorded him, in marked contrast to that bestowed on his predecessor, Morris. The Convention decided to receive him, as a body, and Monroe's ensuing speech, although it lasted only ten minutes, was marked by an effusion of friendly sentiment unbecoming in a diplomat on such an occasion.

As soon as the report of Monroe's reception by the French reached America, there was an outburst of criticism against him especially by the Federalists, who were predominantly pro-English. He was warmly attacked in the House and chided by the Secretary of State, who wrote: "But the range of a public minister's mind will go to all the relations of our country with the whole world. We do not perceive that your instructions have imposed upon you the extreme glow of some parts of your address; and my letter, in behalf of the House of Representatives, which has been considered by some gentlemen as too strong, was not to be viewed in any other light than as executing the task assigned by that body.

"After these remarks, which are never to be interpreted into any dereliction of the French cause, I must observe to you that they are made principally to recommend caution; lest we should be obliged at some time or other, to explain away or disavow an excess of fervor, so as to reduce it down to the cool system of neutrality. You have it still in charge to cultivate the French Republic with zeal but without any unnecessary éclat; besides the dictates of sincerity do not demand that we should render notorious all our feelings in favor of that nation."

Later, Randolph again wrote to Monroe: "We are fully sensible of the importance of the friendship of the French Republic. Cultivate it with zeal, proportioned to the value we set upon it. Remember to remove every suspicion of our preferring a connection with Great Britain or in any manner weakening our old attachment to France. The caution suggested in my letter of the 30th ultimo arises solely from an honorable wish to sustain our character of neutrality, in a style which may be a pattern for the morality of nations. The Republic, while they approve of the purity of your conduct, cannot but be persuaded of the purity of our affection."

During his mission he was instrumental in obtaining the release from prison of Thomas Paine and of Mme. de Lafayette. The influence of the former, who lived in Monroe's Paris residence for a year and a half after his liberation, upon the American Minister was probably unfortunate, and in part responsible for Monroe's over-zealous sponsorship of the French Revolution, and also for his unfriendliness to Washington. His chivalrous attitude to General Lafayette's wife won him the undying friendship of her family. Many years later, when Monroe, then an ex-President, was in financial difficulties the generous Lafayette placed his purse at his friend's disposal, an offer for which Monroe was deeply grateful but of which he did not take advantage.

However, his great popularity with the French was comparatively short-lived; for they held him, as an American public man, partly responsible for the Jay treaty, which he denounced as "the most shameful transaction I have ever known of the kind." The French felt that he should have kept their government advised of the prog-

ress of Jay's negotiations, which would have been impossible since
he had no current knowledge of them.

He had spoken of France as "our ally and sister republican," and
had extolled the "wisdom and firmness" of a government that placed
less faith in laws than in the guillotine. In the dark himself as to
the real purposes of the Jay treaty, he had assured the French that
Jay was only authorized to demand "reparation for injuries." When
the full import of the treaty was made known at Paris, Monroe was
as astonished, and almost as indignant as the French. His position
became even more embarrassing when Secretary Pickering instructed
him to defend the very agreement which he asserted had never been
under negotiation. He tardily did so, but Washington had already
determined upon his recall.

Pickering, who succeeded Randolph as Secretary of State, visited
on the envoy to France a considerable portion of his great store of
malice, complaining that Monroe had not made a suitable vindica-
tion of the Jay treaty, or done anything to reconcile the French people to it at a time when the faith and honor of the United States
were questioned. Monroe was curtly informed of his impending
replacement by C. C. Pinckney.

Upon the arrival of Mr. Pinckney in Paris he was presented by
Monroe to the Minister for Foreign Affairs, but was not recognized
by the Directory or permitted to remain in Paris. This action by the
French was, no doubt, somewhat soothing to Monroe's ruffled feelings, and he was pleased to find that the French government on the
eve his his departure began to renew those civilities formerly accorded him.

He returned to the United States in the spring of 1797. At the end
of that year he published a defense of his career abroad, in a five-
hundred-page pamphlet, entitled *A View of the Conduct of the Executive in the Foreign Affairs of the United States Etc.*, in which he
printed his instructions, speeches and correspondence. The pamphlet served no useful purpose, and the attack upon Washington
elicited from the retired President the comment: "The truth is, Mr.
Monroe was cajoled, flattered, and made to believe strange things.
In return, he did, or was disposed to do, whatever was pleasing to
that nation, reluctantly urging the rights of his own." During the
short remainder of his life Washington preserved for his former
appointee a feeling of antipathy.

The wound to Monroe's self-esteem, caused by his recall, was soon

partially salved by his election as Governor of Virginia. The Jeffersonian Republicans rallied around him, attributing his treatment by
the Federalists to partisan motives. He was twice re-elected Governor, and served in that capacity until 1802. In January 1803 he was
appointed by President Jefferson Envoy Extraordinary and Minister
Plenipotentiary to France, to aid Robert R. Livingston, the resident
Minister. At the same time he was instructed to co-operate with
Charles Pinckney, the Minister to Spain, in securing from that country the cession of the two Floridas. Three months later he was commissioned the regular Minister to Great Britain.

The first of these comprehensive diplomatic appointments was
speedily and gloriously concluded by the purchase of Louisiana, a
transaction well under way before Monroe's arrival in Paris, and for
the consummation of which his presence was probably superfluous.
His association with Livingston in this affair gave rise to jealousy
between them, in which neither man showed to advantage. The
negotiations for the acquisition of the Floridas were markedly unsuccessful, since Spain had no intention of parting with that territory,
and treated the overtures of the American envoys with contemptuous
disdain. The French had promised to assist the American cause in
Spain but failed to do so, and the American Ministers were completely frustrated.

It was as Minister to England that Monroe's career as a diplomatist
came to an unsuccessful and humiliating close. At the end of 1806
he was so ill advised as to conclude a treaty with the English in
violation of his instructions. He failed to secure any provision against
the impressment of American seamen, or any indemnity for losses
incurred by the Americans in connection with British seizures of
their vessels or goods. Jefferson took the responsibility of not submit-
ting the unsatisfactory treaty to Congress, and let it die as quietly
as possible; he wrote kindly to Monroe, but observed: "Depend on
it, my dear Sir, that it will be considered as a hard treaty when it is
known. The British Commissioners appear to have screwed every
Article as far as it would bear,—to have taken everything and yielded
nothing."

In spite of the luster attaching to his name as a result of the Louisiana Purchase, Monroe returned to America, near the close of 1807,
a disappointed man, conscious of the failure of his diplomatic career
as a consequence of his English negotiations.

He immediately proceeded in a lengthy letter to Madison to lay down an elaborate defense of his diplomatic endeavors in England, but his friend, the Secretary of State, was unconvinced by his arguments. Jefferson had previously pressed upon him the office of Governor of New Orleans Territory. "It is," he said, "the second office in the United States in importance, and I am still in hopes you will accept it; it is impossible to let you stay at home while the public has so much need of talents." Monroe, however, declined the offer, and in defense of his rejected treaty declared: "Under such circumstances, it seemed to me to be highly for the interest of our country and to the credit of our government to get out of the general scrape on the best terms we could, and with that view to accommodate our differences with the great maritime Power on what might be called fair and reasonable conditions, if such could be obtained."

In spite of his reverses he was seriously considered as a Republican candidate for President in succession to Jefferson, but the Legislature of Virginia settled the matter by deciding upon Madison as its nominee.

Never happy out of public office, he was, in 1810, for the third time elected to the Virginia House of Delegates. The following year, for the fourth time, he was chosen as Governor. He had the resiliency of a rubber ball, and, despite any adversity of fortune he seldom experienced difficulty in regaining the favor of the electorate. The Virginia Federalists greeted his election as Governor with dismay. Their leading paper announced the election day as one of mourning. "Virginia's misfortunes," it said, "may be comprised in one short sentence: Monroe is elected Governor."

Part of his strength, as a possible candidate for the Presidency in 1808, had been derived from the popular impression that he leaned toward reconciliation with England, whereas Madison inclined toward friendship with France. When the governorship of Virginia was in prospect, he abandoned, in part, his previous position of opposition to Madison. As a consequence he drew from John Randolph of Roanoke a letter, on January 14, 1811, telling him reports were being circulated "that in order to promote your selection to the chief magistracy of this Commonwealth, you have descended to unbecoming compliances with the members of the Assembly, not excepting your bitterest personal enemies; that you have volunteered explanations to them of the differences heretofore subsisting between yourself and the Administration which amount to a dereliction of the ground which you took after your return from England, and even

of your warmest personal friends." When Monroe entered Madison's Cabinet, John Randolph saw his worst fears realized, and thereafter had little esteem for his former friend.

Having become Secretary of State, it was not long before Monroe
adopted Madison's views of foreign policy. He soon abandoned any
hope of obtaining justice from England through the writing of con-
ciliatory notes. After war was declared, he continued in the same
office and on September 27, 1814, following the capture of Washington, also became Secretary of War. He was vigorous and determined
in the latter office, his policy in marked contrast to that of his predecessors. He even pledged his personal credit, always insufficient for
his own needs, to support the exhausted financial resources of the
government in carrying on the war.

Upon retirement of Madison, Monroe succeeded him as President,
having received 183 electoral votes to 34 for Rufus King. In 1820 he
was re-elected without opposition, obtaining all votes cast except
that of Mr. Plumer of New Hampshire, who polled his for John
Quincy Adams. During both of his terms, D. D. Tompkins of New
York served as Vice-President.

Monroe was the logical successor of Madison, not due to unusual
popularity but because he was the strongest member of the Madison
Cabinet, a close friend of the retiring President and a believer in the
Jeffersonian program of government. His Cabinet contained four
men who remained in it during both his presidential terms: John
Quincy Adams, as Secretary of State; John C. Calhoun as Secretary
of War; William H. Crawford as Secretary of the Treasury; and
William Wirt as Attorney General. Henry Clay and Andrew Jackson
had both declined an offer to be his Secretary of War.

The chief events of Monroe's administration were the signing of
an American-Canadian treaty, the Seminole War, the acquisition of
the Floridas, the Missouri Compromise, the veto of the Cumberland
Road Bill, and the promulgation of the Monroe Doctrine. It was also
during his term of office that Lafayette made a farewell visit to the
United States which resolved itself into an almost royal progress.

In spite of various controversial subjects arising during his administration and breeding the usual degree of party strife, his tenure
of the presidency was on the whole so tranquil that it was contem-
poraneously referred to as the "Era of Good Feeling." The old lines
of cleavage between Federalists and Republicans were almost oblit-
erated. Before he was inducted into office the first American pro-

tective tariff had been passed. The "American System," sponsored by Clay, providing for a home market and better transportation for the farmers, a protective tariff for manufacturers, and internal improvements, was in the ascendancy, although Monroe himself approved of a tariff primarily for the sake of revenue, and did not favor federal patronage of internal improvements in the absence of a constitutional amendment expressly permitting it.

In the year 1817 the Bank of the United States had resumed operation, with the power to establish branches in all important cities and towns, the government being the owner of twenty per cent of its capital stock and its principal customer.

It seemed, in short, as if an eight-year truce had been declared between all opposing political elements, which was only to be broken, and then permanently, after the accession of John Quincy Adams to the chief magistracy. Underneath the surface the old animosity of agrarianism versus industrialism smoldered, and sectionalism was rampant, but there were few open indications of such divisions of sentiment. By 1820 the population of the states and territories west of the Appalachians had increased, in ten years, from 1,080,000 to 2,234,000, and during the decade from 1810 to 1820 the states of Indiana, Mississippi, Illinois, Alabama and Louisiana had been admitted to the Union. The prosperity that followed the conclusion of the War of 1812 had been replaced by an era of depression which lasted during much of Monroe's regime and was only concluded in 1824, but in spite of it the financial condition of the country was not a cause for much concern.

By 1820 sectional lines on the question of a protective tariff were clearly drawn; the manufacturing Middle states and the West were in favor of it, while the South, with its great export crops of tobacco and cotton and the New England shipping states, were opposed to it.

Under the skillful handling of John Quincy Adams, a treaty was signed with England, creating complete political amity between the United States and Canada. Its terms provided that the naval forces to be maintained on the Great Lakes by the two governments should be limited on either side to four single-gun vessels of one hundred tons each.

The Seminole War of 1817-18 resulted not only in enhancing the military reputation of Andrew Jackson and eventually in the acquisition of those parts of the Floridas which we had not previously seized, but also almost involved us in another war with England.

Jackson had been instructed to chastise the Seminole Indians, who had killed some American settlers. In pursuing them he crossed into Spanish Florida, where despite the law of nations he proceeded to take possession of St. Marks and Pensacola. In addition, having captured two British subjects, Ambrister and Arbuthnot (the latter a man of seventy), who were perhaps rightly accused of stirring up the Indians to violence against Americans, he gave them short shrift. One was shot by a firing squad and the other hanged from the topsail yard of a naval vessel.

When news of this summary proceeding reached London, it was touch and go whether it would not be a casus belli. "If the Ministry had but held up a finger," said Lord Castlereagh, "there would have been war." Fortunately Parliament was not in session, and the British Government, in spite of press clamors, decided not to declare war for the sake of the deaths of an obscure adventurer and a petty trader.

Jackson's invasion of Florida was the ultimate gesture necessary to convince the Spaniards they had best sell their possession before it was wholly seized. Finally Spain, by a treaty ratified February 22, 1819, ceded all her lands east of the Mississippi, together with any rights to the Oregon country, in return for five million dollars in bonds, to be paid to American citizens in discharge of claims for damages to American commerce committed by Spanish authorities during the recent European war. The territory acquired contained 59,268 square miles, or 37,931,520 acres, and was obtained at a cost, with interest, of seventeen and one-tenth cents per acre.

On the great question of slavery Monroe was in general accord with the views of Jefferson and Madison. With the former, he had as early as 1801 corresponded on the subject of repatriating the free blacks to Africa. Not only was he to contribute largely to the creation of Liberia, the capital of which is named after him, but his attitude toward the other oppressed race, the Indians, was more humane than that of any President since Washington. He also sponsored a slave trade convention with Great Britain, designed to make such commerce piratical, but the treaty was not ratified.

In 1818 the question of slavery assumed a political importance it was never afterwards to lose. Hitherto a balance satisfactory to the Southerners had been preserved between the free and the slave states. But when, in 1818, the territory of Missouri applied for incorporation in the Union as a state, the free states demanded that slavery which had existed there during its territorial status should, as a requisite of the admission of Missouri to statehood, be gradually abolished by a prohibition on the entrance into Missouri of new slaves, and by the freeing of all Negro children born there subsequent to admission.

The ensuing strife alarmed Jefferson. "This momentous question, like a fire bell in the night, awakened and filled me with terror," he wrote; and John Quincy Adams observed: "I take it for granted that the present question is a mere preamble—a title-page to a great tragic volume." At last, in 1820, an agreement was arrived at, unsatisfactory to the extremists of both schools of thought, known as the Missouri Compromise, which, for the time being, prevented a crisis. Maine, detached from Massachusetts, was admitted as a free state, and Missouri as a slave state, making twelve free and twelve slave states. It was additionally agreed that slavery should be excluded from the northern portion of the Louisiana Territory.

On the subject of federal aid for internal improvements, Monroe took the position of a strict constitutional constructionist. He held that the power to establish a system of internal improvements by the building of roads and canals was not possessed by Congress, but he strongly advocated that the states be urged to adopt an amendment conferring such powers upon Congress, together with the right to carry out a program of public education. Since the states had not adopted the suggested amendment, he felt compelled to veto the Cumberland Road Bill, on the ground that the power to pass such a law implied the power to adopt and execute a complete system of internal improvement, and that such a power was neither specifically nor incidentally granted by the Constitution.

The most important event of his administration was, of course, the promulgation of the Monroe Doctrine, in his presidential message of December 2, 1823. Before that time all the Spanish colonies in Central and South America had revolted against their mother country, and some of them had been recognized by the United States. The Holy Alliance, formed by the monarchs of Austria, Russia and Prussia for the perpetuation of the principle of the divine right of kings and for the maintenance of the territorial status quo, was alarmed and outraged by these revolutionary movements. Accordingly it hoped, in conjunction with France, which actually refused to join the coalition, to suppress the new government set up in revolted colonies.

Such an attempt was viewed with the greatest disfavor by Great

Britain, whose Foreign Secretary, George Canning, sensitive to the crescent influence of democracy in England, as well as to the opposition with which British merchants who were deeply involved in trading and investment commitments in Spanish America viewed a restoration there of Spanish rule, sounded out the possibility of an Anglo-American alliance against the imperial ambitions of the continental powers. The United States unwilling to be a tool or ally of English policy formulated its own plan of action, although several years later Canning attempted to claim credit for the result of American policy with the proud boast that he had "called the New World into existence to redress the balance of the Old."

Meanwhile struggles for independence elsewhere in the world had aroused a popular feeling of sympathy in America. The uprising of the Greeks against Turkish rule had evoked particular enthusiasm. The legislature of South Carolina petitioned Congress to acknowledge Greek independence. Albert Gallatin proposed to lend the Greek insurgents a fleet.

It was, therefore, to a public favorable to such expressions of policy that the President's message concerning the independence of the former Spanish colonies was addressed. It was, in effect, a second declaration of independence—independence of the politics of Europe. The doctrine was not only the product of Monroe's thinking, but reflected the views of Jefferson, John Quincy Adams and other philosophical statesmen. Notice was bluntly given to Europe that we would henceforth regard "any attempt on their part to extend their system to any portion of this hemisphere as dangerous to our peace and safety." Moreover, "The American continents" (and this declaration was directed at Russia, which had pretensions to our northwest coast), "by the free and independent condition which they have assumed and maintained," were not to be considered "as subjects for future colonization by any European powers." On the other hand, Monroe expressly disclaimed any intention of interfering with the then existing colonies or dependencies of European powers, and further stated that "in the wars of the European powers in matters relating to themselves, we have never taken any part, nor does it comport with our policy so to do."

The enunciation of this policy put an end to the plans of the Holy Alliance. On April 17, 1824, John Quincy Adams succeeded in negotiating a convention with Russia fixing the southern limit of Russian sovereignty at 54° 40′ north latitude. This treaty was a timely one, for the Russians crossing the Bering Straits from Siberia, had extended their fur trading posts as far south as the Golden Gate, and the Czar had been pleased to designate a large part of the California coast as Russian America.

When Monroe quitted the presidency in 1825, he was still in the flood tide of popularity. A visit from Lafayette, accompanied by his son, George Washington Lafayette, in the summer of 1824, which was to last fourteen months, had marked the end of his administration with a delightful social flavor. Lafayette, financially embarrassed, had been obliged to borrow sufficient money for his voyage. Once arrived, he found himself the guest of a grateful nation, and was fêted and hurrahed from one end of the country to the other. Congress, in tardy recognition of his gallant and generous services, voted him lands and, what was more substantial, the sum of $200,000.

Monroe after his retirement from the presidency became a Justice of the Peace, a Regent of the University of Virginia and a member of the Virginia Constitutional Convention of 1829-30, of which he was chosen President.

In all his presidential career the only important political opposition he had met with had been from Chief Justice John Marshall. In their youth they had been fellow students and friends; in their old age they were friends again, but Marshall had little respect for Monroe's ability and less for his opinions on constitutional questions. Year after year Marshall, in defiance of a succession of Republican Presidents, calmly developed his ideas of national sovereignty. "Let the end be legitimate," he said, "let it be within the scope of the Constitution, and all means which are appropriate, which are plainly adapted to that end, which are not prohibited, but consist with the letter and spirit of the Constitution, are constitutional." Five hundred and nineteen Supreme Court decisions were written by Marshall himself. Their tenor and their influence on the centralization of power at the expense of states rights were anathema to Monroe, who had long before written that the Tory party "has retired into the judiciary in a strong body where it lives on the Treasury and therefore cannot be starved out."

In his youth Monroe had been a strict, even violent, party man. His obstructionist tactics, during Washington's administration, reflected discredit on him. He always remained a Jeffersonian Republican—much more so than did Madison—but, after he reached the presidency, he moderated his partisanship and adopted a generous attitude toward the Federal party. "In the formation of an Administration," he said, "it appears to me that the representation principle ought to be respected, in a certain degree at least, and that a head of a department (there being four) should be taken from the four sections of the Union, the East, the Middle, the South, and the West. This principle should not be always adhered to. Great emergencies and transcendent talents would always justify a departure from it."

In most respects Monroe was a mediocre man. He was almost totally lacking in imagination, in humor and in charm. He wrote and spoke with no facility but Madison said that his "understanding was very much underrated; his judgment was particularly good; few men have made more of what may be called sacrifices in the service of the public."

On the subject of secession he was a unionist. "Satisfied I am," he stated, "that nothing can be so calamitous to every section of the Union as a dismemberment. With such an event our republican system would soon go to wreck; wars would take place between the new States."

Monroe's financial affairs were in chronic disorder. After retiring as President he spent a great deal of time in attempts to secure from Congress adequate reimbursement for the heavy expenses to which he had been subjected while on foreign missions, and was finally granted thirty thousand dollars.

In appearance he was about six feet tall, muscularly compact and rawboned. His powers of physical endurance were great. His countenance was grave, and in later life deeply lined. To his intimates he was unselfish, patient, gentle and affectionate. Although he was an awkward and a diffident man, he was unusually dignified and polite.

While attending Congress in New York he became engaged to, and later married, Eliza Kortwright. During her husband's career as Secretary of State she seldom appeared in Washington society, and even while mistress of the White House secluded herself to a considerable extent because of ill-health. Her manners were too stately, and too much in contrast to Dolly Madison's gay geniality, for her to be a favorite in Washington, but she was admired and conceded to be very gracious, charming and regal-looking." Mrs. Monroe and her daughters attempted to restore formality to White

House etiquette and paid no visits. As a consequence there was a feud between them and the diplomatic corps.

There were two children of this marriage, Eliza and Maria, who became Mrs. George Hay of Virginia, and Mrs. Samuel L. Gouverneur of New York. In the last seven years of his life Monroe divided his time between his own home, Oak Hill, in London County, Virginia, and the New York home of his daughter, Mrs. Gouverneur. Like the preceding Virginia Presidents, he was passionately fond of plantation life, and his house compared favorably in architecture and beauty with Mount Vernon, Monticello and Montpelier.

On July 4, 1831, Monroe died in New York City, thus being the third of our first five Presidents to die on Independence Day.

John Quincy Adams

Born: July 11, 1767.

Accompanied his father to France: 1778.

Private Secretary to Francis Dana, United States Minister to Russia: 1781.

Graduated from Harvard: 1787.

Admitted to Bar: 1790.

Appointed Minister to the Netherlands: 1794.

Appointed Minister to Portugal: 1796.

Appointed Minister to Prussia: 1797.

Returned to America: 1801.

Elected to Massachusetts State Senate: 1802.

Elected United States Senator: February 3, 1803.

Appointed Minister to Russia: 1809.

Appointed a Commissioner to negotiate peace with Great Britain at Ghent: 1814.

Appointed Minister to England: February 8, 1815.

Secretary of State of the United States: 1817-25.

President of the United States: 1825-29.

Member of the House of Representatives: 1831-48.

Died: February 23, 1848.

JOHN QUINCY ADAMS

BEFORE John Adams died, he enjoyed the satisfaction of seeing his son, John Quincy Adams, installed as President of the United States. The younger Adams' elevation to this office was not due to any influence exercised by his father on his behalf; unhappily the father's unpopularity, even with the members of the Federalist party, was such that a blood connection with him was a liability rather than an advantage. The election was a striking reward for the merit displayed by John Quincy Adams for so long and in so many capacities in the service of his country.

While a child of eleven, he had accompanied his parent on that eventful journey to France in the course of which has father had signed a treaty of peace with England, recognizing the independence of the former British colonies in America. A few years later, at the tender age of fourteen, the younger Adams went with Francis Dana, as private secretary, on that envoy's diplomatic mission to Russia. Thirteen years later he was honored by George Washington with an appointment as Minister to the Netherlands.

From that time onward he was, with the exception of brief intervals, seldom out of the public service. For a time he served as Minister to Prussia, he became a member of the Massachusetts State Senate, was a United States Senator, was appointed by Madison Minister to Russia, presided over the American delegation which negotiated peace with England at Ghent, became Minister to England, and was, for eight years, Monroe's Secretary of State, before succeeding his chief as President.

After his defeat for a second term as President his political career appeared terminated, but the electors of his native constituency returned him to Washington as their representative in Congress, where for seventeen years he maintained an independent course of action that did honor alike to himself and to his electorate. During this period his fiery speeches won for him the title of "Old Man Eloquent"; when the sands of his long life ran out, it was on the floor of Congress that he was stricken, it was in one of the rooms of the Capitol that he breathed his last.

A life so constantly devoted to his country would seem to have deserved for his name grateful pages in history, but it may be questioned whether any public man of equal accomplishments and services has been as forgotten or condemned by posterity. The case of his father provides a striking illustration of the ingratitude of republics, but the son, "a greater bear than the old one," as an enemy remarked of him, was to excel his parent on the score of being unappreciated. The name of John Quincy Adams is to the American public but the shadow of a shade, and that shade the name of his father.

The reasons for this are comparatively simple. When he was elected President, he was not the original choice of a majority of his countrymen. During his term as Chief Executive he strove to disassociate himself from any party ties and to be a true representative of the real interests of the whole people. This policy, admirable in theory, made him the victim of partisan machinations, especially when they were directed toward his replacement by such a vivid personality as Andrew Jackson, whom those who were hungry for the material returns of politics felt could be depended upon to reward the faithful.

But more important still was the fact that Adams possessed no popular appeal. He lacked even personal friends. A frigidity of demeanor, joined with a rigidity of opinion, made it difficult if not impossible for anyone outside of his immediate family circle to love him.

As in the case of John Adams, a persecution complex embittered the life of John Quincy Adams. Instead of exploding, as his father so often did, and giving full, if extravagant, vent to his irritations, the son, able to exercise a greater restraint over his disappointments, turned them inward to brood upon his soul. Only in his remarkable diary, an invaluable document for the psychologist as well as for the historian and general reader, did he express the full measure of his hypercritical attitude toward his fellow men, or the full depth of his pessimism. In that great human revelation he poured out the accumulated bile of his repressions. But to one cause he was always true and to its failings blind, namely that of his country. He loved his country with devotion and with passion, fought for its welfare, was jealous of its dignity, ambitious and confident of its future.

Before he was eight years old, he was to see Charlestown fired by the British troopers, and from a neighboring mount to hear the sounds of the cannon at Bunker Hill. Patriotism and a love of his native soil were inculcated in him by a mother and father who never faltered in their ardent desire for American independence. During those stern times, with his father absent from home, his schooling was not neglected. At the age of nine he reported to John Adams as follows:

Dear Sir,—I love to receive letters very well; much better thant I love to write them. I make but a poor figure at composition. My head is much too fickle. My thoughts are running after bird's eggs, play and trifles, till I get vexed with myself. Mama has a troublesome task to keep me a studying. I own I am ashamed of myself. I have but just entered the third volume of Rollin's history, but designed to have got half through it by this time. I am determined this week to be more diligent. Mr. Thaxter is absent at Court. I have set myself a stint this week, to read the third volume half out. If I can but keep my resolution, I may again at the end of the week give a better account of myself. I wish, sir, you would give me in writing, some instructions with regard to the use of my time, and advise me how to proportion my studies and play, and I will keep them by me, and endeavor to follow them.

With the present determination of growing better, I am, dear sir, your son,

JOHN QUINCY ADAMS

P.S. Sir,—If you will be so good as to favor me with a blank book, I will transcribe the most remarkable passages I meet with in my reading, which will serve to fix them upon my mind.

The thoughts of the boy were soon diverted from bird's eggs, play and trifles, by his father taking him as a companion upon his mission to France in 1778. Their stay was not a long one, but it followed within three months of their return by another trip to Paris.

On this second voyage the French frigate bearing them sprung a leak. They put into the port of Ferrol, in Spain, whence they made the rough overland journey for a thousand miles, in the course of which they passed on muleback over the mountains to Paris. It was not therefore to a youth ignorant of the difficulties of European travel or unfamiliar with diplomatic usages that Francis Dana, when appointed Minister to Russia in 1781, offered the position of private secretary. The private secretary, at the age of fourteen, entered thus precociously upon a diplomatic career that was to culminate in his occupancy of the highest foreign post at the disposal of his country. For fourteen months John Quincy Adams served in Russia with zeal and efficiency, before returning to Paris, where he assisted his father, as secretary, during the negotiations which officially terminated the War of the American Revolution.

Probably no young American of his time could have boasted of being such a traveler, at least on land, as young Adams. Coming from the New World to the Old at such an epoch made a deep impression upon a mind as susceptible to curiosity as his. Fifty years later he remarked: "There is a character of romantic wildness about the memory of my travels in Europe from 1778 to 1785, which gives it a tinge as if it was the recollection of something in another world. Life was new, everything was surprising, everything carried with it a deep interest. . . ."

Instead of living with his father in England, where the elder Adams had been appointed Minister, John Quincy decided to return to America and become a student at Harvard. Already proficient in three living, and two dead, languages, he was, according to his father, well acquainted with English and French poetry, Roman and English history, and mathematics.

During his stay in Russia all forms of communication to that part of Europe were slow, but the postal service was particularly inadequate. Abigail Adams complained that for eighteen months she had received no letter from her son. His silence, however, was due to the slow transit of mails, not to any indisposition for writing, which at this period shared love of reading as objects of his attention. His father wrote to a friend at Harvard concerning the boy's literary accomplishments: "It is rare to find a youth possessed of so much knowledge. He has translated Virgil's Aeneid, Suetonius, the whole of Sallust, and Tacitus's Agricola, his Germany, and several books of his Annals, a great part of Homer, some of Ovid, and some of Caesar's Commentaries, in writing, besides a number of Tully's orations. . . .

"In Greek his progress has not been equal; yet he has studied morsels in Aristotle's Poetics, in Plutarch's Lives, and Lucian's Dialogues, the choice of Hercules, in Zenophon, and lately he has gone through several books in Homer's Iliad."

At any rate he entered the junior class at Harvard without difficulty, being "the oldest young man" who had ever attended that oldest of American colleges. Upon his graduation, with second honors in his class, he studied law and was admitted to the Massachusetts Bar. Before he had secured any standing in his new career, the family love of polemical writing asserted itself. He attacked Thomas Paine's *Rights of Man* in a series of articles, published in a Boston paper under the nom de plume of "Publicola." These articles were sufficiently well phrased to have attracted attention on both sides of the Atlantic. They received the commendation among others of Charles James Fox, although their real authorship was for some time unknown, it being generally supposed they had been produced by John Adams. Having embarked on literary waters, the young man continued on his way; in later journalistic contributions he discussed neutrality and other political topics in a manner pleasing to the Federalists, especially to President Washington.

Washington appointed him, on his twenty-seventh birthday, Minister Resident at The Hague, the capital of a country in the language of which the young man was already proficient. For a time he hesitated to accept the post, since he had not yet won any pecuniary competence for himself, and disliked the idea of being wholly dependent upon the government for his living. However, he accepted the offer, and reported at The Hague with his young brother as secretary. His attitude toward public offices was, he once wrote, "that which philosophers teach us should guide our views of death— never to be desired, never to be feared." His attention to his official duties occupied only a portion of his time; much of the remainder he devoted to study of the classics, of modern languages and of poetry. To poetry he was especially addicted, and himself wrote many indifferent verses.

Unhappily for Adams, his arrival in Holland preceded by only a short time the dissolution of the Dutch Republic. The conquering arms of France reduced that formerly proud nation to the status of a subservient ally, and a hundred thousand French soldiers upheld the integrity of the so-called Batavian Republic.

In May 1796, Washington, after whom Adams later named his eldest son, nominated him as Minister to Portugal, but he was fated never to take up the appointment. A year later his father, who in the interval had succeeded Washington as President, made his son Minister Plenipotentiary to Prussia, where there seemed a greater immediate need of a mission than in Portugal. This step under ordinary circumstances would have been violently attacked as an instance of nepotism, and had been taken by John Adams only after strong misgivings, in the course of which he asked advice of Washington, who expressed a "strong hope that you will not withhold merited promotion from Mr. John (Quincy) Adams because he is your son. For without intending to compliment the father, or the mother, or to censure others, I give it as my decided opinion that Mr. Adams is the most valuable public character we have abroad, and that there remains no doubt, in my mind, that he will prove himself to be the ablest of all our diplomatic corps."

Before going to Berlin, Adams married Louisa Johnson, the daughter of Joshua Johnson, the American Consul in London. Johnson, a Marylander, was the brother of Governor Thomas Johnson, a distinguished politician of that state, who afterwards became a Justice of the Supreme Court of the United States. The new Mrs. Adams was beautiful enough to be known later in Paris as "*la belle Américaine*," and possessed a subtle charm in distinct contrast to her husband's gruffness. "I have," once wrote the elder Adams, "known my son's wife from her earliest infancy; and I have come to realize that his choice of a wife was the wisest choice of his whole career." Louisa Adams' softness and delicacy made a strong impression upon those who knew her. When she became a resident of Massachusetts, her foreign upbringing seemingly prevented her from ever becoming acclimated to the New England social scene. Her grandson, Henry Adams, who admired her enormously, described her, at the end of her days, as still "an exotic rose." The match was a successful and happy one. She was as good a French scholar as Adams himself, of whom his father once complained that he expressed himself better in that language than in his native tongue.

Adams took his bride to Prussia, the arduous trip from London consuming three weeks. He had the humiliating experience of being held up at the Brandenburg gate of the capital by an officious martinet who asked his name and calling. When he answered that he was the Minister of the United States of America, the officer avowed he had never heard of such a nation, and only after considerable parleying was the diplomatic party allowed to enter the city.

While in Prussia, Adams studied incessantly and became sufficiently expert in the language to make metrical translations from German into English, including Wieland's *Oberon*. The duties of his mission were not important, and he found the leisure to make a long trip through Silesia, a region almost unknown in America.

Adams' mission to Prussia was brought to an end by his own father, who before retiring from the presidency recalled his son, in order that his successor Jefferson would not be embarrassed by having to decide upon his continuance in or dismissal from the diplomatic service on party or personal grounds.

Soon after Adams' resumption of legal practice in Boston he was appointed by the Judge of the district court a commissioner in bankruptcy, but was shortly removed from this office by Jefferson, much to the indignation of his mother and father, the former of whom long cherished a bitterness against the President on this account. In after years Jefferson attempted to explain away this unusual action on the ground that he had not realized the identity of the incumbent of the office, but his explanation was never thoroughly credible. However, although John Quincy Adams was later to have a low opinion of Jefferson, he bore his dismissal with good grace.

His legal career was not especially lucrative. In fact, at no time during his life did his private income apparently exceed six thousand dollars a year, of which he always had to pay a part in interest on debts. But with this sum he was generous to his family, and authorized any or all of it to be placed at the disposal of his father. Indeed, in view of his almost continuous public service, it is remarkable that he was able to accumulate any property.

In 1802 he was chosen by the Federalists to represent them in the state Senate. At this period, under the restricted franchise, based on property qualifications, existing in Massachusetts, there were only about forty-five thousand qualified voters, of whom approximately twenty-five thousand were Federalists. His independent course of action in this legislative employment caused him to be considered "unmanageable," but did not prevent him a year later from being elected by the legislature as a United States Senator, after he had been nominated for Congress and defeated by a small margin.

In the United States Senate he speedily dispelled any illusion that he would be subject to the crack of a party whip. He supported the Jeffersonian program in many details, including the acquisition of Louisiana, the Nonimportation Act of 1806, and finally the embargo. The breach between the Federalists and himself became complete, but he could scarcely be counted a Republican, for he was always to remain an Adams.

His senatorial career did not bring him popularity. One of his colleagues said of Adams that he regarded every public measure which came up as he would a problem in Euclid, to be solved with no reference to party considerations. His independence might have won for him a following of sorts if his personality had been more genial.

The Massachusetts Federalists had their revenge on Adams. Without awaiting the end of his term, they elected his successor nine months in advance, and on June 8, 1808, Senator Adams having resigned his seat arrived at home to find himself a political outcast amongst the majority of men of property and high social standing in Boston. However, he had, before his resignation, been named professor of rhetoric and oratory at Harvard. It was a gratification to him to lecture to his students, by whom he was held in high esteem. Before such an audience he was at his best. Although he had none of the graces of an orator, and his speeches were not marked by either fluency or wit, their matter was solid and informative, and their style rolling and sonorous.

Immediately after Madison's inauguration the President requested him to go as Minister to Russia. The nomination was rejected by the Senate, which decided that a mission to the Czar's court was a superfluous expense, but upon his being nominated again later in the year the Senate confirmed the appointment. On August 5, 1809, Adams took ship at Boston. After a direct voyage of over ten weeks he arrived at St. Petersburg with an entourage consisting of four members of his family, two secretaries, a lady's maid and a Negro servant.

The capital of Russia was not only the scene of a brilliant social life but of a very expensive one. The American Minister found himself in the same sad position in which many of our later Ministers and Ambassadors have been placed of being financially unable to keep up the style of living considered appropriate to his official standing. His salary of nine thousand dollars a year was inadequate for his modest expenses, for he found he could not under the Russian system dispense with the attention of a horde of servants. "We have a maître d'hôtel," he wrote, "or steward; a cook who has under him two scullions—mujiks; a Swiss, or porter; two footmen; a mujik to make the fires; a coachman and postilion; and Thomas, the black man, to be my valet-de-chambre; Martha Godfrey, the maid we brought with us from America; a femme-de-chambre of Mrs. Adams, who is the wife of the steward; a house-maid, and a laundry maid. The Swiss, the cook, and one of the footmen are married, and their wives all live in the house. The steward has two children, and the washerwoman a daughter, all of whom are kept in the house."

Under these circumstances the Minister deemed it advisable to dismiss his cook and engage his dinners at a stated price, twenty roubles a day. Although he was obliged to entertain moderately, he met a number of people interesting for a variety of qualities. He was much struck by the Princess Woldemar Galitzin, "venerable by the length and thickness of her beard. This is no uncommon thing among the ladies of this Slavonian breed. There is at the Academy of Sciences the portrait of a woman now dead, but with beard equal to that of Plato. But of living subjects, the Princess Woldemar Galitzin is in this respect, of all the females that I have seen, the one who most resembles a Grecian philosopher."

With the Czar Alexander I, who was then only slightly over thirty years old, Adams was on a footing of more than ordinary friendliness. This monarch at that time entertained liberal sentiments, and was sympathetically inclined toward the United States and its citizens. Adams sometimes met him out walking, where they discoursed upon various topics, including the advisability of wearing flannel underwear and sleeping with open windows, subjects most interesting to those who experienced the rigors of a Russian winter.

With the members of the Foreign Office, Adams was on cordial terms. The Czar and his Ministers, in 1812, offered to mediate between the United States and England, but although the proposal was welcomed in Washington England refused it. Nevertheless, the English later decided to send representatives to Ghent to treat directly with American representatives. This transaction occupied much of Adams' time during his last year in Russia. His routine business had been slight, consisting chiefly in attending to matters affecting American ships. But no business was so pressing as his voracious reading. Each year he was in the habit of reading the Bible through, sometimes in English and once at least in French and German. Numbers of other books occupied his attention.

His interest in astronomy was not neglected while he lived in Russia. In 1814 he rose at three in the morning to have the benefit of seeing a clear sky without moonlight. "I was able to discern two of the stars of the sixth magnitude, in the Lion," he says. "I spent two full hours at the chamber-windows on both sides of the house, and, besides all my former celestial acquaintance, recognized the Crow, Hercules, and head of Ophiuchus, and the star of the second magnitude in the first claw of the Scorpion, from my own chamber, and the Dolphin and Antinoius from the front side of the house."

During his stay, moreover, he was honored by President Madison in having his name sent to the Senate for nomination as a Justice of the Supreme Court of the United States. The nomination was confirmed by the Senate, but Adams declined the appointment. Never fond of legal work, it is probable that he cherished, even at that time, aspirations to occupy someday the highest elective office.

When Adams received instructions from the State Department, in April 1814, to proceed to Gothenburg to carry on as a Commissioner, together with Messrs. Bayard, Clay, Russell and Gallatin, negotiations with England looking to a settlement of the Anglo-American War, he embarked for Stockholm and arrived there, in spite of the season of the year and the shortness of the distance, only after a cold voyage of four weeks. Thereupon he received notice that the place of meeting had been changed to Ghent. Thither he repaired in a hasty journey of three weeks.

Adams was the titular head of the American Commissioners, and the strangely matched group took a house together. Gallatin's tact smoothed over many passages of ill feeling between the irritable Adams and the mettlesome Clay. The chief Commissioner was scarcely a man whom convivial gentlemen would have selected to live with under conditions of close intimacy, if they had been fully aware of his censorious feelings. At one time he complains in his diary: "I dined again at the table d'hôte, at one. The other gentlemen dined together, at four. They sit after dinner and drink bad wine and smoke cigars, which neither suits my habits nor my health, and absorbs time which I cannot spare. I find it impossible, even with the most rigorous economy of time, to do half the writing that I ought." Clay's habit of playing cards for high stakes and for long hours was displeasing to Adams, who sometimes found the Lochinvar of the West leaving the tables for bed at the hour when the New Englander was rising to prosecute his daily reading and writing. However, Adams was not a complete recluse. He went into society and attended the theater, of which he was always genuinely fond, although he had early formed a rule never to make the acquaintance of an actress.

The difficulties of concluding peace with England had, for a long time, appeared insurmountable, and there were grave dissensions among the American Commissioners themselves. But finally an agreement was reached that settled none of the original causes of conflict but which was agreeable to both nations. As negotiators the Americans had displayed great skill, as compared with the second-rate Commissioners who had represented Great Britain. Adams, Gallatin and Clay were instructed to proceed to London and negotiate a treaty of commerce with Great Britain.

On January 26, 1815, Adams, well and rightly pleased with the successful termination of the peace negotiations, left Ghent for Paris. The many years that had intervened since his last visit there had not diminished the attractions of the French capital for him. "The tendency to dissipation at Paris," he observed, "seems to be irresistible. There is a moral incapacity for industry and application, a 'mollesse,' against which I am as ill guarded as I was at the age of twenty."

On February 8, Adams was appointed Minister to England, although he was not apprised of his selection for some time. Meanwhile his wife, released at last from the Russian cold, which had claimed the life of one of her children, was making her way, with her young son and an inefficient courier, across the turbulent Continent to join him. That she arrived safely, after threatening perils, is a tribute to her courage and her initiative. In Paris itself great events were taking place. Napoleon had landed from Elba on March 1, and on the nineteenth was in Paris. For part of the great Hundred Days, Adams was a witness of some of the most stirring episodes in history, but by May 25 he had reported for duty in London.

His position in England, like that of his father before him, was one in which he strove to secure for his country a justice that there was little reasonable expectation of having accorded. England was too occupied with the problem of Napoleon and the rectification of the balance of power in Europe to concern herself overmuch with representations regarding the impressment of American sailors and other transatlantic subjects. George III was a lunatic, and George IV was exercising power as Prince Regent. After meeting the Regent, Adams remarked of him, with considerable justice: "The character of this person is a composition of obtundity and of frivolity. His is a Falstaff without the wit, and a Prince Henry without the compunctions. His only talent is that of mimicry, which he exercises without regard to dignity or decorum, to the fitness of his own character, or to the feelings of others. His supreme delight is to expose persons, dependent upon him, to ridicule, and to enjoy their mortification."

In London he was for the first time to witness the use of gas for illuminating streets at night. After noticing that the lamps were remarkably brilliant and shed a light almost too dazzling for his eyes, he said: "They are also attended with an inconvenience of offensive smell, which I thought perceptible even in the streets, and they are thought to be unhealthy. For lighting streets, however, and open places, it is probable they will supersede the use of oil."

Adams' mission in London was brought to a close by the notice that President Monroe had appointed him Secretary of State. On April 15, 1817, he left the British Isles forever, arriving in New York fifty days later.

Before quitting England, Adams had been offered a gratuity, in accordance with a usage that no longer exists. Mr. Chester (the Assistant Master of Ceremonies) inquired of him in what manner he would choose to receive the usual present, given to foreign Ministers on the termination of their missions, which was for Ambassadors one thousand pounds, and for Ministers of the second order, five hundred pounds. "I told him," said Adams, "that by the Constitution of the United States no person in their service was permitted to accept a present from any foreign sovereign."

Monroe had chosen Adams not for reasons of friendship, but because, in forming his Cabinet, he wished all sections of the country to be represented. Adams not only was a New Englander but by experience and talents was the best-equipped man in the country for the position. The selection was a happy one. For eight years John Quincy Adams filled the office of Secretary of State with the most brilliant success. There have been many great American Secretaries of State, but it is doubtful if any occupant of that office has left behind him a record more useful and admirable than did Monroe's appointee.

The two most important matters handled by Adams while he was head of the State Department were, first, the question of the Floridas, and, second, the Monroe Doctrine. Each was sufficiently complex to have made or broken a statesman's reputation, and of each he disposed in a masterly manner.

The problem of Florida had troubled the American government since the day when Jefferson had first tried to buy the colony from Spain. By spoliation and by treaty we had successively managed to acquire large portions of the Spanish holdings, but a tempting and strategic territory yet remained in alien hands. Spain was too feeble to hold her colonies, too obstinate to sell them. This, then, was the problem to which Adams addressed himself. In so doing, he had to deal through the Spanish Minister at Washington, Onis, whose character is best delineated in the story that one day he came to Adams and complained of having found a dead chicken tied to his bell rope the night before, which, he said, was "a gross insult to his sovereign and the Spanish monarchy, importing that they were of no more consequence than a dead old hen." Adams mollified him by suggesting that the incident might be a prank of mischievous boys.

While Adams was attempting to deal with Spain through diplomatic channels, Andrew Jackson undertook to settle matters with the sword. Pursuing some Indian raiders into Spanish territory, he hung two Indian chiefs and executed two British subjects, seized Spanish towns, submitted high Spanish functionaries to gross indignities and behaved, in general, as if his country was in a state of open warfare with Spain and England. As a result, war with Great Britain was narrowly averted, and, except for the impotency of Spain, war with that country would certainly have ensued. The result of Jackson's bold indiscretion was to make him subject to violent attacks in the Cabinet and in Congress. Ironically enough, Adams, who was later to suffer so severely from Jackson's hatred, was almost his only prominent supporter at this time, and was largely responsible for the condonation of Jackson's highhanded conduct. Adams did not limit his attentions to Jackson to an official defense of his conduct, but in 1824, on the anniversary of the battle of New Orleans, gave a ball, attended by about one thousand people, in the General's honor, which was perhaps the most brilliant social function of the Monroe Administration.

In spite of the wounds inflicted by officers of the United States on Spanish pride, that nation was in no condition to do other than to accede to American demands for the cession of her holdings in Florida. Despite discouraging delays and intrigues Adams pursued this object with the obstinacy of a bulldog, until a treaty was ratified whereby Florida was secured for the United States and the boundaries of Louisiana satisfactorily defined; the United States making the concession, unimportant at that time, of abandoning its unsubstantial claim to Texas.

Because of his official position in Washington, Adams was less of a social recluse than he wished to be. Each week he and his wife gave a Tuesday evening party which was not enlivened by any gaiety on the part of the host. Adams wrote of himself at this period: "I am a man of reserved, cold, austere, and forbidding manners; my political adversaries say, a gloomy misanthropist, and my personal enemies, an unsocial savage. With a knowledge of the actual defects in my character, I have not the pliability to reform it."

The physical appearance of the capital city was, during this epoch, almost as unprepossessing as it had been when Adams' father became the first occupant of the presidential mansion. Mills, a Massachusetts Congressman, had written in 1815 that it was a "miserable desert" and "the first appearance of this seat of the national government has produced in me nothing but absolute loathing and disgust." Snakes two feet long had been found in drawing rooms, the roads were so miry that on one occasion the Secretary of State's carriage could not traverse the crossing at the treasury corner. As for Pennsylvania Avenue, John Randolph as late as 1827 termed it "a long lake of mud." There was no church of any denomination in the city, but religious services were usually held on Sundays at the treasury office and at the Capitol. The only house in which real liveliness prevailed was the French Minister's, where M. de Neuville astonished his guests with fanciful specimens of the Gallic cuisine, such as turkeys without bones, puddings in the form of fowls, fresh cod disguised like a salad, and celery like oysters. The same gallant gentleman gave Saturday night dances eagerly welcomed by Washington society.

In addition to his Florida negotiations, Adams was in active treaty with England over the Oregon country, regarding which he effected a compromise on the basis of a joint occupation for ten years. His relations with the British Minister to the United States, Canning, survived with difficulty the strain of personal contact with him. During one interview the following extraordinary conversation took place in the Secretary's office: "Have you," said Mr. Canning, "any

claim to the Shetland Islands?" "Have you any claim," replied Mr.
Adams, "to the mouth of the Columbia River?" "Why do you not
know," answered Canning, "that we have a claim?" "I do not know,"
responded Adams, "what you claim nor what you do not claim. You
claim India; you claim Africa; you claim——" "Perhaps," interrupted
Canning, "a piece of the moon." "No," said Adams, "I have not heard
that you claim exclusively any part of the moon; but there is not a
spot on this habitable globe that I could affirm you do not claim."

Not so controversial as the Oregon question but of great importance was Adams' success in obtaining the demilitarization of the
American-Canadian border.

Adams was cautious in sanctioning the recognition of the independence of the Spanish republics in South America by the United
States until it was apparent they could maintain their free status.
Meanwhile, reflecting deeply on the whole matter of foreign colonization of the American continents, he felt strongly that the United
States should discourage any situation which might in the future
embroil her in European quarrels. In July 1823 he informed the
Russian Minister that we "should contest the right of Russia to any
territorial establishment on this continent, and that we should assume
distinctly the principle that the American continents are no longer
subjects for any new European colonial establishments."

From the enunciation of this policy the progress to the formula-
tion of the familiar Monroe Doctrine was easy. It is only fair to
state that, although the famous doctrine bears the name of Monroe,
it is Adams who is probably more entitled even than his chief to the
credit for its provisions.

While he was handling important diplomatic subjects, Congress
laid on Adams, in 1817, the onerous burden of drawing up a complete
report on weights and measures. Laboring for four years at this
intricate assignment he finally produced an accurate survey of two
hundred and forty-five printed pages, standardizing the weights and
measures of the country, which has remained a classic and an authority on the subject. No accomplishment of his life better illustrates
the range and tenacity of his mind than his successful disposition
of this highly technical task.

During Adams' secretaryship, the great depression of 1819 took
place. The farmers were in debt to the federal government or to
improperly managed country banks, which were borrowing recklessly from the Bank of the United States. In the East, bankers were

financing industrialists in the building of excess manufacturing facilities. Currency theorists insisted that the ills of the depression could be cured if more paper money were placed in circulation. The optimism and expansiveness bred by the boomtime prosperity which followed the end of the War of 1812 bears a striking analogy to the events preceding the depression of 1929. The Bank of the United States fostered, instead of repressed, inflation, until its directors in belated alarm cut down its credits, whereupon a devastating panic ensued.

Except for walking, Adams' only form of exercise was swimming, for which he had a great relish. He commenced his fifty-seventh year by swimming with his French valet for an hour in the Potomac; on similar occasions he spent as much as two hours a day in that river. Even after he became President, he continued this custom; on one occasion at least he narrowly escaped drowning and was taken home, in the presidential carriage, half naked. Late in his life, while a Congressman, at the age of seventy-nine, he again confided his body to the waters of the Potomac, and drew refreshment from a source that had never failed him.

Long before Monroe finished his second term, the question of who should be named his successor was agitating the politicians. Of those considered for the office, Adams was pre-eminently the best qualified, but his aloofness and lack of charm made him an unpopular candidate and, as he observed of himself, he had neither talent nor inclination for intrigue. But so difficult was it for anyone to attack Adams' qualifications for the office that the hostile press was, in one instance, reduced to criticizing him as being an unfit occupant of the presidential mansion on the ground that he did not wear a cravat or waistcoat, and went barefooted to church. A more ludicrous allegation could scarcely have been conceived than such a one against the prim, well-starched, elastic-booted New Englander.

General Jackson was in the Senate and the idol of the frontier. Crawford, who had been Monroe's Secretary of the Treasury, had an enthusiastic following, but during the campaign suffered a stroke of paralysis from which he never entirely recovered, although this fact was not generally known until after the election. Crawford was disliked by Monroe, whom he had personally threatened when still a member of his Cabinet, calling the President a "damned infernal old scoundrel," while raising his cane as if to strike him. Monroe had seized the fire tongs and told Crawford to leave the house. Crawford later returned and apologized, but was never fully forgiven by the President.

The fourth candidate was Henry Clay, later called the "Judas of the West" by Jackson. As the Federalist party was to all intents nonexistent, the choice had to be made from Republican candidates. Jackson carried Pennsylvania, North and South Carolina, and most of the West, amassing a total of 99 electoral votes. Adams was second with 84 votes, mostly contributed by New England and New York, Crawford was third, and Clay last. Calhoun was chosen Vice-President.

As no presidential candidate had a majority in the electoral college, the contest was thrown into the House of Representatives. This meant, in effect, that Clay could decide whether Adams or Jackson would be President, since the Twelfth Amendment provided for a choice to be made only among the candidates receiving the three greatest number of votes, and the state of Crawford's health removed him from consideration. Clay had long before formed an unfavorable impression of Jackson, considering him a dangerous man. It was, therefore, believed that, although he had no personal affection for Adams, he would throw his influence to the Massachusetts candidate. A few days before the election an anonymous letter was published, the authorship of which was later traced to a dull Pennsylvania Congressman named Kremer, who was chiefly known as the possessor of a leopard-skin overcoat, asserting that Clay's friends had approached Jackson, promising Jackson their support in exchange for his promise to nominate Clay as Secretary of State after his election. It was further asserted that, when Jackson had contemptuously refused the bargain, the same proposition had been made to Adams and accepted by him.

This wretched canard, obviously inspired by the Jacksonites, was ridiculous to anyone who knew Adams' high character. The election was held on February 9, 1825, in the House of Representatives, where, the vote being 13 for Adams, 7 for Jackson, and 4 for Crawford, John Quincy Adams was duly entitled to the presidency.

Adams offered the position of Secretary of State to Clay, the logical choice for that office. After some hesitation, Clay accepted. Jackson's friends at once alleged that the appointment was conclusive proof of previous "bargain and corruption" between the President and his new Secretary, and they never ceased thenceforth, until Jackson's election, to harp upon that subject. A hostile newspaper announced that there had "expired at Washington . . . of poison administered by the assassin hands of John Quincy Adams, the usurper, and Henry Clay, the virtue, liberty, and independence of the United States." Jackson himself appears for the moment to have behaved in a dignified and gracious manner to his successful rival, but his mind was poisoned to such an extent that he opposed Clay's confirmation in the Senate, and came to an unalterably false conviction, that Adams and Clay had engaged in an "unholy coalition."

At least one person received the news of the election of John Quincy Adams with unalloyed joy. The Patriarch of Quincy wrote at once to his son:

> I have received your letter of the 9th. Never did I feel so much solemnity as upon this occasion. The multitude of my thoughts, and the intensity of my feelings are too much for a mind like mine, in its ninetieth year. May the blessing of God Almighty continue to protect you to the end of your life, as it has heretofore protected you, in so remarkable a manner from your cradle! I offer the same prayer for your lady and your family, and am your affectionate father.
>
> JOHN ADAMS

The other members of his Cabinet, besides Clay, were Richard Rush, Secretary of the Treasury; James Barbour, Secretary of War; Samuel L. Southard, Secretary of the Navy; and William Wirt, Attorney General. The new Secretary of the Navy and the Attorney General had served with Adams in the Monroe Cabinet. In making his other appointments Adams acted entirely on merit, determining to "renominate every person against whom there was no complaint which would have warranted his removal." "Efforts had been made," he wrote, "by some of the Senators to obtain different nominations, and to introduce a principle for change or rotation in office at the expiration of these [Monroe's] commissions; which would make the government a perpetual and unintermitting scramble for office. A more pernicious expedient could scarcely have been devised."

It resulted from this admirable attitude that Adams built up no political machine, for during his administration he authorized only twelve removals from office. Even in the case of his Postmaster-General, McLean, whose disloyalty was well known to him, he took no action, and that worthy was later rewarded for his base conduct by Jackson who made him a federal Judge.

In his first annual message Adams announced that "the great object of the institution of civil government is the improvement of those who are parties to the social compact." Favoring a loose construction of the Constitution, he advocated, to the dismay of the strict constructionists, the use of excess revenues for the building of national roads and canals, for the deepening of rivers and harbors, for the establishment of scientific and research institutions, and the founding of a great national university. Moreover, his determined attempt to conserve the Western lands for the benefit of the nation instead of handing them over to speculators and to intriguing and dishonest politicians rendered him unpopular with all those, and their number was legion, who wished to batten on the splendid public domain. The rapacity with which speculators flew at the public lands was compared by Adams to the thirst of a tiger for blood. His domestic policies were thwarted either from constitutional objections or more frequently out of sheer partisan malice by his opponents who thereafter devoted their efforts to discrediting Adams with the object of electing Jackson as his successor.

In one crisis Adams showed an absence of his customary courage, and his indecision in the matter was lamentable. The Cherokees, a peaceable and enlightened tribe of Indians living in western Georgia and Eastern Alabama, had the misfortune to be occupying and succesfully tilling, rich farming lands coveted by their white Georgian neighbors. This reservation had been specifically guaranteed to them by a treaty drafted in 1791 by George Washington. Supported by their Governor, Troup, a man of brutal instincts, the Georgians invaded the Indian territory, seized and held it in the face of the administration's disapproval. John Quincy Adams, like his father, was no friend to Indians, but his clear duty, in which he failed, was to restore to this tribe the lands of which they had been dispossessed.

Adams, happily for himself, was not aware of his lack of force in handling this situation. Years later, in reference to declining to serve on an Indian Committee in the House, he observed: "The policy, from Washington to myself, of all the presidents of the United States had been justice and kindness to the Indian tribes— to civilize and preserve them. With the Creeks and Cherokees, it had been eminently successful. Its success was their misfortune. The States, within whose borders their settlements were, took the alarm, and broke down all the treaties which had pledged the faith of the nation. Georgia extended her jurisdiction over them, took possession of their lands, houses, cattle, furniture, Negroes and drove

them out of their own dwellings. All the Southern States supported
Georgia in this utter prostration of faith and justice; and Andrew
Jackson, by the simultaneous operation of fraudulent treaties and
brutal force, completed the work. The Florida War is one of the
fruits of this policy, the conduct of which exhibits one uninterrupted
scene of the most profligate corruption. All resistance against this
abomination is in vain. It is among the heinous sins of this nation,
for which I believe God will one day bring them to judgment—but
at His own time and by His own means. I turned my eyes away
from this sickening mass of putrefaction, and asked to be excused
from serving as chairman of the committee."

During his administration the national debt was reduced by
$30,373,188, leaving due on January 1, 1829, the sum of $58,362,136.

In the foreign field Adams contented himself with making an un-
precedented number of commercial treaties and maintaining friendly
relations with all nations. He favored our taking an active part in
the Panama Conference, but political motives caused the rejection
of that proposition by his adversaries.

It is sad to read the recital of the constant, bitter and unreflecting
battle waged against Adams during his presidency. His patriotism
was above reproach, as were his character and ability; his conception of his office was that it should be treated as a sacred public
trust. His desire was to improve the moral and intellectual condition
of the electorate to a point where an informed democracy, acting
through delegated authority, could set new standards of his achievement in government. He was almost the last of that great line of
Presidents who considered themselves dedicated to the leadership
of their people, rather than the mere servants of popular majorities
or selfish minorities. But his honesty, ability and high ideals were of
little avail against the political arts of his opponents. The widespread extension of manhood suffrage, bringing a more democratic
element into public life, was producing a crop of office seekers whose
aims were more selfish than had been the case in earlier American
history. In mid-term, Adams entirely lost control over Congress;
from then on he was the butt of every partisan shaft. A new party
line-up came into being—the administration men were known as
National Republicans, a title which some years later was changed
to that of Whigs, while the Jackson oppositionists called themselves
Democrats, a name ever since applied to their party.

Adams' activity as President was remarkable. He rose between four and six in the morning, depending upon the time of year, and usually began the day by reading two or three chapters in the Bible, with Scott's and Hewlett's *Commentaries*. Sometimes, before this mental exercise, he walked by the light of the moon, or the stars, or no light at all, for several hours. If he missed his morning walk, he took it in the afternoon, or else, in the proper season, went swimming in the Potomac. Before breakfast, which was served between nine and ten, he read the morning newspapers and public papers from the several departments, and wrote. After breakfast he had a succession of visitors until four or five o'clock. He dined from about half-past five to seven, and, generally passed the evening (from dark until about eleven) playing billiards or signing land grants or blank patents.

One of his visitors, Mrs. Anderson, came to him with a singular petition for the pardon of her husband. "All importunities," Adams remarked, "are trials of temper. The importunities of women are double trials. I had refused this woman three times and she had now nothing new to allege. I now desired her not to come to me again. She hinted that her husband did not wish to be discharged from prison himself; and that it would be no relaxation of his punishment to turn him over to her. It reminded me of the old song about Orpheus and Euridyce."

During his administration a domestic event of great importance was the completion of the Erie Canal—colloquially known, after Governor De Witt Clinton, as "Clinton's Big Ditch." In October 1825, after eight years work, this source of communication covering the 363 miles from Albany to Buffalo was officially opened, and Clinton headed a fleet which traversed its length between crowded banks. From Albany, Clinton proceeded down the Hudson, and, emptying two kegs of water from Lake Erie into the ocean, boasted that communication had been established between "our Mediterranean Seas and the Atlantic." As a result of this canal being established, the freight rate from Albany to Buffalo fell from one hundred to ten dollars a ton, and New York City became the commercial center of the country.

Adams favored a reasonable tariff for the protection of manufactures, but Congress went far beyond his wishes and passed the "Tariff of Abominations" of 1828. The South voted almost solidly against the bill, the Middle States and the West for it, while the New England vote, as a result of high rates on raw materials necessary for use in that section, was split. The whole matter was one of political jockeying and succeeded only in embittering the South against Congress and the President; for, as John Randolph, of Roanoke, said, the only manufacture it was really concerned with was "the manufacture of a President." Adams, near the end of his term, was powerless to influence Congress; he accepted its decision and signed the bill, but later caused its removal from the statute books.

Adams' most vituperative and brilliant critic in Congress was John Randolph, of Roanoke, one of the most eccentric and gifted individuals who has ever crossed the American political stage. His talents were tinged at times with madness, his prejudices were always stronger than his reasoning faculties. Dislike of the Adams family was a creed with him. "I bore some part," he said, "in putting down the dynasty of John the First, and, by the Grace of God, I hope to aid in putting down the dynasty of John the Second."

Randolph at once became a violent supporter of the Jacksonian faction of Congress, indulging in the most intemperate attacks on the President and his friends. In the course of one of his tirades he referred to Henry Clay as "this being, so brilliant yet so corrupt, which, like a rotten mackerel by moonlight, shines and stinks, and stinks and shines." He then continued by characterizing the relation between the President and his Secretary of State as "the coalition of Blifil and Black George—the combination, unheard of until then, of the Puritan and the Blackleg." This language was too extreme for the spirited Clay to disregard, and he challenged Randolph to a duel. The resulting affair, according to a noted connoisseur of the code, was the last high-toned duel in America.

Pistols were the weapons selected. They each fired once, and neither discharge took effect. At the second fire Clay's ball passed through the skirt of Randolph's long coat.

Randolph, who had reserved his bullet, pointed his pistol skyward, fired and walked toward Clay with his hand extended, saying, "Mr. Clay, you owe me a new coat." "I'm glad the debt is no greater," responded Clay, and the two Virginians heartily shook hands.

The attacks of Randolph upon the administration did not abate as a result of this incident, but Adams, who had, as Rufus Choate once remarked, the instinct of a wild beast for the carotid artery, was not silent under them although most of his abuse of Randolph was confided to his diary. As early as 1820 he had there recorded his impressions of the Southerner as follows: "I soon passed into the House of Representatives, where John Randolph was speaking upon one of the Missouri slave questions. I heard him between three and four hours. His speech, as usual, had neither beginning, middle, nor end. Egotism, Virginian aristocracy, slave-scourging liberty, religion, literature, science, wit, fancy, generous feelings and malignant passions constitute a chaos in his mind, from which nothing orderly can ever flow."

Again he described Randolph, Ingham and their group as "skunks of party slander who had been squirting round the House of Representatives thence to issue and perfume the atmosphere of the Union." By 1828 he had decided that "Randolph is the image and superscription of a great man stamped upon base metal. His mind is a jumble of sense, wit, and absurdity."

Before the end of Adams' term he had determined that "the besotted violence of John Randolph excluded him thenceforward from all right to personal civility from me. Half a dozen other frequenters of gin lane and beer alley . . . put themselves into the same position, and two or three slanderers drunk with faction though not with alcohol must be added to the gang."

As late as 1831 the mention of Randolph's name still aroused intense bitterness in Adams' bosom. In speaking of his short residence as Minister to Russia, Adams said of him: "Randolph, who turns his diseases to commodity, stipulated before he went that if his health should require it he should have permission to pass the winter in a more genial climate; went to Russia in a frigate, behaved for a few weeks at St. Petersburg like a crazy man, then sent home a servant with his baggage, and went to spend his winter in London, where he is figuring in speeches at the turtlefeasts of the Lord Mayor, and he is now announced as a candidate in his district for election to the next Congress, where there is no doubt he will be chosen; for the people of his district are as much enamored with him as the Queen of the Fairies was with the ass's head of Bottom after the drop of juice from love-in-idleness had been squeezed upon her eyelids in her sleep."

Long before the expiration of Adams' term, it was realized that the next presidential contest would be between himself and Jackson, with the odds in overwhelming favor of the latter. Martin Van Buren, the skillful political leader of New York State, and James Buchanan, of Pennsylvania, were in practical control of the Jackson campaign, although it is doubtful whether they can be held responsible for the scurrilous attacks made on the President by the Jacksonites. Actually Van Buren entertained a feeling of respect for Adams, of whom he once said: "Mr. Adams was an honest man, not only incorruptible himself, but . . . an enemy to venality in every department of public service."

Adams had no such adept managers to inveigle voters to his support. Indeed, many of his followers, championed him out of "a cold sense of duty"; one of them, Ezekiel Webster, wrote: "We do not entertain for him one personal kind feeling, nor cannot unless we disembowel ourselves like a trussed turkey of all that is human nature within us."

The adminstration party, entirely without Adams' sanction, heaped the most scabrous abuse upon Jackson, lampooning his lawlessness and his military career, and stooped to allegations regarding his premarital relations with Mrs. Jackson and the irregularity of their marriage. The Democratic press carried on an equally unprincipled campaign of invective. It portrayed Adams as a stingy Puritan, a selfish aristocrat, and a corruptionist. One Jackson handbill had a broad-ax cut of Adams driving off with a horsewhip a crippled old soldier who had asked alms of him.

The election of 1828 brought this unsavory spectacle to an end. Jackson had 178 electoral votes to Adams' 83, although Adams' popular vote was 44 per cent of the total. Calhoun continued as Vice-President by 171 votes, showing that, although nominally there were two political parties, actually the choice of a President had been an issue between two personalities, in which one had been elected, according to Channing, by the overrepresentation of the South, combined with the employment of unjustifiable methods by Jackson's partisans in New York and Pennsylvania.

This contest left deep scars on Adams' soul. He had been defeated by a man whose own political career he had saved when no other prominent public man had dared to defend him. Knowing himself to be actuated by the purest ideals of public service, he had witnessed the sabotage for partisan motives of every cause he had championed. Friendless, he had entered the President's house, and almost friendless he left it. Loving his country passionately, he had been unable to inspire popular affection for himself or his program. A lonely, bald-headed, suspicious-faced, ungracious-looking, disappointed man, sixty-one years old, he returned to private life, saying:

"The sun of my political life sets in the deepest gloom. But that of my country shines unclouded."

Like his father he refused to witness the triumph of his opponent. Instead, leaving the White House on the evening of March 3 he withdrew to a house which he had leased on Meridian Hill, in the suburbs of Washington, to ponder over the ingratitude of Republics.

During his presidency Adams had little leisure for reading or writing poetry, and in that respect his enforced retirement was pleasing to him. Immediately returning to his beloved books and to gardening, he began to amass materials for a projected life of his father. Though flattered by election to the Board of Overseers of Harvard University, his political career appeared closed.

But if Adams had not great personal popularity in the nation, the constituents of his own district were enamored of his abilities. In September 1830 he was invited to be a candidate for the House of Representatives from the district of Plymouth. He replied that if the voters desired he would represent them, but added: "I shall not ask their votes. I wish them to act their pleasure." Of the 2565 votes cast, he received 1817. He promptly announced that he would hold himself accountable to no party and to no section. From that time until his death he continued to represent this district. "My election as President of the United States," he recorded, "was not half so gratifying to my inmost soul. No election or appointment conferred upon me ever gave me so much pleasure."

Ten days after Jackson's induction into office the ex-President found that the manner in which the new administration was commencing its operations portended no good. However, criticism of the administration did not occupy his mind nearly as much as did the composition of poetry. Four weeks after he left the White House, he rode on horseback for two hours, and mused "upon the construction of half a dozen elegiac stanzas to versify a similitude upon Corinthian brass. I accomplished it in part, and very much to my satisfaction. It is with poetry as with chess and billiards; there is a certain degree of attainment which labor and practice will reach, and beyond which no vigils and no vows will go."

Throughout his long service in Congress he was conspicuous for his opposition to the "gag rule," passed in 1836 through the influence of Southern members, which resolved that "all petitions, memorials, resolutions, propositions, or papers, relating in any way, or to any extent whatever, to the subject of slavery, or the abolition of slavery, shall, without being either printed or referred, be laid upon the table, and that no further action whatever shall be had thereon."

His concern in this matter was for freedom of speech and petition, for he was never technically an abolitionist, although he opposed the extension of slavery, terming it "the great and foul stain upon the North American Union," and he further said of it: "it is a contemplation, worthy of the most exalted soul whether its total abolition is or is not practicable: if practicable, by what it may be effected, and if a choice of means be within the scope of the object, what means would accomplish it at the smallest cost of human suffering. A dissolution, at least temporary, of the Union, as now constituted, would be certainly necessary. . . . The Union might then be reorganized on the fundamental principle of emancipation. This object is vast in its compass, awful in its prospects, sublime and beautiful in its issue." When South Carolina threatened nullification in 1832, Adams favored a conclusive settlement of the issue at that time, even if it necessitated martial measures.

He was not in agreement with Monroe on the latter's scheme gradually to abolish slavery by colonizing the American Negroes in Africa; for he thought such a plan visionary.

His struggle for the rescission of the gag rule was one of the most dramatic fights ever made by a public man. At each session he moved its abrogation, and exposed himself anew to the fury of the proslavery Congressmen. His voice, high and shrill, often cracked with emotion, his figure was too rotund for his height of five feet seven inches, his hands shook with palsy, his eyes and cheeks were suffused with a rheumy affliction, yet he impressed the House by the majesty of his courage.

It was not against the constitutionality of the institution of slavery that he fought, for he regarded it as established by the Constituion, but against the unconstitutionality of abridging the right of petition and of free speech. In the course of his long struggle he succeeded, however, in focusing the attention of the nation on the evils of slavery as no other individual or group had done.

In his diary he observed, in 1842, that "not a day passes but I receive letters from the North, and sometimes the West, asking for an autograph and a scrap of poetry or of prose, and from the South almost daily letters of insult, profanity, obscenity, and filth. These are indices to the various estimation in which I am held in the free and servile sections of this Union; indices to the moral sensibilities of free and of slavery-trained communities. Threats of lynching and of assassination are the natural off-spring of slave-breeders and slave-traders; profanity and obscenity are their natural associates. Such dross the fire must purge."

Adams became a greater figure in the country than he had ever been as President. Strangers admired him, acquaintances offered him civilities, to which he had been previously unaccustomed.

By a process of attrition he wore down opposition to the abrogation of the gag rule. At last, aged seventy-eight on December 3, 1845, he heard it rescinded by a vote of 108 to 80: "Blessed, forever blessed, be the name of God," was his diary entry for that day.

Four years before this time he had championed the cause of human freedom in another striking manner, when he appeared before the Supreme Court of the United States as the unpaid lawyer of the Amistead Negroes. This complicated case involved certain Negroes kidnaped and imported into Cuba, who had committed mutiny on the high seas, killing the Captain of a Spanish schooner and some of her crew. The Spanish Minister to the United States had demanded the return to their reputed owners of the Negroes, who, in the course of their Odyssey, had drifted upon the Long Island coast. Adams presented their defense before the Supreme Court, actuated by the same unselfish motives that had inspired Voltaire in his famous defense of the Calas family.

As was usual with him, he exaggerated in his imagination the difficulties with which he would be faced in winning an acquittal. "In merely glancing over the slave-trade papers lent me by Mr. Fox," he wrote, "I find impulses of duty upon my own conscience which I cannot resist, while on the other hand are the magnitude, the danger, the insurmountable burden of labor to be encountered in the undertaking to touch upon the slave-trade. No one else will undertake it; no one but a spirit unconquerable by man, woman or fiend can undertake it but with the heart of martyrdom. The world, the flesh, and all the devils in hell are arrayed against any man who now in this North American Union shall dare to join the standard of Almighty God to put down the African slave-trade; and what can I, upon the verge of my seventy-fourth birthday, with a shaking hand, a darkening eye, drowsy brain, and with all my faculties dropping from me one by one, as the teeth are dropping from my head— what can I do for the cause of God and man, for the progress of human emancipation, for the suppression of the African slave-trade?

Yet my conscience presses me on; let me but die upon the breach."

He spoke for four hours and a half on one day before the Court, and concluded, on another day, with a speech of three hours, constituting an argument which Mr. Justice Sorty said was one of the most remarkable presented to the Court during his occupancy of the Bench. The Court decided in favor of the Negroes, who through private contributions were returned to Africa.

While a Congressman, he participated in many debates on various topics, including that of the annexation of Texas, and made a great and successful fight for the sound establishment of the Smithsonian Institution. He also found time to travel about and deliver orations, chiefly on American historical subjects, such as the lives and times of Madison and Monroe.

Although he despised Jackson, whom he considered a shallow, intemperate demagogue, he supported his policies if he felt they deserved it. The most notable of such occasions was when Jackson, in reply to the delay of the French in satisfying the so-called spoliation claims during the Napoleonic Wars, remarked it was a principle of international law that if one nation refused to pay a just debt, the aggrieved nation may "seize on the property belonging to the citizens of the defaulting nation," and that, if France did not arrange for payment at the next session of her Parliament, the United States ought to delay no longer to "take by force what it could not get by negotiation."

Adams' speech, delivered during the debate on this controversy, left the House "lost in excitement," and the "very walls shook with the thundering applause he had awakened." In part he said: "This treaty has been ratified on both sides of the ocean; it has received the sign manual of the sovereign of France through his Majesty's principal Minister of State; it has been ratified by the Senate of this Republic; and still we are told that the arrogance of France, the insolence of the French Chambers, must be submitted to, and we must come down to the lower degradation of re-opening negotiations to attain that which has already been acknowledged to be our due."

At this very time Adams was a candidate for the Senate from Massachusetts, and his course in regard to the controversy with France was used to secure the election of his opponent. The French, it will be remembered, decided to make the payments. But if Adams did, when his sense of duty impelled him, support some of Jackson's public measures he did not compromise in his personal opinion that the President was little better than an ignoramus. When it was proposed that Harvard College should confer on Jackson an honorary degree, he wrote in protest: "As myself an affectionate child of our Alma Mater, I would not be present to witness her disgrace in conferring her highest literary honors upon a barbarian who could not write a sentence of grammar and hardly could spell his own name."

Adams must have been an uncomfortable colleague for his fellow Congressmen. When he did not excoriate them in public, he impaled them in his diary for the contemplation of posterity. He accused Daniel Webster of having a "gigantic intellect, envious temper, ravenous ambition and rotten heart. . . . His treatment of me," he further wrote, "has been, is, and will be, an improved edition of Andrew Jackson's gratitude." He described the brother of James Barbour, who had been his Secretary of War, as "a shallow-pated wildcat, fit for nothing but to tear the Union to rags and tatters." He once fell foul of James Polk, who "started up and fell into an idolizing and mawkish glorification of Doctor Andrew Jackson, with some coarse and equally dull invective against me. . . . I rose," writes Adams, "and said I should not reply to his speech, and gave notice once for all that whenever any admirer of the President of the United States should think fit to pay his court to him in the House, either by a flaming panegyric upon him or by a rancorous invective against me, he should never elicit one word of reply from me.

'No! let the candied tongue lick absurd pomp,
And crook the pregnant hinges of the knee,
Where THRIFT may follow fawning.'

Polk shrunk back abashed into his shell, and said not a word. The lines from Hamlet struck the House like a spark of electricity."

He denounced three of his assailants in the House in unmeasured terms—Wise as a murderer, Marshall as a drunkard, and Gilmer as an inciter of his assassination. It was Wise who once protested, after a long day and night session, that the House was "too sleepy, too tired and too drunk" to consider important business seriously. Wise lamented that Adams should "have outlived his fame! That one who had served his country so long should cancel her debt of gratitude for all his many services." He assured his audience that Adams was "politically dead; dead as Burr, dead as Arnold." He concluded with an expression of the "personal loathing, dread, and contempt I feel for the man." When Wise had finished his speech, Adams rose and said he had "determined not to interrupt the speaker till he had discharged his whole cargo of filthy invective." Tom Marshall retired worsted from his exchange of abuse with Adams and, when asked by his friends to attack him again, replied: "Not I! You left me to fight the lion alone; you can skin your skunks yourselves!"

On February 14, 1844, Stephen A. Douglas, of Illinois, later Lincoln's famous opponent, was described in the diary as having raved out an hour in abusive invectives. "His face was convulsed, his gesticulation frantic, and he lashed himself into such a heat that if his body had been made of combustible matter it would have been burnt out. In the midst of his roaring, to save himself from choking, he stripped and cast away his cravat, unbuttoned his waistcoat, and had the air and aspect of a half-naked pugilist. And this man comes from a judicial bench, and passes for an eloquent orator."

Adams' diary commenced on November 12, 1779, continued, with some lapses and irregularity, to January 4, 1848, less than two months before the writer's death. As one of Adams' biographers expressed it: "Sooner or later every man of any note in the United States was mentioned in his pages, and there is scarcely one of them, who, if he could have read what was said of him, would not have preferred the ignominy of the omission. As one turns the leaves, he feels as though he were walking through a graveyard of slaughtered reputations."

In 1834 he wrote: "New Hampshire is governed by a knave of the name of Isaac Hill, editor of a newspaper, mail contractor, and now a Senator of the United States—just cunning enough to grow rich by railing against the rich, and to fatten upon the public spoils, bawling Democracy. This is the besetting sin of popular governments, and it is now as it always has been. Van Buren is a demagogue of the same school, with a tincture of aristocracy—an amalgamated metal of lead and copper."

In 1804 he was a frequent guest of Jefferson whom he found told "large stories. . . . You never can be an hour in this man's company without something of the marvellous like these stories. His genius is of the French school. It conceives better than it combines." Twenty-seven years later, he was intensely bitter against Jefferson and found that "his treatment of Washington, of Knox, of my father, of Hamilton, of Bayard, who made him President of the United States, and lastly, of me, is marked with features of perfidy worthy of Tiberius Caesar or Louis the Eleventh of France." In connection

with Jefferson, Adams throws an interesting sidelight upon one feature of diplomatic life in Washington, in 1806, when he dined at the
President's in company with the Tunisian Ambassador and his two
secretaries. "By the invitation," he says, "dinner was to have been
on the table precisely at sunset—it being in the midst of Ramadan,
during which the Turks fast while the sun is above the horizon. He
did not arrive until half an hour after sunset, and immediately after
greeting the President and the company, proposed to retire and
smoke his pipe. The President requested him to smoke it there,
which he accordingly did, taking at the same time snuff deeply
scented with otto of roses."

The diary also contains general observations and statements of
interest on various topics. "Conversation," Adams thought, "is an art
of the highest importance, and a school, in which, for the business
in life, more may perhaps be learnt than from books. It is, indeed,
and must be, desultory and superficial; and, as a school, consists
more in making others talk than in talking. Therein has been, and
ever will be, my deficiency—the talent of starting the game." He had
a very low opinion of newspaper editors. "There is not one of them,"
he wrote, "whose friendship is worth buying, nor one whose enmity
is not formidable. They are a sort of assassins who sit with loaded
blunderbusses at the corner of streets and fire them off for hire or
sport at any passenger whom they select." In 1844 he announced,
"James K. Polk of Tennessee is to be President of the United States
for four years from the fourth of March, 1845. What the further
events of this issue may be is not clear, but it will be the signal for
my retirement from public life. It is the victory of the slavery element in the Constitution of the United States."

The severity of Washington winters and the absence of any arti-
ficial heating arrangements sometimes interfered with the transaction
of public business. On January 22, 1805, Adams noted that the
weather was excessively cold and the members of the House spent
almost all the day at the firesides in the lobby. In February of the
following year, another cold spell made life even more uncomfortable
for Congress, with the assistance of a violent wind which obliged
both Houses "to adjourn at an early hour, their windows having
been blown in."

At the time of Van Buren's first candidacy for the presidency,
Adams found the "opposition divided between three talented aspir-
ants . . . neither of whom would yield subordination to either of

the others have been driven in mere desperation to set up men of straw in their places, and they have taken up Hugh Lawson White and William Henry Harriscn, as the Israelites set up a calf, and as the Egyptians worshipped oxen and monkeys." In 1837, Adams called on President Van Buren and "spent half an hour in conversation with him, respecting the weather, the climate, and Queen Victoria, the girl of eighteen, sovereign of all the British dominions—'Youth at the prow, and Pleasure at the helm.'" A few years later, the paunchy Mr. Adams announced that "Mr. Van Buren is growing inordinately fat."

Although Van Buren and Adams were never what one would ordinarily call friends, Van Buren seemed to take a genuine pleasure in occasional conversation with the ex-President, of whom he said: "In a small and agreeable party, he was one of the most entertaining table companions of his day. . . . I . . . always derived [on such occasions] unqualified delight from his society and valuable information from his conversation."

Adams spent a good deal of time in gardening and planting trees. In 1833 he was to be found, "reading and making petty annotations upon the Book of Leviticus, strolling about my garden and nursery, hoeing and plucking up weeds—a never-ceasing occupation." Mrs. Adams was also an agriculturist, and we learn that she wound silk from several hundred silkworms which she had reared, while her husband engaged in a long correspondence with his son Charles and gave the boy an analysis of Cicero's "Oration for Roscius of Ameria." Upon a particularly harassing day Adams received some comfort when he found "a tamarind heaving up the earth, in the centre of tumbler No. 2; and I planted in tumbler No. 1 three whole Hautboy strawberries."

While he was President, he had ordered in London, a signet ring. The device was "a very simple one," said Adams, "of which a sixpenny seal had been given me—a cock with the motto, 'Watch.' I wished it in better garb and execution. But the precept of Jesus is to pray as well as watch, and he used the cock as a monitor to recall to duty the faithful disciple who denied him at the crisis of his fate. To fix the fleeting solemnity of these thoughts, I threw them this morning, before breakfast, into a sonnet to Chanticleer, which is here in the margin, and of which, when I come to be ashamed of the poetry, I may still adhere to the morality."

The great passions of Adams' life were his library and his writing.

"To live without a Cicero and a Tacitus at hand," he said, "seems to me as if it was a privation of one of my limbs." Again he said, "There is such seduction in a library of good books that I cannot resist the temptation to luxuriate in reading; and, because I have so much to write, I count all time lost that is not spent in writing."

"Literature," he once concluded, "has been the charm of my life, and, could I have carved out my own fortunes, to literature would my whole life have been devoted. I have been a lawyer for bread, and a statesman at the call of my country. In the practice of the law I never should have attained the highest eminence, for the want of natural and spontaneous eloquence. The operations of my mind are slow, my imagination sluggish, and my powers of extemporaneous speaking very insufficient. But I have much capacity for, and love of, labor, habits on the whole of industry and temperance, and a strong and almost innate passion for literary pursuits. The business and sometimes the dissipations of my life have in a great measure withdrawn me from it. The summit of my ambition would have been by some great work of literature to have done honor to my age and country, and to have lived in the gratitude of future ages. This consummation of happiness has been denied me."

Adams' own literary work, with the exception of his diary, is not distinguished by any evidence of such art, talent, originality or utility that one can honestly wish he had been able to devote himself wholly to letters. His taste in literature changed, as does that of almost everyone, with the years. In youth he was delighted with fairy tales, *The Arabian Nights* and fictitious adventures of every kind. "And the more there was in them of invention," he said, "the more pleasing they were. My imagination pictured them all as realities, and I dreamed of enchantments as if there was a world in which they existed. At ten years of age I read Shakespeare's Tempest, As You Like It, Merry Wives of Windsor, Much Ado About Nothing, and King Lear. The humors of Falstaff scarcely affected me at all. Bardolph and Pistol and Nym were personages quite unintelligible to me; and the lesson of Sir Hugh Evans to the boy William was too serious an affair. But the incantations of Prospero, the loves of Ferdinand and Miranda, the more than ethereal brightness of Ariel, and the worse than beastly grossness of Caliban, made for me a world of revels, and lapped me in Elysium. With these books, in a closet of my mother's bedchamber, there was also a small edition, in two volumes, of Milton's Paradise Lost, which, I believe, I attempted ten times to read, and never could get through half a book. I might as well have attempted to read Homer before I had learnt the Greek alphabet. . . . I smoked tobacco and read Milton at the same time, and from the same motive—to find out what was the recondite charm in them which gave my father so much pleasure. After making myself four or five times sick with smoking, I mastered that accomplishment, and acquired a habit which, thirty years afterwards, I had much more difficulty in breaking off. But I did not master Milton. I was nearly thirty when I first read the Paradise Lost with delight and astonishment. But of late years I have lost the relish for fiction. I see nothing with sympathy but men, women, and children of flesh and blood."

"I have literary tastes peculiar to myself," he observed on another occasion, "and the correctness of which I distrust, because they differ from the general voice. There is no lyric poet of ancient or modern times who so deeply affects my feelings as Gray. Every one of his odes is to me an inestimable jewel, and nothing in all Dr. Johnson's writings is so disgusting to me as his criticisms upon them."

Adams informed ex-Chancellor Kent, during the course of a conversation on English literature, that he took "little interest in the character of Desdemona, whose sensual passions I thought overardent, so as to reconcile her to a passion for a black man; and although faithful to him I thought the poet had painted her as a lady of rather easy virtue—very different from the innocence of Miranda or the rosy pudency of Imogen."

He regretted growing old because he felt that one of the decays of age was a falling off of the discipline of the mind. "The operation of the mind in reading," he declared, "should be like that of the leech upon the body; but the leech sometimes wanders over the veins without taking hold of any one; and so it is in the dissipation of spirits which comes on with the lassitude of the years."

There was little enduring literature, ancient or modern, with which Adams was not familiar. He was a splendid linguist, although he never seems to have succeeded in mastering the Hebrew alphabet, a task he used to set himself when he wished to compose his mind. With music and art, with science and travels, he was closely familiar, as he was with almost every other department of intellectual or artistic culture.

One of the most striking features of Adams' personality was his feeling of being persecuted by malevolent rivals or enemies. This perhaps accounts for much of his censoriousness. "Among the dark spots in human nature," he complained in 1836, "which, in the course of my life, I have observed, the devices of rivals to ruin me have been sorry pictures of the heart of man. They first exhibited themselves at college, but in the short time that I was there their operation could not be of much effect. But from the day that I quitted the walls of Harvard, Harrison Gray Otis, Theophilus Parsons, Timothy Pickering, James A. Bayard, Henry Clay, Jonathan Russell, William H. Crawford, John C. Calhoun, Andrew Jackson, Daniel Webster, and John Davis, W. B. Giles, and John Randolph, have used up their faculties in base and dirty tricks to thwart my progress in life and destroy my character." Again he wrote: "In the multitudinous whimseys of a disabled mind and body, the thick-coming fancies often occur to me that the events which affect my life and adventures are specially shaped to disappoint my purposes. I can scarcely recollect a single instance of success to anything that I ever undertook. Yet, with fervent gratitude to God, I confess that my life has been equally marked by great and signal successes which I neither aimed at nor anticipated."

Even his successful termination of the Florida treaty was not, in his estimation, appreciated. Instead, "It had at once disconcerted and stimulated my personal antagonists and rivals. It promised well for my reputation in the public opinion. Under the petals of this garland of roses, the Scapin, Onis, had hidden a viper. His mock sickness, his use of De Neuville as a tool to perpetrate a fraud which he did not dare attempt to carry through himself, his double dealings before and after the signature, his fradulent declarations to me, and his shuffling equivocations here and in Spain, to acquire the reputation of having duped the President and me, were but materials in the hands of my enemies to dose me with poison extracted from the laurels of the treaty itself."

While he was in Congress he was once convinced that "the most insignificant error of conduct in me at this time would be my irredeemable ruin in this world, and both the ruling political parties are watching with intense anxiety for some overt act by me to set the whole pack of their hireling press upon me."

Although a devoted Bible reader and the author of many psalms and hymns, Adams was not until late in life a member of any sect. As an old man he joined the Congregationalist Church, at Quincy.

Adams' remarkable health was no doubt due, in large part, to temperate habits and active exercise. He particularly liked walking, and, even as an old man, was known to have walked seven miles to his son's residence in Boston before breakfast. While President, he sometimes made the journey from Washington to Quincy on horseback, accompanied by a servant.

In 1844 he feared that he would have to abandon the writing of his diary because of physical debility. "I have now struggled nearly five years," he said, "without the interval of a day, while mind and body have been wearing away under the daily, silent, but unremitting erosion of time. I rose this morning at four, and, with smarting, bloodshot eye and shivering hand, still sat down and wrote to fill up the chasm of the closing days of the last week; but my stern chase after Time is, to borrow a simile from Tom Paine, like the race of a man with a wooden leg after a horse."

Adams' popularity toward the end of his life was great in the North and Middle West. He made a trip into western New York, for the benefit of the health of his daughter-in-law, Mrs. Charles Francis Adams, which developed into a personal triumph for him. He followed it with a trip to Cincinnati, to dedicate a new astronomical laboratory there, and was greeted most enthusiastically on this excursion.

Within a year of the rescission of the gag rule Adams was stricken in Boston with paralysis. For four months afterwards he made no entries in his diary. The next one was headed "Posthumous Memoir." After describing his recent illness he continued: "From that hour, I date my decease, and consider myself, for every useful purpose, to myself and fellow creatures, dead; and hence I call this, and what I may hereafter write, a posthumous memoir." He recovered sufficiently to return to Congress, and, when he entered that body, every member rose and stood, while the stricken old gladiator was led to his chair by two of his colleagues. He spoke only once more although he was diligent in his attendance. On February 21, 1848, he started to rise from his seat. The Speaker was putting a question when cries of "Stop! Stop! Mr. Adams!" were heard. He had fallen unconscious. He was placed on a sofa, and removed, first to the hall of the rotunda and then to the Speaker's room. Doctors could do nothing to avert the end, and he was not moved again. He lingered through Washington's Birthday, and on the afternoon of the twenty-third murmured: "Thank the officers of the House." A little later he spoke his final words: "This is the last of earth!" In the evening he died. Mrs. Adams survived him until May 15, 1852.

Andrew Jackson

Born: March 15, 1767.

Admitted to Bar: 1787.

Appointed Prosecuting Attorney for Western District of North Carolina: 1788.

Married: 1791.

Member federal House of Representatives: Decem-1796-March 1797.

Elected to United States Senate: 1797.

Judge of the Superior Court of Tennessee: 1798-1804.

Killed Charles Dickinson: 1806.

Major General of Militia in Creek campaigns: 1813-14.

Commissioned Major General in regular army: 1814.

Battle of New Orleans: January 8, 1815.

Commander-in-Chief in Seminole War: 1818.

Executed Arbuthnot and Ambrister: 1818.

Military Governor of Florida: 1821.

Elected to the United States Senate: 1823.

Resigned from United States Senate: 1825.

Elected President of the United States: 1828.

Re-elected President of the United States: 1832.

Died: June 8, 1845.

ANDREW JACKSON

THE accession of Andrew Jackson to the presidency marked the beginning of a very definite change in American political history. Before his election, the highest office in the Republic had been occupied by four Virginians and by two Massachusetts men. In spite of the gradual enlargement of the suffrage, a ruling oligarchy, composed of Southern planters and nominees of the conservative interests of the Eastern seaboard, had continued to dictate national policies. The influence of the West had been of some importance, but no one of its politicians, with the exception of Henry Clay, had previously been given serious consideration as a candidate for the chief magistracy. Moreover, the whole conduct of the presidential office by the first six Presidents had been illustrative of truly representative government. Each of them had carefully studied the problems of national administration and had evolved for himself a distinct political philosophy. But Jackson's candidacy had been based less on political than on personal issues, and the choice between Adams and himself had centered on personalities rather than philosophies.

After a campaign distinguished by bitter and unlicensed attacks on both candidates, the voice of the majority had decreed the defeat of the unpopular John Quincy Adams, one of the finest public servants in our history, and his replacement by Andrew Jackson, who had won a position of immense popularity by his military exploits, but whose supposed radicalism had affrighted most of the propertied elements of the country.

The embittered relations between the retiring and succeeding President further emphasized the differences between the two parties of which they were the titular heads. Jackson, still smarting under attacks upon the character of his wife by Adams' supporters, neglected the ordinary civilities due to his predecessor. Adams, always overdisposed to be churlish, refused to attend the inaugural ceremonies and withdrew to a private house, whence he watched with a jaundiced eye for signs of inefficiency and corruption in the new government.

The White House reception following the inauguration of President Jackson was not calculated to diminish the fears of those who believed the change of administration would mark a surrender of the government to the more lawless groups of the democracy. Jackson's admirers had flocked to the city from the remotest hamlets of the frontier. Swelled by additions of the curious from every class of society, they flowed into the drawing rooms of the White House where, unabashed by the presence of foreign diplomats and social leaders of the capital, they jumped upon chairs, overturned tables, trampled linen underfoot, pilfered silverware, broke china and otherwise signified enthusiasm for their idol. White and colored men and women transformed the President's reception into an impromptu barroom scene, but were finally lured from the interior by tubs of alcoholic punch displayed upon the lawns. Jackson withdrew from the scene but was not appalled at the spectacle: "Let the boys have a good time once in four years," he said.

However, if there had seemed any reason to believe that the President would either publicly or privately countenance interference, lawless or otherwise, with his exercise of the presidential prerogatives, such an impression was quickly dispelled. Jackson knew his own mind, and, even if his maxims of political action were often founded on personal prejudices than on deliberate principles, he was not one to brook dictation from any source. Those who had conjectured that he would be the tool of demagogues soon realized their mistake: if there was to be any demagogue he would be called Jackson.

Andrew Jackson's father, a linen draper, had emigrated in 1765 to the American colonies from his Irish home near Belfast, in County Antrim. The future President was born in South Carolina on March 15, 1767, a few weeks after his father's death. With his two elder brothers and his mother, he engaged from early childhood in the hard task of wringing an exiguous living from the soil. When he was fourteen he managed to attach himself to the colonial forces and to embark on a brief military career. Before he could engage in battle, he was captured by a small British detachment. Its officer, thinking his captive more suited to perform menial tasks than to bear a musket, ordered him to clean a pair of boots. When Jackson refused to carry out the order, explaining that he expected the conventional treatment due to a prisoner of war, the officer struck him with a saber, gashing his head and cutting his left hand to the bone. Thenceforth his hatred of England and of Englishmen was inveterate.

His capture by the British and a subsequent attack of smallpox were the immediate consequences of Jackson's military adventure. But the war had laid a heavy hand on him in other respects. Both his brothers had fallen victims to it, as well as his mother, who had contracted ship fever while nursing prisoners at Charleston. Its close, therefore, left the boy an orphan.

What funds he possessed were speedily exhausted by betting at the race track in Charleston; finally, by a lucky coup at dice, he provided himself with enough money to take up his studies, with a view to becoming a lawyer. For two or three years he taught school, but, whatever other instruction he may have conveyed to his pupils, he could scarcely have drilled them properly in English grammar. In the departments of spelling and syntax his own efforts were to remain singularly deficient, and the correct spelling of such words as "seises, anough, lasy, lott, logg, demagouge, valient" was forever to be a profound puzzle to him.

His native intelligence, capacity and industry however were such that he not only, in a short time, succeeded in being admitted to the Bar, but in 1788 was appointed Prosecuting Attorney for the Western District of North Carolina.

This position called not merely for some knowledge of Blackstone's *Commentaries*, but for a readiness to enforce the law, if necessary, by one's bare fists. There is no record of his personal fights at this period, beyond a tradition that, in a society where the rules of the Marquess of Queensberry would have been regarded as the invention of a milksop, and where gouging and biting off an opponent's ears were common occurrences, the young prosecutor acquired a reputation as a man with whom it was unwise to quarrel.

After the ratification of the federal Constitution by North Carolina, Jackson's district became part of the "Territory of the United States of America, South of the River Ohio." He was retained, as public prosecutor of Mero, under the title of Attorney General in a frontier country, the inhabitants of which matched in fierceness the marauding Indians.

His private law practice grew apace. In 1793 he appeared in almost half of the four hundred and thirty-five litigations recorded during the four terms of court at Nashville. Although his cash fees were small, he was frequently paid in land that was soon to rise considerably in value. However, he was not destined to remain permanently on the frontier. He was a member of the convention which framed a Constitution for Tennessee, and after its admission to statehood, on June 1, 1796, was elected its first and sole member of the federal House of Representatives. The following year he was appointed to the United States Senate.

The impression made by Jackson, during this early service at the national capital, upon his colleagues and officers of the government was not favorable. The fastidious Gallatin recalled him, years later, as "a tall, lank, uncouth-looking personage, with long locks of hair hanging over his face, and a cue down his back tied in an eel-skin; his dress singular, his manners and deportment that of a rough backwoodsman." Jefferson said of him in 1824: "When I was President of the Senate, he was a Senator, and he could never speak on account of the rashness of his feelings. I have seen him attempt it repeatedly, and as often choke with rage."

After about a year in the United States Senate he resigned his seat and returned to Tennessee. His personal affairs had for a long period been in an embarrassed condition, although in 1795 he owned over fifty thousand acres of land. Promptly elected a Judge of the Superior Court of Tennessee, he remained in that office from 1798 to 1804. In spite of his impetuous temper he was considered an excellent Judge, dignified in his bearing, just in his decisions. His legal knowledge, though not extensive, was sound. If he was somewhat weak on juridical precedents, he was quick to seize upon the heart of a controversy. Jackson did not consider it beneath his dignity as a Judge to sell calico and other merchandise over the counter of a general store owned by him in common with some of his wife's relatives.

After six years on the bench he returned to private life and looked after his large landed interests. He planted, raised and raced horses, fought gamecocks, practiced law, dealt in slaves, exercised a keen interest in local politics, put his affairs into solvent shape and led, with the exception of an occasional duel, a comparatively peaceful existence.

Perhaps it is a misnomer to term any part of Jackson's life peaceful. His impulses were so strong, his rages so ungovernable, that even the daily round and the common task were of intense import to him. When he raced a horse, he almost projected his own will into the efforts of the animal; when he advocated a cause, he made that cause his own creation, to be championed as such. Nevertheless, in family life he was tractable as a lamb. In no respect did he appear to better advantage than in his marriage.

Rachel Jackson was a daughter of one of the earliest settlers of Tennessee, John Donelson, who had been killed by the Indians. Before the future President met her, she had been married in Kentucky to Lewis Robards. In spite of his wife's exemplary reputation his jealousy led him to make the most outrageous charges against her. On at least two occasions Robards' behavior was so violent that his wife was forced to leave him; during one such quarrel she was taken back to her mother's home, under the protection of Jackson, who had become a boarder there. Robards, at that time, cast a slur upon Jackson's attentions to Rachel, but desisted from further comment when Jackson threatened to cut off his ears.

Later Robards petitioned the Legislature of Virginia to grant him an act of divorce on the plea that his wife was living in adultery with Jackson. The Legislature of Virginia, without passing on the merit of the charge, authorized the Supreme Court of Kentucky to try the case with a jury. The report of the action taken in Virginia appears to have reached Tennessee in garbled form, and Jackson, believing Mrs. Robards to be divorced, married her in 1791, thereby establishing her on an adulterous basis. Two years later Robards, who had delayed until then the institution of his suit, was granted a divorce in Kentucky, on the ground that his wife was openly living with Jackson. In 1794, after learning to their astonishment that they were not legally man and wife, the couple were remarried. Jackson oiled his pistols and prepared to deal with any criticism of Rachel.

His unfortunate remissness in not having confirmed the report of the Virginia divorce was to cost Jackson at least two duels and a lifetime of sensitiveness on the subject of marriage. In the course of his presidential campaigns the foulest aspersions were made against Mrs. Jackson's morals. He ascribed her death, which occurred after his election but before he took the oath of office, to the calumnies spread by the enemy press. The troubles caused him by gossip made him always particularly ready to defend any woman whose character was assailed, and was one of the chief reasons for his championship of Peggy Eaton, when her reputation threatened to disrupt his administration.

Rachel Jackson was of a retiring disposition. Comparatively little is known of her beyond the fact that she was fond of inhaling "a sootherin' draw" from a long clay pipe, and, sometimes, a cigar. In her youth she was said to have been pretty, but in middle age had become so corpulent that a Louisianian, commenting on her appearance, repeated the French saying: "She shows how far the skin can be stretched." She was of a deeply religious nature but not adverse to dancing rustic measures. At a great ball in New Orleans she amused the sophisticated Creoles by performing, with her husband, an animated dance to the music of "Possum up de Gum Tree."

Jackson engaged in fist fights and caning incidents as well as in regular duels. Four times he was implicated in shooting affrays. On two of these occasions he was seriously wounded; in one of them he killed his opponent. Senator Benton once said: "Yes, I had a fight with Jackson; a fellow was hardly in the fashion then who hadn't."

This famous Senator, "Old Bullion," Thomas H. Benton, and his brother Jesse very nearly brought Jackson's career to a close in 1813. There had been ill blood between the three for some time. Jackson, hearing that Thomas Benton was in a tavern in Nashville, entered it, announcing that he would carry out his often expressed intention of horsewhipping him. As soon as the Bentons saw him, the shooting commenced. Jesse's pistol, loaded with two balls and a slug, was true to its aim; one ball entered Jackson's left arm, and the slug shattered his left shoulder. The fight became general. Jackson was extricated more dead than alive. The doctors recommended that his left arm be amputated: "I will keep my arm," said Jackson, and he did.

While still incapacitated by these wounds, he was appointed to the command of the Creek campaign. When a caller expressed his regret that the Commander was not in condition to take the field, the General answered: "The devil in hell, he is not," and, being too weak to mount his horse, was lifted into the saddle. He proceeded to the place of assembly while an attending physician from time to time bathed his inflamed wounds with solutions of sugar of lead.

Only one man seems to have visited an indignity on him without being chastised for it. While he was President, an irate naval officer named Randolph tweaked his nose but made his escape unpunished. Jackson said that had he been prepared for the attack, Randolph "never would have moved with life from the tracks he stood in."

As may be imagined, a man to whom peacetime afforded so many opportunities for bellicose behavior inhaled the breath of war with delight. His own estimate of his military abilities was not an exalted one: "I can command a body of men in a rough way," he once wrote. However, although he was not noted for modesty, he underrated himself in this respect. When occasion demanded, his notions of tactics were excellent, but, above all, his qualities of leadership were superb. Nor was his popularity with soldiers gained at the expense of any relaxation of discipline. "Old Hickory," as he was called because of his powers of endurance, was a stern martinet.

His first campaign, excepting his short services in the Revolutionary War, was against the Creek Indians, known as the "Red-Sticks." They had long menaced the Southwestern frontier and were a source of terror to the borderers who coveted their rich lands. Jackson, in a swift expedition, gained from his enemies the sobriquet of "Sharp Knife," and completely broke their power. The terms of the ensuing treaty were harsh in the extreme. Although he had been aided in his campaign by many friendly Creeks, he disregarded any claims of the conquered savages to compassion, and confiscated one half of the former Creek holdings, an area that now comprises three fifths of Alabama and one fifth of Georgia.

Jackson's success in the Indian War made the acceptance of his services in the regular establishment during the War of 1812, welcome to the federal government. The tale of how he eventually reached New Orleans, and, after the Articles of Peace had been signed at Ghent, defeated the British at the battle of New Orleans, is one of the few military episodes of the War of 1812 that an American can view with pride. The total casualties on the American side during the main assault were 13 killed, 39 wounded and 19 missing, while the British lost 291 killed, 1262 wounded and 484 missing. Among the English officers killed were three Major Generals, including the brother-in-law of the famous Duke of Wellington.

Jackson's demeanor during the war was distinguished by its usual truculence. He addressed the Governor of Pensacola, the representative of Spain, in language such as has doubtless never before or since been used by an American official to a dignitary of a friendly power. "Justice to my government," wrote Jackson, "compels me to remark, if your Excellency had been as industrious in your researches for facts as you have been studious of evasions and unfounded innuendoes, you might have long since acquired a knowledge that Monsieur Le Fete [sic], commander of the piratical band, has been arrested and confined, and is now under legal trial for the multifarious crimes complained of, and such should be your Excellency's conduct toward Francis, McQueen, Peter and others forming that matricidal band for whom your Christian bowels seem to sympathize and bleed so freely." He further accused the Governor of imbecility and falsehood. It is interesting to note that the General, then so bitter against the pirates, whom he called "hellish banditti," came to look upon them as "privateers and gentlemen" after they had thrown in their lot with the American forces.

His conduct at New Orleans was scarcely more tactful than it had been toward the Spanish Governor. For this, however, he had greater excuse. New Orleans was predominantly foreign, and its inhabitants were by no means united in favor of an American victory. To them Jackson seemed a rough backwoodsman, and his soldiers only a slightly lesser menace than the British troops. When a delegation from the local legislature visited his camp, some time before the great battle, to ascertain whether, if forced to retreat, he intended to burn the city, he gave them the cold comfort of this reply: "If I thought the hair on my head knew my thoughts, I would cut it off and burn it." He proclaimed martial law, and jailed a protestant against his measures. The Federal District Judge, Hall, issued a writ of habeas corpus on the prisoner's behalf. Jackson jailed the Judge. The District Attorney protested and was likewise arrested. After the victory and the revocation of martial law, Judge Hall regained his freedom, and during a hearing adjudged the General in contempt of court and fined him one thousand dollars and costs. This was paid by Jackson, but was, many years afterwards, reimbursed with interest by Congress. In the course of the Judge's decision he used language which Jackson might well have recollected, at various times, during his career. "The question was," said the Judge, "whether the Law should bend to the General, or the General to the Law."

The battle of New Orleans made Jackson the most popular man in the country, as well as its leading military figure. During the first Monroe Administration, when it became necessary to send a force to subdue the Creeks and Seminoles in Florida he was naturally selected to command it. He realized, as did the authorities in Washington, that the subjugation of the Indians would never pacify relations between the United States and Florida unless the Spaniards would release their ownership of that colony. His approach to this delicate question was characteristic. During the War of 1812 he had once informed the Secretary of War that his soldiers had no "constitutional scruples" and could be trusted, if so ordered, to run up an American flag over Mobile, Pensacola and St. Augustine. This old idea he now developed in a startling fashion, writing to President Monroe: "Let it be signified to me through any channel (say Mr. J. Rhea), that the possession of the Floridas would be desirable to the United States, and, in sixty days it will be accomplished." Jackson claimed that he soon received, through Rhea, the suggested approval. At any rate, having disposed of the Indians and executed two British subjects, he proceeded into Spanish territory as if he were engaged in war with Spain. He captured Pensacola, St. Mark's, Barrancas and other towns. The Spanish Minister at Washington promptly demanded the return of the cities thus seized and the punishment of the offending General. In the cabinet debate which followed, Jackson's course was defended by John Quincy Adams, and the Cabinet decided to praise Jackson but to disavow any state of war with Spain. Henry Clay and other orators in Congress also assailed the General's actions, but he was vindicated, and his Floridian career only added to his national popularity.

As a reward for his military services, Jackson was, after the purchase of Florida by the United States, appointed its Governor and instructed to effect the transfer of its administrative offices. His stay in that position was brief and inglorious. He was not to remain long in retirement, for in 1823 he was elected to the United States Senate. The same year he had declined an appointment as Minister to Mexico. In violation of ordinary custom regarding the declination of such a proffered honor, he published in a newspaper as his reason for non-acceptance the fact that no such mission was, in his opinion, needed in Mexico. Perhaps his failure to accept a diplomatic post was no loss to his country; on a previous ocassion, when he was under consideration as a possible Minister to Russia, Jefferson had observed to Monroe: "Why, good God, he would breed you a quarrel before he had been there a month."

After two years in the Senate he resigned. In 1824 he had been defeated for the presidency by John Quicy Adams. The charge of Jackson's friends that Adams had secured his election by making a "corrupt bargain" with Henry Clay to appoint the latter Secretary of State in return for his support, was difficult to believe in view of the unblemished honesty of the high-minded New Englander.

In 1828, the Jackson machine functioned perfectly, and "Old Hickory, the Nation's Hero and the People's Friend," obtained 178 electoral votes to 83 for Adams. The popular vote was 648,273 for Jackson, and 508,064 for Adams. John C. Calhoun was elected Vice-President.

Jackson was to serve as President for two full terms, to name his successor, and to retire from office with the record of having succeeded in carrying through every important policy sponsored by him. While President he ruled as an autocrat, and measurably enhanced the power of his office. He depended but little on the advice of his cabinet officers but was responsive to the counsel of a so-called "Kitchen Cabinet," composed of astute politicians who exercised much influence over him. Even they, however, were powerless to sway him from any purpose on which he had set his heart. He was a natural leader of men. He instantaneously translated thought into action; Justice Catron said: "If he had fallen from the clouds into a city on fire, he would have been at the head of the extinguishing hosts in an hour."

During his first term there occurred the most notable social quarrel in American history. Secretary of War Eaton had married Peggy O'Neale Timberlake, the daughter of a Washington innkeeper and the widow of a naval purser. Gossip about Mrs. Eaton was that with Eaton she had anticipated the death of her husband and her subsequent remarriage. When she took her place in official society as the wife of a Cabinet Minister, a storm of scandalmongering broke out. The President, who was, because of his own past troubles, especially sensitive to attacks on a woman's character, warmly championed her cause, warranting her to be as "chaste as a virgin."

The "Eaton malaria" swept over Washington like a plague. Jackson served notice on one foreign Minister that, if he continued to be rude to Mrs. Eaton, his government would be requested to recall him. Martin Van Buren, the Secretary of State, being a widower, faced no domestic complications as a result of befriending the assailed lady, and finally solved the knotty dilemma by resigning with Jackson's consent from the Cabinet. This forced the resignation of the other cabinet officers. Ex-Secretary Eaton was later named Governor of Florida and thereafter Minister to Spain, where his wife won a great success at the strait-laced court of Madrid.

The success of Jackson in being elected President had been in no small degree due to the skill of Van Buren in practical politics. The "Little Magician" of New York at once proceeded to reward the faithful by introducing at Washington the spoils system which had served him so well during his regency at Albany. The corrupting effect of this system was to cast its lengthened shadow over American political life thenceforward, and to constitute a real blemish on Jackson's record.

The great events of Jackson's two administrations were his stand against nullification and his war against the Bank of the United States. For some years the Southerners had been increasingly apprehensive of the growing political power of the North. In Calhoun they found a mouthpiece for their views. Calhoun was no ordinary man. He entertained a passionate belief in what might be called the Greek slave-state form of government. He maintained that the Constitution of the United States was a compact to which each state was a party in its capacity as sovereign, and that, as a sovereign, each state had the right to judge when its agent, the federal government, had exceeded its powers. The Supreme Court should not assume jurisdiction over a dispute between the federal government and a state, and each state should be the sole judge of when and if the compact had been broken. Only an interpretative federal amendment, adopted by three fourths of the states, could be superior to the interpretation of a single state as to whether its rights had been infringed.

This dangerous doctrine occasioned some of the greatest debates ever heard on the floor of Congress. It provoked Webster's famous Reply to Hayne, that oration, delivered by the Senator of whom it was once said that no man was ever so great as Daniel Webster looked, which concluded in words well known to many American schoolboys: "Liberty *and* Union, now and forever, one and inseparable!"

Calhoun's doctrine might have precipitated a disruption of the Union if Jackson had been a weak President. As it was, he scotched the movement. The tariff act of 1828 had incensed the South, where it was felt that Northern merchants would aggrandize themselves, as a result of tariff protection, at the expense of the plantation owners. Vice-President Calhoun had not fully developed his final theories of nullification, but he represented a strong element favoring that principle. He and his friends hoped that on Jefferson's birthday in 1830 Jackson would, at the anniversary dinner, espouse their cause. But their fellow South Carolinian was, decisively, to disappoint them. Rising for a volunteer toast, the President fixed upon the Vice-President his steely blue eyes and gave "Our Federal Union—it must be preserved." Calhoun rallied, as if from a terrible wound, and tendered as his toast, "The Union—next to our liberty, the most dear!" From that time on Jackson and Calhoun were politically estranged.

A personal estrangement was to sever their relations completely. Not only was Calhoun in favor of nullification, not only had he refused to recognize the moral innocence of Peggy Eaton, but it appeared he had for years concealed the crime of having pressed that Jackson be disciplined for his conduct in Florida. The breach was never healed. When Jackson stood for re-election, Van Buren was his running mate.

A new tariff bill was even more obnoxious to the South Carolinians than the preceding one. On November 24, 1832, a state convention declared, in the name of the sovereign people of South Carolina, that the tariff act was "unauthorized by the Constitution of the United States . . . null, void, and no law, nor binding upon this State, its officers or citizens." This Nullification Ordinance also refused to recognize the power of federal officers to collect customs duties in South Carolina after February 1, 1833, and threatened secession from the Union.

Jackson met this situation with his usual firmness. His Nullification Proclamation was a masterful, cogent paper. Before issuing it he had warned the nullifiers that if a drop of blood was shed in South Carolina in defiance of the laws of the United States, he would hang the first nullifier on whom he could get his hand, on the first tree he could find. When Hayne, commenting on this threat, told Benton he doubted whether the President really meant it, the latter replied: "I tell you, Hayne, when Jackson begins to talk about hanging, they can begin to look for the ropes." The Proclamation, in addition to other strong language, stated: "I consider the power to annul a law of the United States, assumed by one State, incompatible with the existence of the Union, contradicted expressly by the letter of the Constitution, unauthorized by its spirit, inconsistent with every principle on which it was founded and destructive of the great object for which it was formed."

Jackson's decisive action was followed by the introduction in Congress of a "force bill," looking toward the armed execution of the revenue laws. Fortunately before matters grew any worse, Clay, the "Great Compromiser," who always claimed he would "rather be right than President," put through his new tariff law providing a gradual reduction in all schedules until, in ten years time, they should reach twenty per cent ad valorem. The South Carolinians professed themselves satisfied. The crisis was over, the President had strengthened the federal authority, but the embers of conflict between North and South still smoldered.

The destruction of the second Bank of the United States, incorporated in 1816 for twenty years, with a capital of thirty-five million dollars, one fifth of which had been subscribed by the government, became an obsession with Jackson even before the expiration of its charter. To the President the bank was a "hydra" and a "mammoth" of corruption, representative of monopoly and of the money power that he thought was seeking to dominate and oppress the people. The bank undoubtedly had a great political influence. It maintained lobbies, it lent money to politicians, it paid retainers to Congressmen, and it controlled most of the issues of new bank notes in the country. Moreover, it was headed by Nicholas Biddle, the most aggressive banker and lobbyist of his period. But that the bank was exercising a baleful influence unfavorable to democracy is at least doubtful. Its greatest supposed sin was its size. Jackson arbitrarily deprived it of its deposits and thereby directed it on the road to ruin. Its demise was one of the deciding factors in precipitating the great financial panic that formed part of Jackson's gift of the presidency to Van Buren.

Before the Van Buren depression commenced, there had been eight years of almost continual prosperity under Jacksonian rule. Adams regarded the public lands as property to be held in trust for posterity: Jackson threw them open to speculators and permitted the public domain to be exploited and looted. The resulting revenue was sufficient to enable him to accomplish one of his dearest objects, the complete payment of the public debt in the year 1835. In spite of his general ignorance of sound financial policy, the President was insistent on government thrift. By 1836 a surplus of twenty-eight million dollars had accumulated in the treasury; by act of Congress it was directed that this surplus should be distributed among the states, where it dangerously inflated the credit structure and no doubt fattened the pockets of local politicians.

Jackson's opinions on the tariff question are, in view of the discussions on that same subject a hundred years later, of very considerable interest.

"Heaven smiled upon, and gave us liberty and independence," he wrote. "That same Providence has blessed us with the means of national independence and national defense. If we omit or refuse to use the gifts which He has extended to us, we deserve not the continuation of His blessings. He has filled our mountains and our plains with minerals—with lead, iron, and copper, and given us a climate and a soil for the growing of hemp and wool. These being the grand materials of our national defense, they ought to have extended to them adequate and fair protection, that our own manufactories and laborers may be placed on a fair competition with those of Europe; and that we may have within our own country a supply of those leading and important articles so essential to war. Beyond this, I look at the Tariff with an eye to the proper distribution of labor and revenue; and with a view to discharge our national debt. I am one of those who do not believe that a national debt is a national blessing, but rather a curse to a republic; inasmuch as it is calculated to raise around the administration a moneyed aristocracy dangerous to the liberties of the country.

"This Tariff—I mean a judicious one—possesses more fanciful than real dangers. I will ask what is the real situation of the agriculturist? Where has the American farmer a market for his surplus products? Except for cotton he has neither a foreign nor a home market. Does not this clearly prove, when there is no market either at home or abroad, that there is too much labor employed in agriculture? and that the channels of labor should be multiplied? Common sense points out at once the remedy. Draw from agriculture the super-abundant labor, employ it in mechanism and manufactures, thereby creating a home market for your breadstuffs, and distributing labor to a most profitable account, and benefits to the country will result. Take from agriculture in the United States six hundred thousand men, women, and children, and you at once give a home market for more breadstuffs than all Europe now furnishes us. In short, sir, we have been too long subject to the policy of the British merchants. It is time we should become a little more *Americanized,* and instead of feeding the paupers and laborers of Europe, feed our own, or else in a short time, by continuing our present policy, we shall all be paupers ourselves.

"It is, therefore, my opinion that a careful Tariff is much wanted to pay our national debt, and afford us a means of that defense within ourselves on which the safety and liberty of our country depend; and last, though not least, to our labor, which must prove beneficial to the happiness, independence, and wealth of the community."

Jackson's second election as President was an unequivocal triumph. The old property qualifications for voting, that had disenfranchised great numbers of Americans, had been liberalized in the original states. They had never existed in most of the territories later raised to statehood. Moreover, the caucus system, by which party representatives in Congress had nominated presidential candidates, had died an unlamented death. In 1832, conventions, essentially the same as our present nominating conventions, met and selected their candidates. Henry Clay, "the Mill Boy of the Slashes," was nominated by the National Republicans, afterwards to be known as Whigs, and Jackson was nominated by the regular Republicans, who shortly changed the party name from Democratic-Republican to Democratic. Moreover, the Jackson convention adopted the two-thirds rule which long continued to be a feature of the Democratic party system. In addition, there was an Anti-Masonic party. The result of the election was overwhelming: Jackson obtained 219 electoral votes to 49 for Clay.

The chief event of Jackson's foreign policy was the settlement of the French spoliation claims. For a time France refused to meet her obligations. The President ordered the navy to prepare for service and recommended to Congress that, if the debt were not paid, we should seize its equivalent in French property. Our minister asked for his passports and quitted Paris. A peaceful settlement of the matter ensued.

Mexican affairs took an acute turn during his administration. He sympathized warmly with Sam Houston in the latter's fight for Texan independence, without, however, openly opposing Mexico. After his retirement he became an advocate of the annexation of Texas, and a fifty-four-forty settlement of the Oregon boundary dispute.

But the strongest feature of his external policy was the knowledge acquired by foreign chancelleries that his personal character was an uncommonly forceful one, and that he could not be bluffed or persuaded into any surrender of national rights. No President since Washington had inspired the foreign offices of Europe with such a wholesome respect for the State Department.

His attitude toward the Indians was typical of that of the frontiersmen—cruel and conscienceless, but effective. By treaty he acquired millions of acres of Indian lands and transported whole tribes to the Far West. When the Georgia case was decided by the Supreme Court against the government and in favor of the Indians, he is reported to have said: "John Marshall has made his decision. Now let him enforce it."

His own relations with the great Chief Justice were strained and unpleasant. Although he recognized Marshall's brilliant legal gifts, he disliked his philosophy of constitutional law. In fact Jackson did not, certainly at one period of his career, believe that the Supreme Court had any authority to annul legislative or executive acts. Yet he made no attempt to undermine the prestige of the judiciary, and once wrote: "Let me tell you that all the rights secured to the citizens under the constitution are worth nothing . . . except guaranteed to them by a virtuous and independent Judiciary."

Several of the early Presidents of the United States were fine horsemen, but none was as devoted to the turf as Jackson. As soon as he was financially able, he established a racing stable and made heavy wagers on his own horses. Although he was fond of cockfighting and was said at times to have attended mains howling drunk, and to have urged on his birds with an envied wealth of blasphemy, it was on the track that his sporting proclivities were usually exercised. His most famous horse was Truxton, whom he matched against Greyhound, a well-known Tennessee animal, for a private bet of five thousand dollars a side. Sections of land and numerous horses, as well as money, were staked by the spectators. In a three-heat race Truxton won, and Jackson purchased Greyhound and added him to his stud.

In 1805, Jackson trained sixteen horses for a five-thousand-dollar race and won it with Greyhound. For twenty years he continued to be a leading owner: Truxton alone won more than twenty thousand dollars in stakes. His Clover Bottom race track, owned by him until he sold it to the Nashville Jockey Club, was the scene of many of his triumphs. It was there that he once "covered the starting post with his pistols to prevent a race he believed had been fixed."

Jackson's personal appearance was one to command attention. His lined face, his firm jaw and mouth, his penetrating blue eyes were indices of the inflexibility of his will. A great shock of white hair, crowned an intellectual forehead. He carried his six feet of spare bone and muscle with a graceful dignity. His manners were those of an aristocrat. Until his means became too straitened to permit it, his hospitality, both at the White House and at the

Hermitage, was literally boundless. He had retained Mr. Adams'
famous French chef, and his table was replete with the finest food
and wines. His own diet was sparing. In his later years he abandoned the use of spirits and drank only wine. He was a great
smoker, preferring to use tobacco in a corncob pipe. In his attire he
was scrupulously neat. His home was furnished tastefully and
luxuriously and he exercised a strict supervision over his household
affairs.

He was a bitter foe but a loving friend and relative. He treated
his niece, Mrs. Donelson, who presided with courtesy and charm
over the White House during his residence there, with the exception
of a period when she was sent home for refusing to accept Mrs.
Eaton, as a daughter. His adopted son, who had a genius for making
bad investments, was rescued by him from ruin again and again.
He was never happier than in the society of children, of whom he
reared and educated at least eleven. To Martin Van Buren he was
almost paternal in his affection. A friend could, in his estimation,
do no wrong.

In explaining his friendship for Burr to his friend, the Secretary
of War, he must have astonished that official by writing: "But, Sir,
when prooff shews him to be a treator, I would cut his throat with
as much pleasure as I would cut yours on equal testimony."

Like Jefferson, Madison and Monroe, Jackson was frequently in
financial straits. His private income was derived chiefly from farming and horse racing, with a smaller revenue sometimes accruing
from slave dealing. When he left the presidency for Tennessee, he
had only ninety dollars in cash, against ten thousand dollars in debts,
but he owned a good plantation and a hundred and forty slaves. It
is pleasant to record that, when one of his slaves longed to be joined
with his children and grandchildren, who were owned elsewhere,
Jackson gathered the family together under his care at an expenditure of eighteen hundred dollars.

The termination of his presidential career left him well satisfied
with his conduct of the office. He had ruled more like a Czar than
an elected magistrate. Every honor that could be bestowed by his
countrymen had been received by him, and his popularity was unbounded. No policy upon which he had set the seal of his approval
had been rejected by Congress, and his only regrets when he left
Washington were that he had never had an opportunity to shoot
Henry Clay or to hang John C. Calhoun.

He had permitted the rapine of the public domain and had de-

bauched the public service by favoring the spoils system of appointment, thereby lowering for all time the whole tone of American
political life; but there were incidents in his career to which he was
completely blind. He had democratized the presidency, and was
proud of it. That in the process much of value in the American
heritage had been destroyed is more apparent now than it was in
his own time. The electorate was to become increasingly less interested in the distinction of its representatives, and more engrossed
in what practical benefits its leaders could extract for it from the
national purse. His predecessors in the White House had dedicated
their talents, ripened by constant study and thought on public questions, to ruling their country. His successors were, the majority of
them, better equipped to win votes by popular arts than they were
to evolve enlightened policies for the best government of their fellow
men.

Until the end of his life, his influence in the councils of the Democratic party remained powerful, and his favorite exclamation, when
aroused, "By the Eternal," still inspired terror in his enemies. He
was patient and courageous to the last, and followed his lifelong
habit of seeking consolation in reading the Bible, of which he had
made a habit for half a century of perusing three chapters daily.

It must be hoped that his ultimate destination, after death, was
one to which "Uncle Alfred," a favorite slave, believed he had been
translated. When Alfred was asked if he thought General Jackson
had gone to heaven, he answered: "Wal, suh, he said he wuz a-goin'
thar, an' when Gineral Jackson say he wuz a goin' any place, he
sho went thar."

Martin Van Buren

Born: December 5, 1782.

Married: 1807.

Surrogate of Columbia County: February 20, 1808.

Member of New York State Senate: November 3, 1812.

Attorney General of New York: February 17, 1815.

Elected to United States Senate: February 1821.

Member of New York State Constitutional Convention: August 1821.

Re-elected to United States Senate: 1827.

Governor of New York: January 1, 1829.

Secretary of State of the United States: March 28, 1829.

Minister to Great Britain: August 1, 1831.

Vice-President of the United States: March 4, 1833.

President of the United States: March 4, 1837.

Defeated for re-election: November 1840.

Defeated as Free-Soil candidate for presidency: November 1848.

Died at Kinderhook, New York: July 24, 1862.

MARTIN VAN BUREN

MARTIN VAN BUREN was the first political boss ever to become President of the United States. Jefferson, as an autocratic leader, had attached his followers to him by outlining for their guidance a set of party principles rather than by distributing patronage to them. Jackson had profited by the political manipulations of his subordinates but was entirely lacking in any inclination to intrigue. Van Buren, however, attained his ends by inciting or restraining his partisans through a system of rewards and punishments, the rewards usually consisting of allocating to them revenues from the public treasury, and the punishments of separating them from political spoils.

But Van Buren was no ordinary boss, with a barroom as his scene of operations and pecuniary graft as his ambition. He was a dandy who loved luxurious surroundings and stimulating companionship. Nor in his ambition was he one whit mercenary. His personal objectives were always the highest elective or appointive offices, and under circumstances where he might with ease have illicitly riched himself, no dishonest dollar ever found its way into his coffers.

The truth is that Van Buren was a courtier, ignoble not in his aspirations, but in his choice of means to gratify them. When his fortune was at the flood, he knew how to ride the tide. The son of a tavern keeper, he was to become the darling of drawing rooms and to be importuned by great New York patroons to counsel them and assist them to political offices. Without any extraordinary qualities, he progressed steadily, step by step, until he seized the glittering prize of the presidency, which such men of genius as Calhoun, Clay, and Webster, all his rivals, had vainly attempted to gain.

His undeniable personal charm and his good temper made it diffi-

195

cult for those whom he habitually outwitted and circumvented to hate him, even when they despised him for his seeming lack of principles. Some of the terms by which he was referred to, such as "the Flying Dutchman," "the Red Fox," "the Little Magician," "the American Talleyrand," indicate an estimate of sly qualities in him that irritated and infuriated the victims of his machinations. He was caricatured as part fox and part man, as half snake and half mink, and in other hybrid forms.

In his early career "the Cautious Dutchman" seldom took a position from which he would be unable to retire gracefully; his skill in picking a winning political side became proverbial. His name passed into currency, in his own time, as a synonym for equivocating noncommittalism, and an ambiguous statement was known as "Vanburenish." John Randolph, who had a high opinion of his abilities, alluding to his crafty conduct, spoke of him as one who "rowed to his object with muffled oars."

Van Buren, during his career, held a great variety of public offices and acquitted himself with distinction in all of them. In addition to occupying minor positions, he was a State Senator, Attorney General of New York, Governor of the Empire State, United States Senator, Secretary of State, Minister to Great Britain (although the Senate refused to confirm his nomination to that post), Vice-President and President. As a boss he was the "Director" of the Albany Regency which controlled New York State politics, and he was the undisputed mentor of the Tammany Hall "Bucktails." More than any other man, he was responsible for the election of Andrew Jackson as President. As a lawyer he was sufficiently competent to retire at a comparatively early age from professional activity with an independent fortune and a high legal reputation. As a newspaper proprietor he was both powerful and prosperous. As Secretary of State he was instrumental in settling the dispute between the United States and Great Britain in regard to the West India trade, and in solving the vexed question of the spoliation claims with France. As Vice-President he presided over the Senate with exemplary dignity and impartiality.

He was born at Kinderhook, New York, on December 5, 1782. His parents were of Dutch extraction; his ancestors had been, since 1633, settled in the Hudson River Valley, without having risen above the level of mediocrity. His father was the indolent proprietor of a pothouse. His mother, a hard-working and sensible woman with a numerous progeny by two husbands, insisted on Martin having as

good an education—it was, in fact, very limited—as the neighbor-
hood afforded.

When Van Buren went to New York City at an early age to continue his studies of the law, he was brought to the notice of Burr,
one of whose few admirable traits was his kindness to able and obscure young men. He was frequently a guest at Richmond Hill,
where he may have perfected the polished fashion of his address,
which like Burr's was artful enough to seem natural.

Van Buren was a devoted son and a loyal husband. He married
a childhood neighbor and distant kinswoman, Hannah Hoes, whose
early death was the greatest personal loss he ever sustained. One of
his sons by her, nicknamed "Prince John," was so handsome in appearance and so captivating in manner that the repute of his personal
attractions became common on two continents.

After Van Buren's return to Kinderhook, having been the recipient
of many kindly favors at the hands of Burr, he was accused of having betrayed his benefactor by openly favoring a rival candidate in
their race for the governorship. This imputation of ingratitude is,
however, somewhat fanciful, since his connection with Burr had
been social rather than political. Nevertheless, during the course of
Van Buren's life, there was a sufficient number of similar examples
of seeming tergiversation to lend color to the belief that his sense of
expediency was stronger than his conception of the obligations of
friendship or of political principle. Nor was he one to cling to an
allegiance to a losing cause. He initially opposed the construction
of the Erie Canal, out of fear that its completion would enhance the
prestige of his political enemy, De Witt Clinton, who was magnilo-
quently dubbed "the Magnus Apollo." But when he realized that a
sustained opposition might be harmful to his own position he became an enthusiastic convert to the scheme. On the other hand,
there are instances where he continued to support candidacies, such
as that of William H. Crawford for the presidency, after the expectation of a successful issue had definitely evaporated, and when he
might have abandoned his efforts without any loss of honor.

Then, too, there were incidents, exclusive of those occurring while
he was President, that belied his reputation for seeking always to
be on the popular side of any contested political question. As a
member of the convention to revise the Constitution of New York
State, he opposed an elective judiciary and likewise the dismissal
of the existing members of the Supreme Court, who were his fervent

enemies. He also advocated a restricted suffrage (that under certain conditions might be extended to Negroes), and in general refused to court public favor by blindly agreeing to proposals for popular constitutional changes. As a United States Senator he substantially followed Jeffersonian principles. Although he voted for several internal improvements, he finally took a firm position against their authorization in the absence of a permissive constitutional amendment.

Van Buren owed his election to the presidency to Andrew Jackson's partiality for him. In 1836 he was chosen President, to succeed "Old Hickory," over three competitors, William Henry Harrison, Hugh L. White and Daniel Webster, by a majority of fifty-seven in the electoral college, and of twenty-five thousand in the popular vote.

Since no candidate had received the necessary majority of votes for the vice-presidency, the Senate, on the only such occasion in our history, had to choose its presiding officer. It selected Richard M. Johnson, of Kentucky, who, it was claimed, had with his own hand slain Tecumseh at the battle of the Thames.

At the outset of his term Van Buren retained as members of his Cabinet almost all those who had lately served under Jackson. John Forsyth was his Secretary of State, Benjamin F. Butler his Attorney General, Levi Woodbury the Secretary of the Treasury, Mahlon Dickerson the Secretary of the Navy, and Amos Kendall the Postmaster General. The only new face in the cabinet circle was that of Joel R. Poinsett, who was appointed Secretary of War.

Van Buren's presidential record is, in essence, the history of the great depression of 1837. That event was one of those profound and almost cyclical disturbances which in varying degrees of intensity have from time to time afflicted our country as a dreadful reminder of our own folly and avarice. Undoubtedly it was brought about in part by Jackson's war on the Bank of the United States and the resulting contraction of credit. In part it was also contributed to by Jackson's specie circular, requiring that purchasers of public lands must, with certain exceptions, meet their obligations to the government in gold and silver instead of bank notes. And in part it was caused by the distribution of the surplus federal revenues to the states.

But its primary cause lay in the irrepressible urge of the American people to speculate. The fever for getting rich quickly had infected all classes of society; a flood of paper money had favored widespread purchases on margin; the development of a vast and thinly populated

continent had engulfed both domestic and foreign capital in unhealthy quantities. Promoters sold lots in projected townships, the
only inhabitants of which were to be the rattlesnake, the coyote and
the buffalo. Actual wealth did not increase in proportion to paper
profits. Public land, which was, by law, sold at a fixed price of $1.25
per acre, had become, in the possession of speculative owners, a
commodity to be resold at inflated values, and the proceeds were
reinvested in further land or security purchases. An eventual collapse was inevitable. As in later periods, so many Americans were
involved in speculative excesses that when the collapse actually took
place, and liquidation ensued, rich and poor were alike prostrated.
To make matters worse, no assistance could be expected from European bankers, for the depression was world-wide.

Indeed, the panic of 1837 presented striking similarities, in many
respects, to the great depression that was to take place almost a
century later. The same sort of propaganda had been used to induce
the citizenry to believe that unless they made immediate placements
of their money the opportunities for advantageous investment might
be completely and forever engrossed by bolder spirits. In a country
where illimitable areas of land awaited settlers, the prices even of
remote farm acreages rose to dizzy and unreal heights. Men freely
borrowed to make speculations in ventures compared with which
the wildest of wildcat schemes were conservative. It was predicted
that the demand for lumber would rapidly denude Maine of its
timber resources, and stands of forest trees were sold at fantastic
figures. Land in the growing industrial centers such as New York
trebled and quadrupled in price, but its descent in value was to be
even more precipitous. Property at Broadway and 100th Street sold
at $480 a lot, and was to change hands seven months later at fifty
dollars. Money poured in from Europe, magnetized by high interest
rates. Its sudden withdrawal, when fear of the stability of the boom
began to spread, was one of the causes of the drastic deflation after
the orgy of overexpansion. The panic was to leave sad and lasting
memories in England, where investors lost heavily as a result of the
permanent repudiation by the states of Mississippi and Michigan
of bonds which had been legally issued and widely distributed in
Great Britain. Many Southerners persuaded themselves that slaves,
even if bought at the exorbitant price of fifteen hundred dollars
apiece, might be expected to produce progeny who could be sold
by their masters for even higher sums in the golden days to come.
Owners who thought they had acquired bargains in "black ivory"

were glad, a few months later, to realize in cash one fifth of what they had paid for the same human commodity.

The social effect of the panic was, of course, devastating. Industrial operations came practically to a standstill. Workmen were discharged by their bankrupt employers and haunted the streets of cities with hopeless faces and starving wives and children. One half of all the property in the country, it is said, changed ownership. Nine tenths of all the factories in the Eastern states closed, and the charitable agencies that were, in future crises, to alleviate at least the most desperate poverty were yet to be organized.

From all quarters pressure was immediately brought to bear upon the President to save the people, by some governmental thaumaturgy, from the consequences of their own mistakes. Public funds were demanded to assist private rehabilitation. But he who so often had conjured political white rabbits from a hat refused to prescribe any dubious panaceas. In a message breathing the purest Jeffersonianism, Van Buren concluded with the admonition: "These who look to this government for specific aid . . . lose sight of the ends for which it was created, and the powers with which it is clothed. . . . It was not intended to confer special favors on individuals or on any classes of them; to create systems of agriculture, manufacturers or trade. . . .

"All communities are apt to look to government for too much . . . especially at periods of sudden embarrassment or distress. But this ought not to be. The framers of our excellent Constitution, and the people who approved it with calm and sagacious deliberation, acted at the time on a sounder principle. They wisely judged that the less government interferes with private pursuits the better for general prosperity. It is not its legitimate object to make men rich, or to repair by direct grants of money or legislation in favor of particular pursuits, losses not incurred in public service.

"Its real duty—that duty the performance of which makes a good government the most precious of human blessings—is to enact and enforce a system of general laws . . . and to leave every citizen and every interest to reap, under its benign protection, the reward of virtue, industry and prudence.

"Let it be indelibly engraved on our minds," he said, "that relief is not to be found in expedients. Indebtedness cannot be lessened by borrowing more money, or by changing the form of the debt."

This statesmanlike stand by Van Buren brought about his defeat for re-election. As the nominee of his party he was to be buried under an avalanche of electoral votes cast for the Whig candidate, William Henry Harrison. The closing of his one term as President was to mark the end of his career as an officeholder.

It is the conflicting elements in Van Buren's character and the contradictions in his record that make him interesting in perspective. His colleague Rufus King wrote to friends when Van Buren was elected to the United States Senate: "He will not be there [Washington] two weeks until he will know every man's opinion, but none will know his." Andrew Jackson spoke of him as "one of the most frank men" he ever knew, and as "a true man with no guile."

We know that Van Buren was largely responsible for the full development of the spoils system in the operations of the federal government. He was not the inventor of that system; indeed, it had been used somewhat by Presidents prior to Andrew Jackson and had been in vogue in his own state, under the respected banners of the Livingstons and the Clintons, whose relatives at one time engrossed almost every office of importance, municipal, state and federal, in the gift of New York. But he had popularized it nationally under Jackson.

Nor can it be forgotten that during a long occupancy of high offices there is not, with the exception of the Subtreasury Act, one successful legislative measure of great merit—for there was not time enough during the War of 1812 to carry through his Classification bill, the forerunner of the Military Draft Acts—which bears the stamp of his origination.

Yet this same man, this manipulator, this spoilsman, this wily Ulysses, this "Northern man with Southern principles," upon becoming President pursued a course of conduct which completely contradicts the impression that his guiding star was expediency, and this under circumstances requiring not only a high degree of judgment but a display of exalted firmness and courage.

Van Buren was far too sensitive to public sentiment, and too aware of the then existing popular hysteria, not to have realized that his do-nothing policy would seal his political doom. When the defeat he had almost invited disrobed him of his authority, he greeted his friends and his enemies with the same smiling composure with which he had been accustomed to welcome his almost unbroken train of success.

The attempt to evaluate the remainder of Van Buren's career, subsequent to his defeat for re-election as President, is entirely baffling. On the eve of another seemingly certain presidential nomination by the Democrats, he lost his opportunity by expressing his objection to the annexation of Texas. He had been fortunate during his presidential term in that the always disturbing problem of slavery although ever menacing had not been politically active. The question of whether Texas should be joined to the United States was, however, one which even as supple a statesman as Van Buren would willingly have consigned to limbo. To favor annexation was to advocate the creation of another great slave state or states, a consummation devoutly wished in the South and bitterly opposed in the North. Van Buren's qualified condemnation of an immediate junction lost him the votes of the Southern delegates, without adding to his following north of the Mason-Dixon line.

When another election ensued, Van Buren went over to the antislavery advocates and became the candidate of the Free-Soilers for the presidency. In this contest he did not secure one electoral vote, and not a single popular vote in the Southern states, except in Virginia, where nine votes were tabulated for him. In this campaign his popular vote in the country reached 291,263, against 1,220,544 for Cass, and 1,360,101 for Taylor.

Did Van Buren, a consummate appraiser of public opinion, really believe there was any hope for him running on such a ticket, did the vanity of an aging man feel gratified at being a presidential nominee on a forlorn platform, after he had held the highest offices in his country, or did he indeed despise the institution of slavery and stand for office as a testimonial of his antipathy to that institution, even though he was later to abandon the antislavery party and return to the Democratic fold?

"Little Van," pink-cheeked, five feet six, with his blue eyes, his cupid's bow mouth, his fluffy fringes of white hair and his muttonchop whiskers, dressed almost as foppishly as Beau Brummel—how he must have smiled in his retirement at the recurring attacks upon him. He had aspired to much, he had achieved much. Let the future students of his time puzzle over his character. Not from any consistency of conduct during his lifetime, not from any published work of his, would they solve the enigma. He had been accused of many things—"the Red Fox" would keep his secrets.

William Henry Harrison

Born: February 9, 1773.

Ensign in United States Army: 1791.

Lieutenant: 1792.

Married: 1795.

Captain: 1797.

Secretary of Territory Northwest of the Ohio: 1798.

Territorial Delegate to Congress: 1799.

Governor of Indiana Territory: 1800-13.

Battle of Tippecanoe: November 7, 1811.

Brigadier General in United States Army: August 22, 1812.

Major General: March 2, 1813.

Battle of Thames: October 5, 1813.

Member of United States House of Representatives: 1816-19.

Member of Ohio Senate: December 6, 1819.

United States Senator: March 4, 1825.

Minister to Colombia: May 24, 1828.

President of the United States: March 4, 1841.

Died: April 4, 1841.

WILLIAM HENRY HARRISON

I F BENJAMIN HARRISON, signer of the Declaration of Independence,
Governor of Virginia, and for twenty-three years member of the
House of Burgesses of his commonwealth, had lived to hear of his
son William Henry being supported as a candidate for the presidency
of the United States as a plain man of the people, whose home was a
log cabin and whose only beverage was hard cider, he would indeed
have wondered whether the Whig managers had taken leave of their
senses. Among the leading families of Virginia, that of the Harrisons had been prominent for generations. By ties of consanguinity
they were connected with the Ludwells, the Lees, the Byrds, the
Pages, the Braxtons, the Carters, the Fitzhughs, the Carys, the Armi-
steads and the Randolphs, and with many other famous tribes of the
Old Dominion. Brandon, Carter's Grove, Shirley, Westover, Rose-
well, Sabine Hall, Nomini and Eagles Nest were but a few of the
manors possessed by their relatives. Their pride and their political
power, their wealth and their aristocratic social position, their hospitality and their patriotism, were bywords, not only in their native
state, but far beyond its borders. The only log cabins they had built
had been for their slaves, and the family predisposition to gout had
never been ascribed to the use of cider.

About 1634, Benjamin Harrison, a direct ancestor of the ninth
President of the United States, had emigrated from England to
America and within a few years had become a delegate to the Virginia House of Burgesses. His eldest son, "Benjamin of West Surry,"
likewise was elected a Burgess, and not only was one of the first
Governors of the College of William and Mary, but was for twelve
years a member of the Council of Virginia, an autocratic body that

ruled the colony. Because of their privileges the Councillors enjoyed unusual opportunities to make their fortunes, and when this Harrison died he was one of the richest men of his period. His eldest son, "Benjamin of Berkeley," after reading law in London, settled in Charles City County and represented it in the House of Burgesses, as well as serving as Speaker and Treasurer of the colony until his death in 1710, at the age of thirty-seven.

His successor, another Benjamin, for ten years a Burgess, was destroyed in 1745 by a bolt of lightning which killed at the same time two of his daughters. But the defunct Harrison had employed his domestic talents to such an extent before this catastrophe occurred that he had, during his marriage with Anne Carter the daughter of "King" Robert Carter of Corotoman, begotten two other daughters and six sons, all of whom survived him. By the custom of primogeniture, the oldest son Benjamin, the father of William Henry, inherited Berkeley the family seat on the James River, and other wide landholdings.

It was at Berkeley, therefore, that the future President was born, on February 9, 1773. In the very year of the boy's birth the elder Harrison was made a member of the Committee of Correspondence, eight years after he had enjoyed the signal honor of being elected to the committee to draft a petition to the King against the Stamp Act. From this time on Benjamin Harrison had taken an active part in the formation of the new nation. He was a delegate to the first and second Continental Congresses; in June 1776 he was Chairman of the committee for the resolution for the independence of the colonies, and on July 4, 1776, he read the Declaration as it was adopted. Elected to the Virginia Legislature in 1778, he defeated Thomas Jefferson for the speakership and was chosen, in 1781, Governor of Virginia, an office to which he was twice re-elected. Although an opponent of the broad powers granted to the federal government by the new Constitution, he became, after the instrument was ratified over his protests, its loyal supporter. His wife, Elizabeth Bassett, was the daughter of Colonel William Bassett of Eltham, and through his marriage with her he acquired kinsmanship with another powerful family group.

William Henry led the usual life of a Virginia boy. He had as companions two older brothers and four sisters, and a swarm of young cousins. After some preliminary schooling he was sent off to Hampden-Sydney College, in Hanover County. Upon leaving there he attended an academy in Southampton and in 1790 went to Richmond, at the age of seventeen, to study medicine.

Owing to his father's connections he went the following year to Philadelphia, to continue his medical program under the tutelage of the celebrated doctors Benjamin Rush and Richard Shippen. However, his father's death in the same year, caused an alteration of his plans. The patrimony of even so wealthy a planter as Benjamin Harrison offered little prospect of pecuniary independence to a younger son, and in spite of the remonstrances of his guardian Robert Morris, he applied for a commission as ensign in the army. Through the sponsorship of General Richard Henry Lee he obtained a post in the 1st Regiment of the United States Infantry, which was stationed at Fort Washington in the Northwestern Territory.

St. Clair had lately suffered the severe defeat at the hands of the Indians which caused Washington such anger and sorrow, and the President had appointed "Mad Anthony" Wayne to defend the frontier. From the boring duties of a rough military post, Harrison was relieved by an appointment as aide-de-camp to the new Commander-in-Chief, and gained Wayne's notice of his bravery at the battle of Fallen Timbers. This campaign was closed by the Treaty of Greenville in 1795, as a result of which a large tract of land north of the Ohio was ceded by the Indians to the government, and the aged Chief Cornplanter optimistically wrote: "We have made peace with the United States as long as water runs."

Having gathered modest laurels, Harrison married Anna, daughter of John Cleves Symmes, known as "The Miami Purchaser," a great land speculator, one of the Associate Judges of the Supreme Court of the Northwestern Territory. Her father, who controlled about a million acres of land, although he was later to relinquish much of it, did not regard with any favor his daughter's marriage to a subaltern, penniless except for his meager army pay, and he absented himself from the wedding. However, as time went on, he reconciled himself to the match; through it he became the grandfather of ten Harrison children, only one of whom died before maturity. Had Judge Symmes been able to gaze into the future, his initial opposition to this union might well have been overcome by the realization that his daughter would be the wife of one President of the United States, and the grandmother of another.

The first few years of the Harrisons' married life were passed at the fort that he commanded, but more exciting prospects were near

at hand. Through the assistance of Robert Goodloe Harper, a Federalist leader in Congress, Harrison induced President Adams to appoint him Secretary of the Territory Northwest of the River Ohio.
A year later he became the Territorial Delegate to the national Congress. This served him as a steppingstone to his appointment in 1800
at the age of twenty-seven, as Governor of the Indiana Territory, an
office which he retained by the successive patronage of various Presidents for almost thirteen years.

The Indiana Territory was created in the year 1800. Until 1809
it included Illinois. It numbered, at the beginning of the nineteenth
century, a white population of about five thousand people and approximately the same number of Indian warriors. Its area embraced
most of the present state of Indiana, some of Minnesota, a large part
of Michigan and all of Illinois and Wisconsin. Its Governor was
vested with powers extensive enough for John Randolph to compare
his position with that of a satrap. Not only did he have the immense
authority appertaining to the privilege of confirming land grants, but
he was authorized to create counties and subdivisions, to appoint
civil officers and militia officers under the grade of general, and to
veto any of the acts of the territorial legislature.

The opportunities thus offered to build up a political organization
by the use of patronage were not neglected by Harrison. Throughout his public career his own attitude toward officeholding was almost naïve. He solicited appointments both for himself and for his
relations, on the plea that their pecuniary needs should be satisfied
at governmental expense.

In his own case he exemplified the passion for political office which
Juvenal likened to "an endless itch." Besides his territorial and military appointments, and his service in the United States Senate, the
United States House of Representatives, and as President, he was at
various times a member of the Ohio Senate, Minister to Colombia,
and a Clerk of the Court of Common Pleas of Hamilton County,
Ohio. In addition he sought, unsuccessfully, to be made Secretary
of War by James Monroe, and to be sent as Minister to Russia. In
1820 he ran for the governorship of Ohio and was defeated. The
next year he failed of election to the United States Senate. Twelve
months later he met a second rebuff in a further quest for that office.
In the same year he was also rejected for the national House of
Representatives.

Elected at last to the United States Senate, he had only occupied his seat two years when he suggested himself as a vice-presidential candidate on the ticket with John Quincy Adams. In 1828, the possibility of securing nine thousand dollars for an outfit as Minister to Colombia, as well as a yearly salary of a like amount, caused him to solicit President Adams for that position. The Chief Executive appointed him, but observed: "This person's thirst for lucrative office is absolutely rabid. Vice-President, Major-General of the Army, Minister to Colombia—for each of these places he has been this very session as hot in pursuit as a hound on the scent of a hare. He is a *Bavard* of a lively and active, but shallow mind, a political adventurer, not without talents, but self-sufficient, vain and indiscreet. He has, withal, a faculty of making friends, and is incessantly importuning them for their influence in his favor."

While he was Governor of the Territory, Harrison used the spoils system of appointment to such an extent that frequent charges of favoritism were made against him, and a strong rival faction would almost certainly have deprived him eventually of his office had the War of 1812 not drawn him off from his civil occupations into military life. In addition to minding his gubernatorial duties he engaged actively in a distillery. He was extremely fond of shooting and fishing, and named his large brick house, which he built at Vincennes, "Grouseland."

In regard to the relations of the Americans with their Indian neighbors Harrison's tenure of the territorial governorship was especially notable. As a federal appointee the Governor was of course dependent on the good will of the Secretary of War, and especially on that of the President whose memoranda on policy toward the natives he was obliged to carry out. But owing to the distance separating the Territory from Washington, questions were frequently presented for his resolution that had to be decided without instructions from his superiors.

Harrison's communications to Thomas Jefferson during the latter's presidency, stop little short of abject flattery and even of subservience. In 1802 he wrote to Jefferson: "If, Sir, it should again happen that in the wide Range which you suffer your thoughts to take for the benefit of mankind the accomplishment of any of your wishes can in the smallest degree be aided by me, I beg you to believe that your Commands shall be executed to the utmost extent of my small talents."

It was not long before Harrison was indeed aiding in the accomplishment of certain of Jefferson's wishes, which could not however, even by the most latitudinarian construction be considered conducive to the benefit of the American Indians. Amongst the most curious instances of the blend in Jefferson's character of a true humanitarian feeling with inhumanitarian practices was his treatment of the Indian tribes. Jefferson was, throughout his life, intensely interested in everything relating to the Indians. But in his desire to acquire their land he was merciless in his rapacity, and recreant to his professions of helpfulness. His policy of claiming for his country the title to all land formerly belonging to tribes become extinct put a premium on extinction, and he commended the enticement of tribal chieftains into debt that they might be obliged to sell their people's lands.

After depriving the Indians of their best hunting grounds and removing them to less desirable surroundings, Jefferson was, however, ready to give them sage and wholesome advice for the regulation of their future, even though such admonition rubbed salt in their wounds.

In carrying out the national policy of absorbing Indian lands, Harrison was both faithful and adroit. By the use of "judicious liberality" he acquired, without payment, for the United States in 1803 about 1,152,000 acres of land from a small number of chiefs, on the pretext that this cession simply defined the frontiers indicated by the Treaty of Greenville. In the same year he acquired from the Kaskaskia seven or eight million acres in lower Illinois. Fifteen months later he made an even greater coup by inducing the Saks and the Foxes to sell about fifty million acres to the United States. With a wizardry in which whisky was a potent ingredient, Harrison achieved this result at an average cost of one to two cents per acre.

The federal government, although gorged with these great accessions, developed an insatiable appetite for more. Large additional surrenders were made, and at last in 1809 some reluctant chieftains of the Miami and other tribes, "mellowed with wine" consented to deed away two and a half million acres of excellent land. This final outrage provoked a warning from the remarkable chieftain Tecumseh, that he would not recognize this or any further purported sales of Indian holdings.

There was, also, a reason other than land hunger for the desire of the government at Washington to take possession as rapidly as possible of Indian lands in the Indiana Territory. Almost from the close of the Revolutionary War, British agents in the Northwest had fomented trouble among the Indians, and the American settlers were fearful, and justly so, that encouraged and armed by the English any strong provocation, especially a declaration of war by the United States against Great Britain, might bring down upon them a horde of enraged savages.

The mere proximity of the whites was almost the same as a sentence of death on the Indians. If they did not denude their territory of game, they were likely to debauch their health by supplying them with firewater. Harrison inveighed against the evils of selling liquor to the Indians, but in spite of casual efforts to stop such commerce a steady flow of contraband entered and percolated through the Territory. The sale of whisky was unlawful in the whole Wabash Valley, but it was believed the six hundred warriors who resided there consumed six thousand gallons of whisky per year.

When the condition of the Indians in the Territory seemed most hopeless, a leader arose among them who was to influence their aspirations to a point where many of them thought it not impossible that the whites would be expelled from all the lands they had appropriated.

This was Tecumseh, called "the Meteor," whose career blazed with glory until he fell honorably on the field of battle, as a Brigadier-General in the British Army.

Tecumseh, born about 1768, was the son of a famous Shawnee Chief, Cornstalk, and a Creek mother. His father and two of his brothers were killed fighting against the whites, and he himself while still a young man had taken a conspicuous part in several battles. In addition to rare personal beauty and magnetism, he was an eloquent orator and a military leader familiar with the best of Indian and European tactics. In contrast to other Indians, he was humane and did not permit the torture or massacre of prisoners. But it was especially his genius for organization that disturbed the American government. He envisaged the possibility of founding a great Indian confederacy beyond the Ohio River, and bent all his energies to the realization of his dream. In this project he received the encouragement of the British, who heartily approved his desire to drive the Americans out of the land northwest of the Ohio.

Tecumseh's first task was to bind together the loosely organized tribes in a common cause. To do this effectively he deemed it advisable to connect, in some way, the Great Spirit with his undertaking. An instrument to be used to this end lay ready to his hand in the person of his twin brother, Elskwatawa, "the Open Door," who had hitherto been little better than a winebibber. By a remarkable transformation the drunkard became a prophet. Elskwatawa convinced the tribesmen that he was the bearer of a revelation from the Master of Life, ordering the Indians to eschew the drinking of liquor and cohabitation with the whites, and especially to cease the alienation of their lands. One of the cardinal tenets of Tecumseh's policy was that joint ownership of Indian lands reposed in the warriors of all the tribes, and that their chiefs were without authority to make sales. By threats and by actual murder he soon cowed most of those sachems who, bribed by the whites, sought to give concessions. Meanwhile the Prophet settled himself at Tippecanoe Creek, where numerous partisans gathered about him, and forsaking the use of whiskey tilled the soil.

A visit made by the Prophet to Harrison at Vincennes in August 1808 elicited from Harrison a letter to the Secretary of War as follows:

Sir: The celebrated Shawnese Prophet has just left me after a visit of more than two weeks. He is rather possessed of considerable talents and the art and address with which he manages the Indians is really astonishing. I was not able to ascertain whether he is, as I at first supposed, a tool of the British or not. His denial of being under any such influence was strong and apparently candid. He says that his sole purpose is to reclaim the Indians from the bad habits they have contracted and to cause them to live in Peace and friendship with all mankind and declares that he is particularly instructed to that effect by the Great Spirit. He frequently harangued his followers in my presence and the evils attendant upon war and the use of ardent spirits was his constant theme. I cannot say how successful he may be in persuading them to lay aside their passion for war but the experiment made to determine whether their refusal to drink whiskey proceeded from principle or was only empty profession, established the former beyond all doubt. Upon the whole, Sir, I am inclined to think that the influence which the Prophet has acquired will prove rather advantageous than otherwise to the United States.

Harrison, in 1809, acted promptly and aggressively by summoning the most degraded of the tribes and buying another three million acres from them. The following year Tecumseh visited him and warned him: "Brother, since the peace was made in 1795 you have killed some of the Shawnee, Winnebagoes, Delawares, and Miamis, and you have taken our land from us; and I do not see how we can remain at peace with you if you continue to do so. . . . You try to force the red people to do some injury; it is you who are pushing them on to do mischief. . . .

"Since my residence at Tippecanoe we have endeavoured to level all distinctions, to destroy village chiefs by whom all mischief is done; it is they who sell our lands to the Americans. Our object is to let all our affairs be transacted by warriors. This land that was sold, and the goods that were given for it, was only done by a few. In future we are prepared to punish those chiefs who may come forward to propose to sell their land. If you continue to purchase of them, it will produce war among the different tribes, and at last I do not know what will be the consequence to the white people."

At the same time Tecumseh warned Harrison that he would be inclined to join forces with the English, unless the President repudiated the late purchases of land and agreed to make no further treaties except with the Confederacy. Many of the Indians began to talk in confident terms of an attack upon the American settlements, but at least one of the old leaders tried to dissuade Tecumseh from committing any overt acts of hostility, saying to him: "Let me tell you, should you defeat the American army, you have not done. Another will come; and if you defeat that, still another—one like waves of the Greatwater, overwhelming and sweeping you from the face of the earth." To all remonstrances Tecumseh was adamant. "I and my people have retreated enough," he nobly answered. "We will yield no more of our land."

Tecumseh's attitude of defiance inflamed the whites to demand that the native village of Tippecanoe be eradicated. Tecumseh himself had gone for a visit to the Southern tribes, but before leaving had requested Harrison to do nothing to alter the existing state of affairs between the two races before his return, a few months later. Harrison had made no promises, but on September 26, 1811, he marched out of Vincennes toward Tippecanoe with an effective force of about nine hundred men, composed of territorial militia, Kentucky volunteers and regular infantrymen. The Prophet sent messages to him, asking that a combat be averted. On November 6, Harrison encamped about a mile or two from the town to await the reply of the Prophet to demands made upon him. Before daybreak his little army was attacked by the natives, and despite darkness and rain beat back its assailants, who finally abandoned the field. The Americans were fortunately using cartridges containing twelve buckshot each, perfectly suitable for a night action. Harrison conducted himself bravely and a bullet passed through his hat. One hundred and eighty-eight of his men were killed or wounded, while the Indians, whose force was probably about one half as large as that of the whites, left thirty-five or more dead behind them. The Prophet himself escaped unharmed. During the attack he had taken up his station on high ground, at a safe distance from the camp, where he chanted a war song and encouraged the waves of advance and retreat, regulating them by a rattling sound made by deer hoofs. His followers had every reason to be displeased at the unhappy refutation of his prophecies, for during the night preceding the action he had assured them that through his incantations half the members of the white army were already dead, and the other half were in so demoralized a condition that they could be felled as easily by the tomahawk as so many stalled oxen.

This border skirmish is now known as the battle of Tippecanoe. It is difficult to appraise its results. The issue discredited the Prophet, but also definitely decided Tecumseh, who upon his return disavowed any knowledge of his brother's actions, to join forces with the English. In the opinion of some historians, his collaboration with the British during the War of 1812 probably prevented the loss of Canada to the United States.

Harrison ordered the destruction of the Prophet's village, then marched his troops back to Vincennes where he received the congratulations of the Legislature of Indiana on "not only the consummate abilities of the General, but the heroism of the man." Not to be outdone by Indiana, the Kentucky Legislature resolved, "that in the late campaign against the Indians on the Wabash, Governor William H. Harrison has, in the opinion of this Legislature, behaved like a hero, a patriot and a general; and that for his cool, deliberate, skillful and gallant conduct in the late battle of Tippecanoe, he well deserves the warmest thanks of the nation." The authorities at Washington were overjoyed, and the Governor of the Territory suddenly found the national spotlight turned full upon him.

In April 1812 Indian hostilities broke out like forest fires along the border. The frontier people were terror-stricken. They realized that a war with England might ensue, since the inhabitants of the territories ascribed all their troubles with the natives to the machinations of British political agents.

The United States declared war against England on June 18, 1812. Chiefly through the influence of Henry Clay, Harrison was made a brevet Major General of the Kentucky militia. On August 22, 1812, he was commissioned by President Madison a Brigadier General in the United States Army. Almost seven months later he was promoted to a major-generalship in the regular establishment. On October 5, 1813, he commanded the American forces at the battle of the Thames, where they overwhelmed the armies of Proctor and Tecumseh, and killed Tecumseh, dooming alike the threat of Canadian incursions onto American soil and Tecumseh's dream of a powerful Indian confederacy.

In the marching and countermarching that preceded the battle of the Thames, Harrison had acquitted himself well. A Kentucky soldier described him as a very plain-looking and plainly clad man, "in whose company we cannot but be perfectly at ease." With due allowance for certain qualities of indecision and of slothfulness he did his work well, and Colonel Johnson declared: "During the late war [he] was longer in active service than any other general officer, was perhaps oftener in action than any of them, and never sustained a defeat."

Bad communications and inefficient handling of supplies were to make difficult Harrison's task of defending the long Northwestern frontier. Luckily for him the whole British population of Upper Canada, not including Indians, was only 77,000, compared with which Kentucky and Ohio alone had over 102,000 men of military age, whose usefulness was, however, seriously handicapped by their lack of discipline and the temporary duration of their enlistment. If the troops were issued sufficient food, they were likely to find themselves lacking in supplies of clothing. If they were both fed and clothed, they were often short of guns and ammunition.

The battle of the Thames was an event of far-reaching importance, for, together with Perry's naval victory, it ended British influence over the Indians of the Northwest and terminated the war in Upper Canada. In the actual number of belligerents involved it was a small affair, since the entire force under Harrison numbered less than twenty-five hundred men, and Proctor commanded only about five hundred British veterans and twelve hundred of Tecumseh's natives. The superiority of American numbers was somewhat compensated for by the advantages of the British position, but the generalship of Harrison was far better than that of Proctor, who was as dilatory as he was incompetent.

Harrison closed his army career by resigning his commission as Major General because of the slights he considered had been put upon him by John Armstrong, the Secretary of War, and also because his family affairs required his closer attention. Andrew Jackson was appointed to fill the vacancy. For some years thereafter Harrison was the object of various partisan attacks upon his military reputation, as well as accusations that he had misused public moneys, but investigations completely exonerated him from any culpability.

He returned to North Bend and took up what proved to be the insoluble problem of how to increase his assets, while at the same time liquidating his debts. The task was made doubly difficult by the demands upon his hospitality, which he never refused to honor. A traveler noted that three hundred and sixty-five hams were consumed yearly at his table.

The log cabin at North Bend, later the theme of so much campaign oratory, was actually a commodious frame house placed within a six-acre lawn adorned by two ponds or tiny lakes. As Harrison once observed, his nursery had filled faster than his strongbox, and the support of eight children and a wife was an obligation that his election to Congress in 1816 helped him to meet. During his two terms in the national House of Representatives he pressed bills for the relief of soldiers and their widows and children, supported plans for internal improvements, and voted against measures to prohibit the extension of slavery, although in a debate on the admission of the new state of Illinois he declared himself to be opposed to slavery.

His next official appearance in Washington was as a United States Senator, a position which he resigned to accept the greater emoluments of a mission to Colombia. Elated by his diplomatic appointment, Harrison borrowed a considerable amount from the Bank of the United States. Leaving New York the middle of November 1828, he arrived at Bogota on February 5, 1829.

Simon Bolivar, "the Liberator," "the Washington of South America," was President of Colombia. He was believed to be planning to convert his office into that of a dictator or a monarch, a supposed ambition which our State Department rather tactlessly suggested he would do well to abandon. But if the Department of State had irritated the pride of Bolivar and his people, the Minister was to blunder about in the internal affairs of the Southern republic like an elephant running amok in a drawing room.

For reasons of political proscription, one of the early moves of Andrew Jackson when he became President was to recall Harrison and appoint Thomas P. Moore his successor, in obedience to the latter gentleman's desire to recoup his fortunes and improve his impaired health in the salubrious air of Bogota.

On September 25, 1829, Harrison ceased officially to be Minister. Two days later, in violation of the most rudimentary requirements of diplomatic etiquette, he addressed a long letter to Bolivar, exhorting the hero of the entire Southern hemisphere to put aside the crown he coveted. Harrison next made some tours through the country districts. During his absence, one of the Colombian cabinet officers openly alleged that he had planned the assassination of certain high government officials. The rumor spread that the ex-Minister was not only planning private murders but was inciting the army to revolt. The new Minister, Colonel Moore, considered Harrison as "rather a weak, vain, garrulous, amiable man, with very little malignity," who had made the mistake, unpardonable in a diplomat, of allying himself with a faction bitterly opposed to the elected powers of the country.

In 1830, Harrison was again settled at North Bend. A heavily indebted son had come to live with him, and another son died and bequeathed a wife and six children to his generosity. With the most admirable fortitude and cheerfulness he struggled under these burdens, which were at last lightened by his appointment, in 1834, as Clerk of the Court of Common Pleas of Hamilton County.

In 1836 he was nominated for the Presidency, and though defeated by Van Buren, obtained 73 electoral votes to his opponent's 170. Instead of being abandoned by the Whigs because of his defeat, Harrison was groomed by astute party managers as an entry for the next election. The nomination was fought for on behalf of three native Virginians—Henry Clay, Winfield Scott and Harrison. The last, being the most obscure, and therefore the least vulnerable politically of the three, was nominated with John Tyler of Virginia as his running mate. As it was difficult to determine what policies would meet with the united approval of the heterogeneous political elements who made up the loosely constituted Whig party, no platform whatever was announced. The great fear of the party stalwarts was that Harrison would talk too much and express unpopular convictions. Before his nomination Nicholas Biddle had advised him to "say not one single word about his principles, or his creed—let him say nothing. Let no Committee, no Convention—no town meeting ever extract from him a single word about what he thinks now or will do hereafter. Let the use of pen and ink be wholly forbidden."

As events transpired, it was necessary for Harrison to say little and to promise almost nothing. American politicians suddenly discovered the uses of propaganda, and the Whig campaign was carried on in the spirit of a great traveling carnival.

A Baltimore newspaper had sneered when the Harrison nomination was announced: "Give him a barrel of hard cider and a pension of two thousand a year, and our word for it, he will sit the remainder of his days in a log cabin by the side of a 'sea coal' fire and study moral philosophy." This gibe was immediately turned into a campaign rallying cry for the Whigs. Their party, really representative of property and conservatism, became, in public estimation, the party of the plebeians. Van Buren, who had started life as a poor boy with no influential connections, was represented as living luxuriously in 'a palace as splendid as that of the Caesars and as richly adorned as the proudest Asiatic mansion."

Harrison, the child of privilege, was depicted as a poor farmer boy become great.

The log cabin suddenly became a feature of the campaign. There were log-cabin newspapers and log-cabin songbooks, log-cabin clubs and badges, there were tremendous floats, drawn by four pairs of horses, surmounted by log cabins, with real smoke coming out of the chimneys and a barrel of cider beside the door. Sometimes the Whigs sat on the roofs of these cabins, drinking toasts as they passed through the crowds, and sometimes they fell, rather drunkenly, into the crowds. Mass meetings became the fashion of the day. It mattered very little what was said at them, but it seemed to matter enormously that they should be well attended. Some of them convened vast aggregations of people; the crowds were measured not by count but surveyed by the acre. The whole country seemed to be on the march, and Clay likened it to "an ocean convulsed by a terrible storm."

The electorate became highly vocal, in prose, and in verse set to music. They sang heartily:

"Oh, know ye the farmer of Tippecanoe?
The gallant old farmer of Tippecanoe?
With an arm that is strong and a heart that is true,
The man of the people is Tippecanoe."

As one historian has said: "It was not a presidential campaign at all, it was simply a contest between two modes of dress, two varieties of diet, two styles of architecture."

At last, the contest over, the singing hordes went home. Harrison had 234 electoral votes to Van Buren's 60, while of the popular vote Harrison received 1,275,017, Van Buren 1,128,702, and Birney the Abolitionist 7059.

John Quincy Adams, as usual, was not sanguine of the future: "Harrison comes in upon a hurricane," he wrote; "God grant he may not go out upon a wreck." Calhoun was almost equally doubtful, and remarked that the new President was "as unconscious as a child of his difficulties and those of his country."

Harrison appointed Daniel Webster Secretary of State; Thomas Ewing, of Ohio, Secretary of the Treasury; John Bell, of Tennessee, Secretary of War; George E. Badger, of North Carolina, Secretary of the Navy; Francis Granger, of New York, Postmaster General; and John J. Crittenden, of Kentucky, Attorney General.

The inauguration ceremonies, on March 4, 1841, were very entertaining, with log cabins and cider kegs a feature of the procession. The day was dreary and cold, yet the President rode his white charger for two hours without an overcoat, to refute, so it was said, the rumor that his health was feeble. In his address he promised to hold office for only one term. He stated that Congress had no right to abolish slavery in the District of Columbia without the consent of its residents, and on the same subject remarked that "the attempts of those [citizens] of one State to control the domestic institutions of another can only result in feelings of distrust and jealousy, the certain harbingers of disunion, violence and civil war, and the ultimate destruction of our free institutions."

The President was too kindly to treat office seekers unceremoniously. As a result he was literally besieged in the White House; numbers of applicants slept on the doorsteps of the mansion and lined up each morning, like a queue for a World Series baseball game. Harrison had been used to go to bed at cockcrow; now he was kept awake by importunities and excitements until after midnight. His good nature was exercised at the expense of his health and his reputation.

President Harrison's most striking characteristic was his affectionate nature. He was generous to excess, sociable, even-tempered and moderately witty. His abilities were of a mediocre order. He was not a statesman, his political horizon was limited and narrow. As a General he occupies a high place in American history, for though his successes were gained in minor engagements, their importance was far-reaching. How he would have met the demands of his last high office will never be known, for a month after his inauguration he was dead of bilious pneumonia, uttering as his dying words: "Sir, I wish you to understand the principles of government. I wish them carried out. I ask nothing more."

Being the first President who had died in office, he was given a magnificent state funeral, and his body was interred in the Congressional Cemetery at Washington, whence it was removed a few years later to North Bend. Mrs. Harrison survived him until 1864, dying at the age of eighty-eight.

John Tyler

Born: March 29, 1790.

Graduated from William and Mary College: 1807.

Elected to the Virginia State Legislature: 1811.

Married Letitia Christian: 1813.

Member of United States House of Representatives: 1816-21.

Re-elected to the Virginia State Legislature: 1823.

Governor of Virginia: 1825.

Re-elected Governor: 1826.

Elected to United States Senate: 1827.

Member of Virginia Constitutional Convention: 1829-30.

Re-elected to United States Senate: 1833.

Resigned from Senate: 1836.

Elected Vice-President of the United States: 1840.

President of the United States: 1841-45.

Married Julia Gardiner: 1844.

Elected Chancellor of William and Mary College: 1860.

President of the Peace Convention: 1861.

Elected to Confederate Congress: 1861.

Died: January 18, 1862.

JOHN TYLER

Jᴏʜɴ Tʏʟᴇʀ was the first Vice-President of the United States to succeed to the office of President as the result of the death of its incumbent. He was absent from the capital at the time of Harrison's decease. Upon his notification of that event, he rode on horseback from Williamsburg to Washington, a distance of two hundred and thirty miles, in twenty-one hours, which for a man of fifty-one betokened an enviable state of physical vigor.

When he arrived there, he found a Tweedledum and Tweedledee dispute raging amongst the bereaved statesmen as to whether he had become President or merely Acting President. In the midst of the controversy he sent a message to Congress signed "John Tyler, President," and thereby disposed of this question. A discussion then arose as to whether, since the Constitution was silent on the subject, the President pro tempore of the Senate had succeeded to the vacated vice-presidency, and that matter was settled by the office being left unclaimed.

However, a more delicate problem confronted him. At the first cabinet meeting following Harrison's death the Jovelike Daniel Webster, Secretary of State, addressed Mr. Tyler as follows: "Mr. President, it was the custom in our cabinet meetings of President Harrison that he should preside over them. All measures relating to the administration were to be brought before the Cabinet and their settlement was to be decided by the majority of votes, each member of the Cabinet and the President having but one vote." According to Tyler's son, his private secretary, the President's response dispelled any doubt as to who was to make decisions, for he replied to Webster's observation with the statement: "Gentlemen, I am proud to have in my Cabinet such able statesmen as you have proved your-selves to be. I shall be pleased to avail myself of your counsel and advice, but I can never consent to being dictated to as to what I shall or shall not do. I am the President, and I shall be held respon-sible for my administration. I hope I shall have your hearty co-op-eration in carrying out its measures. So long as you see fit to do this I shall be glad to have you with me. When you think otherwise I will be equally glad to receive your resignation."

For the moment Tyler was to be the master of his Cabinet, but he had almost immediately to reckon with a personage who, though nominally his ally, expected the new President to be his pawn. Henry Clay had been defeated for the Whig nomination by Har-rison, and upon the latter's death arrogated to himself the leadership of that party without regard to the position of Tyler as its titular head. The situation thus brought about was to wreck the party at the next election and to bury its chief sponsors in its ruin.

Clay's immediate objective was to revive the program, popularly known as "the American System," of a national bank, a protective tariff and internal improvements. Even before Harrison's death he had, by his importunities, annoyed that old gentleman, who com-mented: "The Federal portion of the Whig party are making des-perate efforts to seize the reins of government. They are urging the most unmerciful proscription, and if they continue to do so much longer, they will drive me mad." Since Tyler's convictions, as well as his entire public record, were absolutely opposed to such a pro-gram, a collision between the two men was inevitable. Clay did not fear its result: "Tyler dares not resist," he confidently declared; "I will drive him before me." A long acquaintance with Tyler should have taught the Senator from Kentucky that if the President, who had the reputation of being "as obstinate as a bull," had failed to yield to the persuasive powers of Clay's moving eloquence, he would prove adamant to blustering threats. The President's reply to Clay's prediction was: "I pray you to believe that my back is to the wall, and that while I shall deplore the assaults I shall, if practicable, beat back the assailants."

The struggle thus joined between the Executive and the great Whig leader was, as often happens in a battle between two wild animals, destined to prove fatal to both adversaries. As a result of it Tyler was excommunicated by the Whigs and became, as his opponent said, a "President without a party," while the "parties of the country were without a President." But cursed as he was, with bell, book and candle, he retained a following at the next presidential election sufficient to bring about the election of Polk, the Democratic candidate, over Clay, the Whig nominee. The ultimate outcome of their duel was that some future historians were inclined to treat Tyler as an apostate from his political faith, whereas, in truth, he was probably one of the most consistent statesmen of his generation.

It might almost be said that President John Tyler, Jr., acquired the appellation of "Honest John" by descent. His father, a friend of Thomas Jefferson, with whom he shared a love of liberty, literature, and the violin, was one of those incorruptible Virginians whose antique virtues were reminiscent of those attributed to the most distinguished Roman senators during the great days of the republic. In the veins of the elder John Tyler the blood of Saxons commingled with that of French Huguenots. From his mother he inherited a Gallic grace which made him a figure so popular that not only was he elected Speaker of the Virginia House of Delegates over Richard Henry Lee, but later was chosen Governor of the Commonwealth. At the earnest solicitation of Jefferson, who asserted that he was the only man strong enough to preserve his independence on a circuit bench with John Marshall, he was appointed by President Madison a United States District Judge, and died while occupying that position.

He was typical of the Virginia planting class, hospitable and genial, a lover of agriculture and country life. He was sufficiently fond of horses to have imported at least two from England, Romulus and Pantaloon. In politics he was a Jeffersonian Republican. He had disapproved the adoption of the federal Constitution, on the ground that it permitted the continuance of the slave trade, which he despised.

John Tyler, Jr., was born on March 29, 1790, at Greenway, his father's house in Charles City County, Virginia, a region with which his family had been intimately identified since his first American ancestor had settled near Jamestown prior to 1650.

The first school attended by him was a small private one. Its master believed so firmly in the uses of flogging as an aid to education that Tyler later remarked: "It was a wonder he did not whip all the sense out of his scholars." His harassed pupils finally set upon their preceptor and trussed him up like a fowl, after which his curriculum was administered in a gentler fashion.

Tyler was graduated at seventeen from the College of William and Mary, and admitted to the Bar before he reached his majority. A few days later he was elected to the Virginia House of Delegates.

There he introduced a resolution condemning the two United States Senators from his native state for disregarding the formal orders of the General Assembly to vote against the reincorporation of the Bank of the United States. In view of the furore aroused at a later period by his own opposition to the bank, it is interesting to recall how early his convictions on this subject had crystallized.

At the age of twenty-three he married Letitia Christian, the daughter of a prominent Virginian, Robert Christian. Shortly afterwards he joined the Virginia militia but saw no action during the War of 1812. To support his family he applied himself to the practice of law. He was so successful as an advocate that at the age of twenty-six his annual professional income was two thousand dollars, which for those days represented an unusually extensive business.

Like his father, the junior Tyler had a winning personality. After five years in the General Assembly he was elected to the national House of Representatives over Andrew Stevenson, at that time Speaker of the House of Delegates, and subsequently Speaker of the House of Representatives and Minister to England. He was to remain a Congressman until ill health and the necessity of augmenting his income forced him to retire to private life at the age of thirty-one.

During his service in Congress, Tyler took an unflinching position as an upholder of state rights. To this doctrine he remained true until the day of his death. He felt, as did many Southerners, that only by strictly respecting the reserved powers of the states would his section of the country preserve its cherished political and social concepts.

In the Fourteenth Congress a bill was passed changing the per diem remuneration of members to an annual payment of fifteen hundred dollars. Tyler opposed this increase and at the next session it was repealed.

The paramount issue confronting the Sixteenth Congress was the application for the admission of Missouri to statehood. Although Tyler was personally opposed to the perpetuation of slavery, he maintained that Congress had no constitutional authority to restrict the extension of slavery either in the states or in the territories, or to impose any limitations on the grant of statehood. He believed that time and the colonization in Africa of Negroes would abolish slavery if Northern abolitionists would leave the South free to settle its own great problem. The passage of the Missouri Compromise Bill, that he was one of the minority of forty-two to vote against, sounded, as we can now realize, the death knell of slavery. If the South, which at that time exercised complete political control over the country, had been united and firm in opposition to Northern demands, it could no doubt have seceded peaceably from the Union, whereas forty years later it had been outstripped in power and wealth, and to some extent in political influence, by those portions of the Republic implacably hostile to its "Peculiar Institution."

When Calhoun introduced his bill in favor of internal improvements, Taylor voted against it, as he was thereafter to vote against all bills for internal improvements, with unimportant exceptions. He regarded them as a means of building up special interests in the states with national funds, and as tending to favor graft and speculation. He was also, while in Congress, uncompromisingly opposed to protective tariffs, which he considered unfavorable to the prosperity of the agricultural South, "where," he complained, "we sell cheap and are made to buy dear." As a strict constructionist he believed the incorporation of the Bank of the United States to have been an unconstitutional act.

In 1823, Tyler's constituents sent him back to the House of Delegates. Two years later the legislature elected him Governor of the state. Another year, and he was selected to succeed himself as Governor by a unanimous vote. Before the expiration of this term he defeated John Randolph of Roanoke for election to the United States Senate, and was re-elected to that body in 1833. Meanwhile he had served as a member of the Virginia Constitutional Convention of 1829-1830.

In the presidential election of 1828 Tyler had originally been a supporter of Crawford, but upon his elimination from the contest had voted for Jackson. He, together with many other state-rights Southerners, reprobated those of Jackson's measures which tended to a centralization of power in the federal government. Nevertheless he again voted for Jackson in 1832 in preference to Henry Clay, the National Republican nominee.

During Jackson's first administration Tyler advised the Senate that he would not sacrifice his interpretation of the Constitution to any demands of party expediency. Soon after Jackson commenced his second administration, Tyler saw with alarm what he considered the attempt by the Executive to usurp powers not pertaining to the chief magistracy. Although he disapproved of nullification, and condemned South Carolina's agitation against the Tariff Act of 1832, he denounced unsparingly the Force Bill, authorizing the President to execute the provisions of the tariff law in that state by power of arms. On this measure, when all its other opponents found it convenient to absent themselves from the senate chamber, he cast the only negative vote, there being thirty-two Senators recorded in its favor. However, he was instrumental in bringing about a concert between Calhoun and Clay which resulted in the passage of the compromise tariff bill that obviated the danger of civil war threatened by the Force Bill.

When Jackson removed the government deposits from the Bank of the United States, Tyler disapproved of the President's action, although he never ceased to declare that he believed the bank itself to be "the original sin against the Constitution, which, in the progress of our history, has called into existence a numerous progeny of usurpations." Sentiment in Virginia became strongly anti-Jackson, and Tyler was applauded for voting in favor of a resolution to censure the President for removing the deposits. When in turn the Jacksonites again obtained control of the Virginia legislature, and instructed their Senators to vote in favor of expunging the minute of censure from the *Senate Journal*, Tyler, although acknowledging the right of the legislature to instruct him, refused to obey its directions on this subject and resigned his seat.

He had now definitely broken with those elements in the Democratic party dominated by Jackson. In the election of 1836 he was supported for the vice-presidency on a state-rights ticket, headed by Judge Hugh L. White of Tennessee, and received forty-seven electoral votes for that office.

The Southern states were now, as Tyler said, "in constant apprehension lest the government should be converted into a mere majority machine." In unison with many other conservative state-rights Democrats he went over to the Whig party. The name "Whig" had originally been applied during the Revolution to persons embracing the colonial cause. The Jeffersonians had often called themselves

"Whigs," while terming their Federalist opponents "Tories." During the Jackson administration certain of the President's adversaries, representing him as a self-opinionated tyrant, called his adherents Tories and themselves Whigs.

The Whig party which Tyler had decided to support was constituted of the most heterogeneous elements. The state-rights Democrats, who included the Nullifiers, amalgamated with the National Republicans, with whom they differed at least theoretically on the policies of the tariff, the bank and internal improvements, because of a common hatred and fear of Jackson and all his works. To their standard flocked the majority of conservative men of property both North and South. The most diverse voters united under the motto of "The Union of the Whigs for the sake of the Union." Of this coalition, Emerson commented that the Democrats had the best principles and the Whigs the best men.

When Harrison instead of Clay was nominated for the presidency by the Whigs, it seemed desirable to the Whig leaders to couple with him, as his running mate, a man who would conciliate Clay's friends and attract the state-rights votes of the South. Tyler was their logical choice.

One historian alleges that Taylor knew that the cardinal principle of Whig doctrine was the establishment of a national bank, and if he were not a Whig at heart he should have come out in his true colors before the election. Even a cursory review of the circumstances surrounding the Harrison-Van Buren campaign is sufficient to dispose of this criticism. The Whig party in many places, and particularly in Virginia, was anti-bank at the time of the election of 1840. In fact Tyler's known aversion to a national bank was used as bait by Whigs to attract former Jackson men. Little was said of "the American System," and Clay himself considered most of his old and favorite political tenets "obsolete." Webster declared himself a "Jeffersonian Democrat." Harrison, as befitted a chronic office seeker, was silent on controversial subjects. No promise whatever was exacted of Tyler as to his future course; the very differences between his opinions and those formerly held by Clay were used as an argument to win support for his ticket. The inability of the Whigs to write a platform is an additional indication that the state-rights Democrats had not jettisoned their political opinions in order to trim the Whig ship.

Soon after Tyler became President, Clay reviewed his "obsolete" program and breathed new life into the Bank of the United States. The Chief Executive took up Clay's gage of battle. "Go you now, then, Mr. Clay," he said, "to your end of the avenue, where stands the Capitol, and there perform your duty to the country as you shall think proper. So help me God, I shall do mine at this end of it as I shall think proper." The two men never again wrote or spoke to each other.

When Clay and the Whigs passed the Fiscal Bank bill, clothing the old Bank of the United States in new habiliments, President Tyler vetoed the act. His own suggestions as to a banking bill which would, in his opinion, be free from constitutional objections were ignored by the Whig majority. When they submitted to him a Fiscal Corporation bill, he promptly vetoed it. His second veto message was sent to Congress on September 9; on September 11 his Cabinet, composed of the holdover members of the Harrison Cabinet, resigned with the exception of Webster, the Secretary of State, who wished to finish his negotiations with England over the delimitation of the Northern boundary. The resignation of the Cabinet unloosed the floodgates of abuse against the Executive. The Whigs, in caucus, announced that "all political connection between them and John Tyler was at an end." This pronunciamento must have been a surprise to Andrew Jackson, who, expecting that Tyler would assent to a Whig bank bill, had with his usual impetuosity declared from his retreat at the Hermitage that the President was "an imbecile in the Executive Chair, a mere puppet for Clay, Webster and their unpublished clike."

One of the reasons why the Whigs felt they had been betrayed by the President was the whispered information put abroad to the effect that the President had agreed to sign a bank bill. The resigned Secretary of the Treasury, Ewing, stated in a letter to Tyler: "This bill, framed and fashioned according to your own suggestion, in the initiation of which I and other members of your Cabinet were made by you the agents and negotiators, was passed by large majorities through the two Houses of Congress, and sent to you, and you rejected it, . . . the veto message attacks in an especial manner the very provisions which were inserted at your request."

This charge of duplicity is indeed a grave one, but was indignantly denied by Tyler and given no support by the other members of the Cabinet who had resigned. In any event the bank issue was now as dead as mutton, for the Whigs did not have the power to pass such a measure over the President's veto. Popular excitement in regard to the measure flamed and was extinguished, although the day after the second veto a discontented assemblage of people marched to the White House, where they beat drums, hissed, and rang bells. The following night they burned the President in effigy. At a Whig meeting held in Albany posters were displayed, reading: "The people betrayed . . . John Tyler no Whig, but a Benedict Arnold—What Washington approved Judas Iscariot vetoed." Resolutions for the impeachment of the President were offered in the House but were defeated. At the next election the Whig platform was entirely silent on the bank and did not even mention that contentious word.

To replace the members of his former Cabinet, the President named Walter Forward, of Pennsylvania, Secretary of the Treasury; John McLean, of Ohio, Secretary of War; Abel P. Upshur, of Virginia, Secretary of the Navy; Hugh S. Legaré, of South Carolina, Attorney General; and Charles A. Wickliffe, of Kentucky, Postmaster General.

Tyler vetoed the first and second tariff bills presented to him; he particularly objected to the provisions contained in them for distribution of the proceeds from public land sales. Finally he did approve in 1842, a tariff bill for revenue, with incidental protection of manufacturing industry and a stipulation that the land surplus was never to be distributed unless the tariff fell below twenty per cent. This tariff was a partial victory for the Whigs, since the duties were changed from *ad valorem* to *specific,* and were increased from twenty to thirty per cent.

Tyler's name was now anathema to the Whigs. The Democrats, who had gained decidedly in strength at the mid-term elections, were inclined, in spite of the Jacksonian complexion of his new Cabinet, to regard him as a renegade from their ranks. However he remained steadfast to his own convictions. He vetoed all bills for internal improvements at national expense, except one relating to the Mississippi River, which he approved on the ground that the Mississippi was a great common highway for the commerce of the entire country.

In 1842, the Webster-Ashburton Treaty was completed and ratified. By this treaty the twelve thousand square miles of territory which had been in dispute between Maine and New Brunswick were divided; seven twelfths was awarded to Maine and the remainder to Great Britain. Webster had finished, under Tyler's direction, what he considered his most necessary task in the State Department. In May 1843, no doubt influenced by Whig political pressure and by his lack of sympathy for the administration program concerning the annexation of Texas, he laid down his portfolio. He was temporarily replaced by Hugh S. Legaré, who died a few weeks later. Legaré was, in turn, succeeded by Abel P. Upshur. On March 31, 1842, Clay had retired from the Senate, leaving that Whig body without a leader. The House was Democratic, but Calhoun's retirement in 1843 deprived the Democrats in Congress of the services of their champion.

The great measure of Tyler's administration was now pushed to a conclusion. Webster had once written that "the port of San Francisco was twenty times as valuable to us as all Texas," but this was far from being the President's opinion, or that of Upshur. The relations of the United States with Mexico were at this time in a most unsatisfactory condition. The Mexicans themselves, by a liberal policy of land grants, had favored the emigration of Americans to their province of Texas. Both John Quincy Adams and Andrew Jackson had attempted to purchase the whole, or a part, of Texas, but their offers were refused. In 1829, when slavery was abolished throughout the Mexican Republic, the Texans refused to obey the edict, and the Mexican authorities were too feeble to coerce them into obedience. In 1835, Mexico proclaimed a new Constitution, striking down all state rights; the American settlers rebelled and established a provisional government.

Santa Anna, the President of Mexico, led a punitive expedition against the revolting province. On March 5, 1836, after having, with his 3000 troops, bottled up 180 Texans in the Alamo fortress, he captured that stronghold and massacred all the survivors, with the exception of three women, two children and a Negro slave.

Texas pride was exalted by the noble defense and revolted by the conqueror's cruelty. Santa Anna ordered another slaughter of about three hundred and fifty captured troops at Goliad. At this juncture the Texans found a heaven-sent leader in the person of Sam Houston. A more picturesque figure never illuminated the pages of our history. He was a native Virginian. At fifteen he ran away from home and lived for three years with the Cherokee Indians. Upon his return to civilization he became a member of Congress from Tennessee, and afterwards Governor. Unfortunate domestic complications were responsible for his resigning that office. Again he took refuge with the Cherokees. Upon being formally adopted a member of their nation, they named him "the Raven." He finally gravitated to Texas, where, soon after the outbreak of the War of Texan Independence, he was chosen Commander-in-Chief of the insurgent army. On April 21, 1836, he led 743 raw Texan troops against double that number of Mexican veterans at San Jacinto. Dispersing the Mexican army, they captured Santa Anna, who had disguised himself as a peasant. The independence of Texas was thus won, and Houston elected its first President.

Although we acknowledged the independence of Texas, the Mexican government still regarded it as a rebellious province. Great Britain recognized the republic, hoping to have it continue as an independent power and as a source of cotton supply to Lancashire looms, which had hitherto been at the mercy of the American cotton monopoly. The abolitionists in England were opposed to the possible annexation of the republic by the United States, on the theory that such an event would result in the indefinite perpetuation of slavery there. Meanwhile there was embodied in the Texas Constitution a provision forbidding the legislature ever to proclaim a general liberation of slaves. Southern statesmen were inclined to view as a political asset of enormous potential value this tremendous region, which might be carved into several states and used to offset any elevation of Northern antislavery territory to statehood. They feared, however, that unless Texas were speedily annexed, European nations might, by loans or a protectorate, gain control over it, abolish slavery and set it up as a buffer between the United States and Mexico.

Tyler was resolved to annex Texas. In 1843 he instructed the Secretary of State to submit such a proposal to the Texan Minister at Washington. The ensuing debate was violent. In a proclamation inspired by John Quincy Adams, the consummation of the Texas annexation measure was declared "so injurious as . . . not only inevitably to result in a dissolution of the Union, but fully to justify it." On the other hand, because of the rapid growth of the West, Southern opinion declared that without Texas the South could not much longer maintain its equilibrium in the Senate. The abolitionists breathed fire and thunder.

The President was nevertheless to derive powerful assistance for his project from some of the most conservative Northern Whigs, whose antipathy to slavery was not as strong as their financial self-interest. The government of Texas was deeply embarrassed by the existence of great quantities of its bonds and notes, which had been issued wholesale during the early days of the Lone Star Republic. By 1845 bonds and notes bearing eight per cent interest were for sale as low as three cents on the dollar. Original holders and speculators alike looked to annexation to make good their losses or to enrich them.

A formal treaty of annexation was finally drafted, but when submitted to the Senate, failed of the necessary two-thirds vote for passage. This treaty provided that the United States should assume the public debt of Texas up to ten million dollars and should become the owner of the public lands of the former republic. But the will of the people was to be expressed, during the following presidential campaign. Many felt, as did Andrew Jackson, that Texas annexation was "the most important question, as it relates to the defense, the security, and safety of the most important interests of the whole Union that has ever been presented to us. It is a great national, and not a party question." Polk's election settled the matter; Tyler and Calhoun, the Secretary of State, were able to secure the passage of a joint resolution by a majority of both Houses of Congress, authorizing annexation and providing that Texas should be made a state as soon as she had presented an acceptable constitution. On his last day in office Tyler sent to Texas the instructions, drawn by the Secretary of State, covering the subject, and at approximately the same period he signed bills admitting Florida and Iowa to statehood.

Among Tyler's other successful measures were the termination of the Seminole War and the execution of various diplomatic, fiscal and administrative policies. He endeavored to compromise the contention regarding the Oregon boundary, but the matter was carried over into the next administration.

One great tragedy was to mark his term. In February 1844 the President had gone down the Potomac River, with about one hundred persons, on a new battleship, the *Princeton*. The guests were entertained by the firing of salvos of cannon balls, which threw up sprays and geysers of water. A great gun, "the Peacemaker," exploded. The President had gone below, and thus escaped injury, but the deck was turned into a shambles. Among the dead were

Mr. Upshur the Secretary of State, Mr. Gilmer the Secretary of the Navy; and the Hon. David Gardiner of New York, whose daughter Tyler subsequently married.

The death of Upshur made necessary the appointment of a new Secretary of State; Tyler gave the position to John C. Calhoun.

Outlawed by the Whigs and spurned by the Democrats, Tyler was nominated for a second term by a rump convention, representing eighteen states, in Baltimore. Clay was nominated by the Whigs, James K. Polk by the Democrats. Tyler, realizing that he had no chance of election, withdrew from the race in favor of Polk.

When Tyler left office, the finances of the country were in a sound condition. Webster said of Tyler that "in all things respecting the expenditure of public moneys he was remarkably cautious, exact and particular."

Soon after Polk's inauguration the ex-President retired to Sherwood Forest, his twelve-hundred-acre plantation on the James River, not far from his birthplace. Occasionally he delivered political addresses. In 1860 he became the first Chancellor of the College of William and Mary since George Washington. When, in January 1861, at the behest of Virginia, a Peace Convention was called at Washington to agree, if possible, on some plan to avert civil war, Tyler attended it, being named its President. After its proceedings had aborted, he returned to Richmond, where he advocated the immediate passage of an ordinance of secession by his native state. He then became a member, first of the Provisional, and later of the Permanent Congress of the Confederate States. He died on January 18, 1862, and was buried in Hollywood Cemetery at Richmond.

Tyler was twice married. His first wife died in 1842. In 1844, Tyler married Miss Julia Gardiner, a member of the family which owned Gardiners Island, near Easthampton, New York.

Tyler was spare of person, and six feet tall. He had blue eyes, silky brown hair, a lofty brow and a firm-set mouth; his nose would almost have entitled him to walk the boards as Cyrano de Bergerac. Charles Dickens, who lampooned most Americans, recorded that: "The expression of his face was mild and pleasant, and his manner was remarkably unaffected, gentlemanly, and agreeable. I thought that in his whole carriage and demaenour he became his station singularly Well."

John Tyler was not a genius like Randolph, nor did he have an intellect or personality nearly as remarkable as that of each of his extraordinarily gifted contemporaries, Clay, Calhoun and Webster. He was, however, perhaps better equipped, because of his lifelong adherence to established political principles, than any of those four statesmen to meet the problems which presented themselves during the term of his presidency.

James K. Polk

Born: November 2, 1795.

Admitted to Bar: 1820.

Member of House of Representatives of Tennessee: 1823-25.

Married Miss Sarah Childress: January 1, 1824.

Member of House of Representatives of United States: 1825-39.

Speaker of the House of Representatives: 1835-39.

Governor of Tennessee for one term: 1839.

President of the United States: 1845-49.

War with Mexico: 1846-48.

Died: June 5, 1849.

JAMES K. POLK

"WHO is James K. Polk?" was a popular interrogation when he was nominated by the Democratic party for the presidency. But his name is now intimately associated with one of the greatest periods of national expansion our country has known. The Polk administration added more than five hundred thousand square miles to the federal domain. This cold and seemingly unimaginative politician was as greedy of territorial acquisition as any of the great Spanish conquistadors.

Polk faithfully reflected the desires of the majority of his countrymen. To men exasperated by the recalcitrant and exhausted soil of many sections of the Eastern states the mere thought of the fallow Mexican territory was alluring.

There were other factors, too. Not least was the imperial ambition of the Southern planters to have an additional great expanse where Negro slavery would flourish, unchecked by the opposition of Northern antislavery sentiment.

"Polk the Mendacious" and "Polk the Mediocre" are terms used by his detractors in describing the eleventh President. The first appellation is inaccurate and unjust. Polk was inclined to be evasive and cautious in making commitments, but he was a man of truth. Although suspicious and secretive, his political and moral courage were undeniable. His mind was indeed mediocre; nevertheless, his governmental program was farsighted and crowned by success. He was endowed with sound judgment and sense in practical affairs far above the ordinary. His Secretary of the Navy, the historian George Bancroft, called him "one of the very best, most honest, and most successful presidents the country ever had." Vice-President Dallas, his colleague in office, described him as "temperate but not unsocial, industrious but accessible, punctual but patient, moral without austerity, and devotional though not bigoted."

Even if Dallas did not find Polk austere, other contemporaries often did. His very appearance was frigid. His body was stiff and angular, his gray eyes set in a face lean of outline and almost morose in expression. Grizzled hair, brushed back from his fine forehead, fell lankly upon his neck.

Mrs. Polk was a woman of exceptional personal attractions. In contrast to her husband she was highly popular, as was her excellent French chef. The President was of little assistance to her on social occasions, for he was incapable of relaxation and conviviality.

It is difficult to reconcile Polk's seeming lack of humor while President with his early reputation as an entertaining orator. When still young he was noted as a witty and sarcastic speaker, and was one of the earliest of that long line of politicians who have been denominated "Napoleons of the Stump."

He owed his success to the pertinacity, the diligence and the determination of his character. He dominated infinitely more gifted men by his rigidity and positiveness of purpose. His political principles were partisan and narrow, but they were fixed and lucid. Having set himself a goal, he never lost sight of it nor doubted the certainty of reaching it. At the outset of his term he announced the four great objectives of his administration were a reduction of the tariff, the re-establishment of the independent treasury, the settlement of the Oregon boundary and the acquisition of California. He attained them all, with a great slice of foreign territory added for good measure. He was opposed to internal improvements and vetoed any such bills. In spite of his Southern birth and training and the fact he was a slaveholder, his attitude on that great question was remarkably free from sectional bias.

In certain respects his character was petty. He was jealous, though not vindictive. His conduct toward Generals Winfield Scott and Zachary Taylor was marked by fear that the Whig party might derive political benefits, as it ultimately did, from their victories. On occasion he displayed great patience and forbearance, as in his relations with James Buchanan, whose frequent vacillation while Secretary of State was enough to madden a less phlegmatic chief. On the other hand, he had little sympathy with human foibles and lacked true generosity of heart.

His marriage was childless, and the legacy of his estate "to the worthiest of the name forever," was declared void by the courts, as violating the rule against perpetuities. His real legacy, however, was the gift in perpetuity by his administration to the American people of that splendid area which made the national boundaries extend from the Atlantic to the Pacific Ocean.

James Knox Polk was born in Mecklenburg County, North Carolina, on November 2, 1795, the eldest of the ten children of Samuel Polk and Jane Knox, both of whose fathers had been officers in the Revolutionary army. His mother was of Scotch descent. His father, the descendant of seventeenth-century emigrants from Ireland, was an enterprising farmer. When Samuel Polk's oldest son was eleven, he removed the family over the mountains to Maury County, Tennessee. In the autumn of 1815, James was sent back to the University of North Carolina, of which one of his Polk cousins had for many years been a trustee. There his industrious habits were manifested by his graduation with highest honors in the often incompatible departments of mathematics and the classics.

The practice of law was the profession to which the college-educated sons of Southern farmers were most likely to turn, and Polk was admitted to the Tennessee Bar at the age of twenty-two. Three years later he was elected to the state legislature; after two years in that body he was rewarded by a promotion to the national House of Representatives.

He celebrated New Year's Day of 1824 by marrying Sarah Childress, aged nineteen, the daughter of a prosperous Tennessee farmer. Like his mother, his wife was a strict Presbyterian and Sabbatarian, but never succeeded in bringing her husband into the fold of the Church in spite of his exemplary personal habits.

Polk's congressional career was respectable but not brilliant. He early developed a dislike for the incessant disputation that raged in Congress over the slavery question and declared his regret at finding "that scarcely any subject of general concern can be agitated here, without having this important subject of slavery either collaterally, or incidentally, brought into view, and made to mingle in our deliberations."

Polk's political fortunes were made by his fellow Tennessean Andrew Jackson, at whose behest he led the fight on the Bank of the United States as Chairman of the House Ways and Means Committee. His opinion of Jackson was flattering to Old Hickory, who was, Polk once wrote, "the greatest man of the age in which he lived —a man whose confidence and friendship I was so happy as to have enjoyed from my youth to the latest." Consequently he was assailed as a sycophant of the President.

Riding on the wave of Jackson's power, he was swept into the Speakership, an office almost as powerful as the Presidency, and he only relinquished his post to return to Tennessee where he was elected Governor. During his term as a Democratic Governor the prestige of the Whigs everywhere steadily increased, and he was twice defeated for re-election by "Lean Jimmy" Jones, whom Andrew Jackson refused to call by his assumed title of Major, on the ground that "he never was a corporal."

Polk had shown himself such an able campaigner in his various congressional and gubernatorial contests that his friends advocated his selection as Vice-President at the next convention. Meanwhile he had declined an invitation from Tyler to accept a seat in the Cabinet. He was, therefore, free to oppose Tyler's pretensions to another term, and thanks to the efforts of Senator Robert J. Walker of Mississippi, and other political managers, instead of being nominated as Vice-President was chosen for the higher office, thereby becoming the first "dark horse" candidate for the presidency. It was soon proved that the combination of Polk, a low-tariff sponsor, and of his running mate, Dallas of Pennsylvania, a protectionist, was a formidable entry. In vain Henry Clay, like a rabbit closely pursued by a pack of beagles, turned and twisted in his effort to please all factions on the issue of Texan annexation. Polk frankly declared for the measure.

In his statements on slavery Clay had been as impolitic as in those on Texas. "Whether Texas be independent," he said, "or incorporated in the United States, I do not believe it will prolong or shorten the duration of that institution [slavery]. It is destined to become extinct, at some distant day, in my opinion, by the operation of the inevitable law of population." Obviously this speech by a Kentuckian was not balm of Gilead to Southern slaveholders; they, at least, preferred Polk who was bored by the discussion of this question. Although he lost his own state, Polk was victorious by 170 electoral votes to 105 for Clay, and a popular vote of 1,337,242 to Clay's 1,299,068.

The new President formed a Cabinet consisting of James Buchanan of Pennsylvania, Secretary of State; Robert J. Walker of

Mississippi, Secretary of the Treasury; William L. Marcy of New York, Secretary of War; George Bancroft of Massachusetts, Secretary of the Navy; Cave Johnson of Tennessee, Postmaster General; and John Y. Mason of Virginia, Attorney General. Being, as one of his admirers declared, "a pure, whole-hogged Democrat," he proceeded to purge the minor offices of unorthodox placemen.

Four months after he entered the White House a Texas convention, against the active opposition of British government agents, accepted annexation. Two weeks later the President of Mexico recommended to his Congress a declaration of war against the United States as soon as it should be apparent that Texas had been invaded or that annexation had been concluded. The Mexican Minister at Washington demanded and received his passports. War with Mexico seemed inevitable.

To complicate matters still further, the impending controversy over the Oregon boundary boded no peaceful prospect in the direction of England. But Polk had already taken an aggressive initiative in regard to both nations. In his inaugural address he had shaken his fist in the face of the British lion. In the same year he reaffirmed the Democratic party's claim to the whole of Oregon and asked Congress to permit him to terminate the joint occupation agreement under which that territory had long been administered.

His actions in regard to Mexico were equally emphatic. He ordered General Zachary Taylor to transport an army force to the southwestern border of Texas. Exactly what limits constituted this border was a moot question. To begin with, from the Mexican point of view, any claim by the United States regarding the boundaries of Texas was phantom, since Mexico still considered Texas a province in revolt. Secondly, so our neighbors argued, even if Mexico should surrender Texas, the border would be the Nueces River, and not, as the Texans claimed, the Rio Grande.

This argument rested on a rather sound historical basis. The barren land between the Nueces and the Rio Grande had always been under Mexican jurisdiction, and Texan pride was almost the only ingredient of title to it possessed by the Americans. It was, however, natural that Polk, in obedience to the fanatical feelings of the residents of the Lone Star State on the subject, should command Taylor to push forward to the Rio Grande. This maneuver, accomplished in March 1846, was regarded by the Mexicans as constituting a definite invasion of their country. Their saber-rattling President directed the Commanding General of the Mexican army to "attack the army which is attacking us; to answer with war the enemy who makes war upon us." A skirmish ensued on April 25, in the course of which two companies of American dragoons were assaulted by a Mexican force and were defeated with a loss of sixteen killed and wounded, as well as the capture of numerous prisoners.

On May 11, 1846, Polk sent a message to Congress, declaring: "After reiterated menaces, Mexico has passed the boundary of the United States, has invaded our territory, and shed American blood upon the American soil. She has proclaimed that hostilities have commenced, and that the two nations are now at war.

"As war exists, and, notwithstanding all our efforts to avoid it, exists by the act of Mexico herself, we are called upon by every consideration of duty and patriotism to vindicate with decision and honor, the rights, and the interests of our country."

Although this message was approved by a majority in Congress, the Whigs were in general opposed to war, and a great body of Americans considered it an operation designed only to advance the interests of the Southern slavocracy. Abraham Lincoln, then an inconspicuous member of the House, introduced what were called the "spot resolutions," requesting the President to point out the spot of American territory on which the purported aggressions had taken place, and proof of its ownership. Lincoln's hostility to war was such that at its close he voted for a resolution which actually passed, thanking the American officers for their behavior "in a war unnecessarily and unconstitutionally begun by the President of the United States."

Our provocations had been great indeed. Disraeli once remarked that every government of Mexico was "born in a revolution and expired in a riot." The country was peopled by about four million Indians, two million half-breeds, and one million whites. The standard of education was low, that of political morality almost nonexistent. It is a melancholy comment on a nation's capacity to produce leaders that Santa Anna was for decades the most powerful individual in his country.

The handsome person of this lover of pomp, women and cockfighting concealed a paucity of talents. Even his loss of one leg in a minor engagement was capitalized to his advantage. The amputated member was interred with the ceremony due to a departed hero, and was, until its ignominious exhumation during a period of his unpopularity, the central feature of a shrine. Several times he had to flee for his life from his infuriated fellow citizens, but discredit, like dishonor, did not seem to stick to him. Neither his promises nor his patriotism were to be trusted, yet so powerful was his ambition, so masterly his egotism and so ruthless his cynicism, that whenever the cause of his people seemed most desperate they turned for leadership to this gaudy adventurer, who always deceived their hopes in the grand manner.

The friction between the two nations was accentuated by the circumstance that Mexico owed our people almost three million dollars in acknowledged but unpaid claims. A crisis resulted when service on this indebtedness was suspended, and an empty treasury offered no hope of its resumption. In an attempt to solve it, Polk sent John Slidell as Minister Plenipotentiary to Mexico City, where his credentials were refused on the quibble that the government had offered to receive a Commissioner but not a Minister.

Shortly thereafter the existing regime was overthrown by General Paredes, who headed a bellicose, anti-American party. The refusal to receive Slidell was unfortunate for all concerned, since he had been authorized to trade the unpaid American claims against Mexican recognition of the Rio Grande as our boundary, and had been additionally instructed to purchase, if possible, New Mexico and California; these areas included, besides our present states of those names, what are now the states of Arizona, Utah, Nevada, and part of Colorado.

Slidell's rejection was a certain portent of war. Polk immediately began to plan the achievement of what may have been his long-cherished project—the alienation of California from Mexican rule and its subsequent absorption into the United States. This tempting territory had for long been Mexican in name only. The body of Mexico was feeble enough, but its extremities were so inert as to seem lifeless. The republic's army in California consisted of about six hundred nondescript warriors, and its navy of one vessel little better than a derelict. Munitions being scarce, Mexican seaport commanders were sometimes forced to borrow powder from a saluting foreign ship in order to fire a return salvo.

The Americans had discovered, some time before, the profitable possibilities of exploiting this neglected domain. Yankee shipowners despatched there cargoes of cheap goods, such as beads and cotton garments, which they traded to the natives for furs. The furs were in turn sold in China, whence Eastern silks and spices were brought home. The gains resulting from such voyages were often stupendous.

In vain the Mexican and Californian authorities sought legally to exclude foreign, and especially American, traders and settlers. They might as well have attempted to stay the tides of the ocean. It was evident that the province was ripe for revolt, but it was hard to predict whether its fate would be independence or its subjection to the United States or another foreign power. In May 1846 the President of Mexico offered to sell California to Great Britain, but Palmerston, unwilling to provoke the wrath of the United States, answered that "Her Majesty's Government would not at present feel disposed to enter into any treaty for the acquisition of California."

About the same time Polk and his Cabinet agreed that an expedition should be fitted out against the upper part of the province. This step was not taken without previous preparations for annexation. The only American Consul in the territory had already been secretly advised that the government at Washington would look with favor upon a revolt against Mexico. Commodore Sloat, our naval commander in the Pacific, had received his orders to take possession of the province if and when we should declare war against its owner. But even earlier the ground for our intervention had been fortuitously prepared by the visits to California, on surveying trips, of John C. Frémont. This American army officer was variously celebrated as "the Pathfinder" and "the West's Greatest Adventurer."

His later career as Senator from California, as millionaire, as pauper, and as a nominee for the presidency need not now concern us. He was born in Georgia, the illegitimate child of a French father and a Virginian mother, whose elopement from the home of her husband had provided one of the celebrated scandals of the Old Dominion. Young Frémont, by his marriage with Jessie Benton, daughter of the influential Senator Thomas H. Benton, incidentally secured the political backing necessary for the accomplishment of his plans of Western exploration. Again and again he led expeditions across arid desert wastes and over fierce mountain ranges to the interior of California. There he discussed with the leading foreign settlers the possibilities of wresting control of the province from Mexico. He became a familiar of the extraordinary Swiss, Sutter, the "Governor of the Fortress of New Helvetia," who occupied a stronghold in the midst of his well-farmed principality, defended by twelve Russian cannon and a uniformed army of personal retainers. It was on Sutter's land that gold was later discovered, and had his titles been protected he would have become the richest man in the world. Instead he lost home and family, and was driven, an outcast, from his state.

Frémont fell into sympathy with those who wished to make California independent. As an American officer, his participation in the events leading up to the American conquest was subject to grave criticism, but his actions were useful and daring.

He aided and abetted the Bear Flag Revolt, on June 14, 1846, in which forty men set up the "Republic of California"; on their standard was painted a large star and a grizzly bear. This movement initiated a series of demonstrations ending in the conquest of California by the Americans, and in the termination by the end of the year of that phase of the Mexican War. Mexico had refused with indignation and scorn the suggestion she sell her province—instead she was forced to let it go almost by default.

Soon after January 14, 1848, the world realized what a loss Mexico had really suffered in being deprived of Upper California, for on that date gold was discovered in Sutter's millrace, and a mad rush began to the Pacific Coast.

After considerable bluster on the part of both nations we agreed with England, in 1846, to a settlement of the thorny Oregon question. Abandoning our demands for the whole of Oregon, and our cry of "54° 40/or fight," we accepted a compromise, fixing the boundary line at the forty-ninth parallel, which allotted us most of the Columbia River. The territory of three future states, Oregon, Washington and Idaho, was thereby confirmed to our ownership.

The settlement was a fortunate one for both Great Britain and America. It satisfied most of the ten thousand Americans who had settled in Oregon, and it removed a potential source of war that neither nation wished to wage. The future development of Oregon proved the perspicacity of Senator Benton, who had insisted on the importance of the territory, to the scorn of many of his colleagues.

Meanwhile, in Mexico, war was on. The success gained by the Mexicans in the initial skirmish was to be their only victory. Congress had authorized the President to raise a military force not to exceed fifty thousand men, and the Whigs although reprobating the war were always ready to vote any necessary supplies. Enlistments were satisfactory. However, Polk himself displayed no anxiety to hasten aggressive action. Long after the declaration of hostilities he still expected to bring about peace by purchase rather than by conquest. On August 8, 1846, he requested that an appropriation of thirty-two million dollars be put at his disposition for negotiations with Mexico. David Wilmot, a Democratic Congressman from Pennsylvania, offered to this appropriation bill the following amendment which became famous as the Wilmot Proviso: "Provided, that as an express and fundamental condition to the acquisition of any territory from the Republic of Mexico by the United States, by virtue of any treaty that may be negotiated between them, and to the use by the Executive of the moneys herein appropriated, neither slavery nor involuntary servitude shall ever exist in any part of said territory except for crime whereof the party shall be first duly convicted."

This amendment passed the House and died in the Senate, but it was to be a burning issue in the next presidential campaign. As a second arrow to his bow Polk, deceived by an alleged emissary of Santa Anna, gave orders that the exile should be allowed to pass through the American blockade and regain his native land; there, if raised to authority, it was represented that he would make peace by selling the United States the territory we coveted. Santa Anna did everything except what had been promised. He reached home, was proclaimed dictator and energetically set forth to wage a vigorous war against us. Optimism ran high at Mexico City. It was said the Americans were too parsimonious to support war taxation. Furthermore, Mexican authorities expected the active intervention of European powers on their side, a belief given color by some of the pungently anti-American English newspapers. And the Whig newspapers in the United States were to prove throughout the war almost as bitter in their denunciation of Polk as the English journals.

It was, at length, evident that little could be expected from further negotiations and Slidell had been correct when he warned Buchanan: "Be assured that nothing is to be done with these people, until they shall have been chastised." To administer chastisement two instruments were ready for use; one was General Zachary Taylor, the other General Winfield Scott—both were native Virginians.

Taylor won a decisive battle at Monterey in September 1846; his resulting popularity caused Polk to feel that the commander of the army of occupation was a "narrow-minded bigoted partisan" who had been "made giddy with the idea of the presidency." Meanwhile Scott, who was stationed in Washington, had injured his standing with the War Department and the President by making various indiscreet and insubordinate complaints concerning the conduct of the war. He was, however, finally selected for want of another officer of suitable rank to lead an army of invasion against Mexico City, by way of Vera Cruz.

Although Scott was pompous, and not inaptly called "Fuss and Feathers," he was famous for his personal bravery and was the ablest officer in our country. Throughout his long army career he never lost a battle, but he never won the confidence of James K. Polk.

The march of General Scott, with only about ten thousand troops, from Vera Cruz to Mexico City and his capture of the capital is one of the most brilliant feats of arms in American history. Taylor had defeated Santa Anna at the bloody battle of Buena Vista, and the very existence of the Mexican nation was now threatened by Scott's invading force, which included such officers as Robert E. Lee, U. S. Grant, George G. Meade, George B. McClellan and P. G. T. Beauregard. The Mexicans fought bravely and well, but their leadership was inadequate. When Scott finally occupied Mexico City, with about six thousand men, Santa Anna fled in disgrace, and the President of the Supreme Court assumed his powers. Political intrigues on the part of certain subordinate officers, which were not discountenanced by the Executive, had hampered Scott throughout the campaign; after bringing it to a successful close he was summarily recalled to Washington, and there, as Robert E. Lee said, "turned out as an old horse to die."

The fighting was over, but peace was yet to be made. This was a difficult task, for there was no government in Mexico fully competent to make a binding treaty, and the American Peace Commissioner had been disowned by the President who had appointed him. The first dilemma was solved by the appointment of a Mexican delegation to draft a peace treaty, and the second by our Commissioner proceeding with the negotiations in spite of the revocation of his authority to do so.

The difficulties of Nicholas P. Trist in Mexico are not without interest. He had married the granddaughter of Thomas Jefferson, had served as private secretary to Andrew Jackson, and for years had been Consul at Havana, Cuba. Polk had appointed him Chief Clerk of the Department of State, and afterwards Minister Pleni-potentiary to make peace with Mexico, in which capacity it was expected that his knowledge of the Spanish language and his famil-iarity with Spanish-American characteristics would make him a use-ful agent of the President.

He set out for his destination with careful instructions from the Secretary of State as to the form of the desired treaty. As soon as he entered into communication with General Scott, there was a clash between two well-developed vanities. Scott, who had lately remarked that he regarded Polk as "an enemy more to be dreaded than Santa Anna and all his hosts," was not predisposed to regard the President's agent with affection.

But the schism between the two prideful men was bridged by Trist's adventitious illness. The kindhearted General sent the dis-tressed diplomat a courteous message, accompanied by the gift of a box of guava marmalade, and a mutual admiration soon replaced their previous relations. Putting their heads together, they evolved the remarkable scheme of attempting to put an end to the war by bribery. "We are both convinced," wrote Trist, "beyond the shadow of a doubt, that the only way in which the indefinite protraction of this war can possibly be prevented . . . is by secret expenditure of money at the city of Mexico." Scott actually disbursed from the secret fund at his disposal the sum of ten thousand dollars, with the pledge of an additional million when a satisfactory treaty should be ratified.

The wine of power was coursing through the veins of Trist, but Polk, unsympathetic to his novel diplomatic methods, sobered him by ordering his recall. Fortunately, as events proved, the Commis-sioner was neither able nor willing to obey. Transport was tem-porarily lacking, and events were marching to a swift conclusion. The capital fell to the Americans, and the head of the Mexican gov-ernment, as well as the British chargé d'affaires, convinced Mr. Trist that if he failed to represent his country in negotiating a treaty a revolution would certainly overthrow the existing Mexican officials and replace them by a less tractable coterie. Under the circum-stances the Commissioner acted courageously and wisely, realizing that due to inevitable delays in transmitting despatches there was no hope of apprising Washington of the true situation in Mexico. His personal opinion of Polk, whom he considered an "imbecile," strengthened his decision to disobey the order of recall.

The Treaty of Guadalupe Hidalgo was signed by Trist on February 2, 1848. By a vote of 38 ayes to 14 nays the Senate of the United States ratified it on March 10, 1848, in spite of strong opposition from Northern Whigs, who objected to the addition of so much potential slave territory, and from expansionists who desired the acquisition of all, not part, of Mexico. By its terms the line of the Rio Grande was fixed, and the ownership of the provinces of New Mexico and Upper California was secured to us. The American government undertook to satisfy the claims of its citizens against the Mexican government, and also to pay Mexico the sum of fifteen million dollars.

The war being gloriously concluded, Polk now looked about for new worlds to conquer or to purchase. Manifest Destiny seemed to point to Cuba, which was being covetously eyed by European powers. The Mexican adventure had cost, in all, about one hundred million dollars; Polk offered that same sum to Spain for the cession of the Pearl of the Antilles. But badly as Spain needed the money, and feeble as was her hold upon her island possession, Castilian pride revolted against the proposal. The Spanish Foreign Minister asserted that his government would rather see Cuba sink beneath the waves than to transfer its ownership.

The remainder of Polk's term passed comparatively uneventfully. He wished to avoid a contest over slavery in the newly acquired Mexican territories by extending the Missouri Compromise line westward to the Pacific, but a decision on this was not to be reached during his presidency.

In the field of foreign affairs he is still remembered as the author of the so-called "Polk Doctrine," which in effect restated the Monroe Doctrine and enlarged it to declare that the United States would not permit "any interference" from abroad in American affairs, and that "no future European colony or dominion shall, with our consent, be planted or established on any part of the North American continent."

In his last annual message the President adverted to the necessity of giving New Mexico and California territorial governments, and to the folly of permitting the slavery issue to disrupt the country.

The news of Zachary Taylor's probable election as President filled him with gloomy forebodings.

Only a little more than three months after leaving the presidency, Polk was dead. The end came in his new home at Nashville, Tennessee, where his remains now lie in the grounds of the State Capitol. "Polk the Mediocre" gave us the provinces of New Mexico and Upper California—few Presidents can be credited with equal accomplishments.

Zachary Taylor

Born: September 24, 1784.
Lieutenant in United States Army: 1808.
Captain in Army: 1810.
Married: June 18, 1810.
War of 1812: Commissioned Major.
Black Hawk War in 1832: Served as Colonel.
Battle of Lake Okeechobee: December 25, 1837.
Major General: June 19, 1846.
Battle of Buena Vista: February 22-23, 1847.
President of the United States: March 4, 1849.
Died: July 9, 1850.

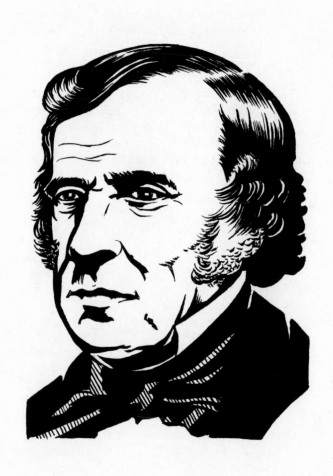

ZACHARY TAYLOR

Virginia, the Mother of Presidents, produced another of that line before lapsing into a long period of sterility. Zachary Taylor, the twelfth President of the United States, was born in Orange County, Virginia, on September 24, 1784. About a hundred years before his birth his ancestor, James Taylor, had emigrated from Carlisle, England, and had settled on the Mattapony River. His grandfather Zachary, after whom he was named, was the owner of twenty-six slaves, and his father, Richard Taylor, a Colonel in the Virginia infantry during the Revolutionary War. Zachary was the third son of Colonel Taylor and his wife, Sarah Strother, who bore five sons and three daughters. Both his father and mother were connected with prominent Virginia families and could name as cousins members of the Barbour, Pendleton and Lee clans. James Madison was their relative, and Colonel Taylor had a strain of New England blood by virtue of his descent from Elder William Brewster, of *Mayflower* fame.

When young Zachary was still a baby, his father quitted Virginia proper, crossing the mountains into the "dark and bloody" ground of Kentucky, where the cheap and productive soil seemed to offer better prospects than the somewhat depleted lands of the Old Dominion. There the Colonel built a log habitation, five miles distant from the site of Louisville, and was later appointed Collector of that port by his friend George Washington.

The white population of Kentucky numbered little more than twenty thousand persons. Indians roamed through the territory at will, taking scalps so freely that every farmer tilled his fields with a gun ready to his hand. Zachary's uncle Hancock was one of the victims, and the boy grew up in an atmosphere of constant danger.

Like his brothers, he assisted in the family farming operations and secured only a rudimentary education from a Connecticut schoolmaster. When he was seventeen he swam the Ohio River while it was filled with floating cakes of ice, and he was skilled in the rude sports of the frontier. Upon the death of his brother, a lieutenant in the United States Army, President Jefferson appointed Zachary to the vacancy. From that time for many years to come, his house was, to use his own expression, "the tent, and my home the battle-field."

At the age of twenty-five he married Margaret Smith, the daughter of a Maryland farmer, who cheerfully shared his life in the dismal army posts to which he was assigned. Like his, her tastes were simple. When she lived in the White House, she shrank from society, preferring to it the seclusion of her room and the companionship of a corncob pipe, while her attractive daughter, Betty Bliss, presided graciously as the President's hostess.

Of their six children, two died in childhood. Their three surviving daughters married army officers: Robert C. Wood, Jefferson Davis, the President of the Confederate States, and William Bliss, Taylor's brilliant Adjutant during the Mexican War. Their only son, Richard, after being educated at Edinburgh, in France and at Yale University, carried on the family tradition of soldiering and became a Lieutenant General in the Confederate army.

Like Winfield Scott, Taylor never lost a battle. His first brush with an enemy occurred during the War of 1812. He was in command of Fort Harrison, on the Wabash River, in Indiana. It was garrisoned by only fifty men, most of whom were disabled by illness, when it was attacked by almost five hundred Indian warriors. Night and day they were besieged. Their situation was so desperate that it seemed impossible for them to be saved from certain destruction except by an act of God. More than once their blockhouse was set on fire, and, as sorrow's crown of sorrow, their store of barreled whisky vanished in flames. In a final, desperate, hand-to-hand encounter they beat back the redskins, among whose leaders were the famous fighters, Negro Legs and Stone Eater, and the savages withdrew sullenly from the vicinity. Throughout this trying period Taylor had never lost courage, nor, as he rather naïvely commented in his official report, did his presence of mind for a moment forsake him.

Taylor's services were rewarded with a majority, but on June 15,

1815, he was honorably discharged from the army and went home to "make a crop of corn." In less than a year he was again an officer, being commissioned a Major in the 3rd Infantry by President Madison.

There now followed for Taylor a long period of routine military life, the tedium of which was first broken by his success in the Black Hawk War of 1832. After that diversion, another dull four years of garrison duty descended like a pall upon him. In 1836 he was sent from Wisconsin to Florida, to prosecute the Seminole War. The difficulties of the terrain made the pursuit of the Florida Indians almost as unsatisfactory as an attempt to exterminate mosquitos in a tropical swamp with bayonets. Osceola, the Indian chieftain, was not only brave but wily. His ultimate capture, for which Taylor bears no responsibility, discredited American honor. While visiting General Thomas Sidney Jesup under the protection of a flag of truce, Osceola was detained and later incarcerated in Fort Moultrie, at Charleston, South Carolina, where he died.

During the Seminole War, Taylor won a brevet as Birgadier General by defeating the Seminoles, on December 25, 1837, at the battle of Lake Okeechobee. He successfully maintained his supremacy in the Everglades for another four years until he was detailed to the command of the First Department, with headquarters in Louisiana.

Taylor was always a passionate farmer, and snatched enough time from his military obligations to operate a cotton plantation in Mississippi. From this tranquil retreat he was drawn into the vortex of Texan-Mexican political troubles, under instructions to protect the Lone Star State from foreign aggression. His orders from the War Department gave him a wide latitude of discretion, for he was advised: "Should Mexico assemble a large body of troops on the Rio Grande, and cross it with a considerable force, such a movement must be added, any personal fear of its dangers. With the same commencement of hostilities. You will, of course, use all the authority which has been, or may be, given you, to meet such a state of things. Texas must be protected from hostile invasion, and for that purpose, you will, of course, employ, to the utmost extent, all the means you possess, or can command."

Taylor seems to have had little curiosity or knowledge regarding the political background of the Mexican War. He hated to leave his cotton crop, and he had no relish for the excitement of war, nor, it must be added, any personal fear of its dangers. With the same com-

posure that he would have displayed on the parade ground (or perhaps with more, for he was notably inefficient at drill), he marched
to Corpus Christi and thereafter to the Rio Grande, which he proceeded phlegmatically to blockade. The capture of a small body of
American dragoons by the Mexicans led to a declaration of war.
Taylor came into collision with the enemy and won the double-
headed victory of Palo Alto and Resaca de la Palma. Some months
later he occupied Monterrey after fierce fighting, and proceeded to
conquer the northeastern states of Mexico. For his successes he was
mildly thanked by the administration, and showered with praise,
adulation and gold medals by the American people and by Congress.

The crucial test of Taylor's military career was now approaching.
President Polk, having decided to entrust the attempt to capture
Mexico City to Winfield Scott, detached from Taylor's command
most of his regular troops. Although Scott himself behaved on this
occasion in the most magnanimous and sympathetic way, General
Taylor's feathers were ruffled, and he included Scott, the President
and the War Department in a comprehensive malediction. He suffered his soldiers to depart, but instead of conferring with Scott he
went off in the opposite direction and was soon threatened by the
rapid northward advance of Santa Anna, who, lured by the depleted
state of his enemy, was optimistically hastening the attack. In truth
Taylor's position, if he had been of an apprehensive state of mind,
was alarming.

Santa Anna was in his element. At the head of twenty thousand
men, he anticipated an easy victory over the small American army
of about forty-five hundred officers and soldiers (of whom only one
tenth were regular troops) and a triumphant and melodramatic return to Mexico City. Never were illusions more rudely dispelled.
The flower of the Mexican army was thrown against the American
forces at the battle of Beuna Vista, on Washington's Birthday, in
1847. For two days the outcome hung in the balance, but on the
second night the Mexicans retired, defeated, from 'the field. The
Americans lost only 673 officers and men, killed and wounded, while
the Mexican losses were great. Santa Anna was headed home for
disaster, Taylor was on the highroad to the White House.

The battle of Buena Vista concluded Taylor's military career.
Judged by results accomplished, it entitles him to be ranked with
the greatest American commanders. Upon examination, however, it
is apparent that his victories were due not to his skill as a tactician,

but to his character as a man, and to the shortcomings of his adversaries. Like Clemenceau, he was regarded as Père le Victoire by his countrymen, who were accustomed to say of him: "Taylor never surrenders." Not only did he never surrender, but he never admitted the possibility of defeat. His outlook was unimaginative. He was not the prey of those doubts and misgivings which afflict the General who envisages all the possibilities of a military situation. His nonchalance under enemy fire had in it no element of bravado, for hostile bullets were to him simply the annoying but inevitable risks of his trade. His favorite position in battle was to sit on his charger, Whitey, with both pudgy legs dangling on one side of the horse's neck, while he surveyed the progress of events from whatever eminence afforded him the best view. During one engagement, while bullets whistled about him, his subordinates remonstrated with him at the unnecessary exposure of his person. "Let us ride up nearer," he replied, "and then their balls will go over us."

During the most intense firing he never became excited, nor was he contagiously affected by the fears of others. At Buena Vista, after listening patiently to various predictions of disaster from his aides, he calmly turned to a commander of artillery and observed: "A little more grape, Captain Bragg." For his failure to use artillery more effectively he was much, and probably rightly, criticized. He always underrated the possibilities of any arms except cold steel. Nor was his disposition of forces for battle such as would meet with the approval of a sound tactician. Some of his subordinates never understood why his troops were not invariably defeated; one of them gloomily remarked: "Whether an idea, strategic or of any other description, has had the rudeness to invade the mind or imagination of our chief is a matter of doubt. We are literally a huge body without a head." He had little regard for military students and no respect for a West Point degree, which may have been the reason why some West Pointers belittled him. Neither did he like war. "I sincerely rejoice," he once wrote, "at the prospect of peace. My life has been devoted to arms, yet I look upon war at all times, and under all circumstances, as a national calamity, to be avoided if compatible with the national honor."

When on foreign soil he apparently felt as secure in his camp as if he had been seated in front of a library fire on his plantation. In vain the War Department tried to have him spy out the enemy country and make suggestions as to a possible course of campaign. Considerations of strategy and detail did not disturb him—they simply bored him. If he needed a mule train or more ammunition, he instructed his Adjutant to write home for them, and then dismissed the subject from his mind until it was next brought to his attention by a worried officer. Most of his officers loved him, and his men idolized him. To the latter he was as indicative of good fortune as a rabbit's foot to a Georgian Negro. Ulysses Grant said, in speaking of Scott and Taylor: "Both were pleasant to serve under—Taylor was pleasant to serve with." His soldiers felt that he was one of them and represented their collective good luck. Rival politicians later complained that he was the luckiest man who ever lived.

Taylor's appearance was highly unmilitary. Only on the rarest occasions did he don a regular uniform or wear insignia of rank. If the weather was hot, his favorite covering was a straw hat. He liked homespun clothes, linen coats and ragged pantaloons, the bottoms of which were stuffed into his boots. When he was inaugurated as President, he was prevailed upon to order a frock coat, but insisted on its being made much too large for him so it would be comfortable. He disliked silk hats but found that by tilting them far back on his head they could be suffered. His spectacles were usually buried in his iron-gray and uncombed hair, from which retreat he would pull them down, when needed, to the bridge of his nose. At one time he wore a full beard but gradually whittled it down until it gave the effect of glorified side whiskers. He was unkempt, slovenly and sometimes dirty, yet when General Sherman met him for the first time, he was "most agreeably surprised at his fine personal appearance and his pleasant, easy manner." His legs were short in proportion to his body, but they supported a weight of about two hundred pounds; when he mounted a horse, an orderly had to boost one leg over the saddle. His physical vigor and strength were remarkable. In spite of his unconventional dress and his habit of conversing freely and informally with everyone who approached him, his native dignity was great. He playfully tweaked his soldiers' ears, as did Napoleon, but they never presumed on his familiarity with them.

The hostility between Polk and Taylor was unfortunate but understandable. Apart from Polk's jealousy of his General's growing political prominence, it was exasperating to have a commander in the field who was sometimes insubordinate, was palpably inefficient as an administrator, and who never seemed to take any initiative, except upon a day of battle.

Taylor returned this dislike with interest. When it was rumored that Polk had died, he said: "While I regret to hear of the death of any one, I would as soon have heard of his death if true, as that of any other individual in the whole Union."

Taylor, singularly free of rancor against the Mexicans, was a generous enemy. At the time of the occupation of Matamoras he handed back the sword of the surrendered Mexican leader, La Vega, to its owner, saying: "General, I do assure you I deeply regret that this misfortune has fallen upon you. I regret it sincerely and I take great pleasure in returning you the sword which you have this day worn with so much gallantry."

"Old Rough and Ready," as Taylor was called by his soldiers, was very unlike the usual presidential candidate. He had never voted, although he professed to be a Whig. The fact that he was a military hero and had no political record for his opponents to criticize made him appear to many politicians an ideal candidate for the Whig nomination. In due course he was preferred over Henry Clay and Winfield Scott. The Democrats selected General Lewis Cass, of Michigan to oppose him. Cass was a man of considerable ability, but a poor campaigner. Later in life, while a member of the United States Senate, he developed the habit of making prolix speeches. When the question arose of hanging gas chandeliers in one of the committee rooms of the Senate, Hamlin, a solon from Maine, suggested it would be better to hang "Old Cass" there, as he would answer the same purpose.

Jefferson Davis, the Mississippi leader, took the stump against Taylor in his own state and in Louisiana, but always conceded that the Whig nominee was a great man and a great general. The personal relations between Taylor and Davis had been unusual. Davis was a West Pointer and during his early army career was assigned to Colonel Taylor's regiment where he fell in love with his commander's daughter Sarah. Despite her father's express prohibition of the match, he married her and gave up his profession, returning to his plantation in Mississippi. The Colonel refused any reconciliation with the young couple stating "no honorable man would thus defy the wishes of parents, and no truly affectionate daughter be so regardless of her duty." Three months after their marriage Sarah Davis died of malarial fever. Upon the outbreak of the Mexican War, Davis recruited and was made Colonel of the "Mississippi Rifles." He was sent with this elite body of soldiers to serve under Taylor, who, however, refused to acknowledge his existence, except in his official capacity. A spectacular charge at Monterrey failed to melt the obduracy of the General toward his son-in-law. But when, in spite of a severe wound, Davis stayed in his saddle throughout the battle of Buena Vista and contributed largely to the American success in that engagement, the older man was completely mollified and, it is said, burst into tears as he publicly embraced Davis on the battlefield.

The election was bitterly contested. After the ballots were tabulated, it was found that Taylor, the Whig, had received 1,360,101 popular votes; Cass, the Democrat, 1,220,554; and Van Buren, the Free-Soiler, 291,263. In the electoral college Taylor was given 163 votes to 127 for Cass.

As Polk and Taylor rode together down Pennsylvania Avenue on inauguration day, the new President shocked the retiring Executive by his slapdash observations on political matters. "Gen'l Taylor is, I have no doubt, a well meaning old man," Polk recorded in his diary. "He is, however, exceedingly ignorant of public affairs, and, I should judge, of very ordinary capacity. He will be in the hands of others, and must rely wholly upon his Cabinet to administer the Government."

Taylor appointed John M. Clayton of Delaware, Secretary of State; William M. Meredith of Pennsylvania, Secretary of the Treasury; George W. Crawford of Georgia, Secretary of War; W. Ballard Preston of Virginia, Secretary of the Navy; Reverdy Johnson of Maryland, Attorney General; and Alexander H. H. Stuart of Virginia, Secretary of the Interior.

The immediate problem of the administration was to determine what policy should be adopted on the subject of slavery in the lands lately acquired from Mexico. This question, fiercely discussed during the agitation over the Wilmot Proviso, was a matter of vital interest in all parts of the country. The President, who had, before his nomination, viewed the Wilmot Proviso as a "mere bugbear," was apparently unaware of the extent of the cleavage existing between the proponents of slavery and its opponents. Although he was a Southerner and a slaveowner, he was an ardent unionist and deprecated the secession movement. As vainly as King Canute attempted to stay the tides did he plead that slavery discussions be discontinued in Congress. In his inaugural address he said: "By awaiting their action" (application of California and New Mexico for statehood) "all causes for uneasiness may be avoided, and confidence and kind feeling be preserved. With a view of maintaining the harmony and tranquillity so dear to all, we should abstain from the introduction of those exciting topics of a sectional character which have hitherto produced painful apprehensions in the public mind; and I repeat the solemn warning of the first and most illustrious of my predecessors, against furnishing 'any ground for characterizing parties by geographical discriminations.' "

Congress paid no heed to the President's admonitions. The House of Representatives, which convened in December 1849, used up three contentious weeks before Howell Cobb of Georgia could be chosen Speaker, and no topic was long discussed except that of slavery. One Congressman remarked: "Passions are so high that I have of late gone every day to the hall of the House with a pistol in my bosom." California had never been organized as a territory, but now, ignoring that intermediate step, applied for admission as a state, with a free Constitution which had been ratified by a great majority of her people. The Chief Executive recommended immediate admission. The resulting debate almost rent the Union asunder. Many Southerners, especially those from the Deep South, were infuriated; they demanded that the line of the Missouri Compromise be extended to the Pacific Ocean, splitting California into two states —one servile and the other free. Otherwise, they threatened secession. The President declared himself inveterately opposed to secession, warning its advocates that he would take the field at the head of the army to crush any rebellious movement. Taylor, although a Southerner, became very unpopular in that section of the country, where he was regarded as an apostate from its traditions and principles.

The direction of affairs as regarded slavery was taken out of the President's hands. The great orators, Calhoun, Webster and Clay, were back in the Senate, ready for the fray. Clay came forward with a series of compromise measures supported by Webster but unsatisfactory to Calhoun. They were finally passed during Fillmore's administration. Although they composed a crazy quilt of legislative proposals, they sufficiently conciliated all factions to insure peace between the North and the South for another decade. The President himself was bewildered by the violence of the slavery debate, and floated about in the sea of words like a straw in a whirlpool. He actively opposed the suggested fugitive slave law and contemptuously called the compromise measures the "Omnibus Bill."

In the field of foreign affairs the Taylor administration was responsible for the Clayton-Bulwer Treaty, signed on April 19, 1850, which, in addition to other provisions, guaranteed the neutralization by the United States and Great Britain of any inter-oceanic canal across Central America. At that time there was a proposal for the building of a Nicaragua canal, and the two nations mutually agreed to abstain from fortifying or acquiring exclusive control over it. Taylor also sent a consul to the Sandwich Islands, stating: "The position of the Sandwich Islands in reference to the territory of the United States in the Pacific . . . renders their destiny peculiarly interesting to us . . . we could in no event be indifferent to their passing under the domination of any other power."

A scandal known as the Galphin Claim, which bade fair to besmirch the name of his Secretary of War and indirectly involve other members of his official family, so distressed the President, that he resolved to reorganize his Cabinet. Before he could carry out this intention, his own life was brought to a close. On the fourth of July 1850 while attending dedication ceremonies at the laying of the cornerstone of the Washington Monument, he had exposed himself to a broiling sun. Upon returning to the White House, he drank a quantity of iced milk and ate handfuls of fruit. In less than an hour he suffered a violent attack of cholera morbis. It was soon apparent that his recovery was doubtful. On the third day of his illness he said: "I should not be surprised if this were to terminate in death. I did not expect to encounter what has beset me since my elevation to the presidency. God knows, I have endeavored to fulfill what I considered to be an honest duty; but I have been mistaken, my motives have been misconstrued, and my feelings grossly betrayed." On the day of his death he remarked: "I am about to die. I expect the summons soon. I have endeavored to discharge all my official duties faithfully. I regret nothing, but that I am about to leave my friends."

"Old Zach's" summons came on July 9. Whitey, his Mexican War steed, appeared in the funeral cortege, bearing an empty saddle, and this eloquent reminder of the departed President's military services to his country moved onlookers to a dramatic display of sorrow. The American people sincerely mourned his departure; it was as if a familiar and rugged landmark had been suddenly eliminated from their view.

Millard Fillmore

Born: February 7, 1800.
Admitted to Bar: 1823.
Married: 1826.
State Assembly: 1829-32.
United States House of Representatives: 1833-35,
    1837-43.
Comptroller of New York State: 1848.
Vice-President of the United States: 1849-50.
President of the United States: July 10, 1850-
    March 4, 1853.
Defeated as American party candidate for President:
    November 4, 1856.
Married for second time: 1858.
Died: March 8, 1874.

MILLARD FILLMORE

WHEN Millard Fillmore became President as the result of Zachary Taylor's fatal attack of indigestion, he must have experienced somewhat the same feelings as Byron, when he awoke one morning to find himself famous. The Vice-President of the United States is not a conspicuous figure; almost his sole official duty is to preside over the Senate, where he is often overshadowed in importance by many members of that body. In Fillmore's case this was particularly true, for the great slavery debate of 1850 had summoned to the Capitol, in the persons of Calhoun, Clay and Webster, a triumvirate of talents that can seldom have been equaled in the history of legislative assemblies. Compared with them, their presiding officer was almost a nullity. Calhoun himself predeceased Taylor, but the two surviving giants must have been jealous of the quirk of fate which had enabled the gentleman from New York to inherit so easily a position that each of them had futilely coveted.

What Fillmore's reflections were when he took the oath of office on July 10, 1850, we can only surmise. He should be pardoned if his thoughts dwelt with pride on his spectacular rise from the humblest of beginnings. It is to be hoped he had no gift of prescience, to enable him to foretell that he was to survive in history as probably the most obscure and least celebrated of American Presidents.

The Fillmore family's first known representative in the colonies was one named John, who appears to have been in 1704 a mariner of Ipswich, Massachusetts. His son too was a sailor, for he was captured by pirates and forced to serve under the skull and cross-bones for nine months before with some brave companions he slew his pirate overlords and brought their brig into a friendly port. This stout soul was the grandfather of the future President. Millard's own father, Nathaniel, was a native of Vermont, but the boy's first name derived from his mother, Phoebe Millard.

It is difficult to conceive now of how any part of New York State could have been in the nineteenth century a frontier in the wilderness, but such was Cayuga County on February 7, 1800. Fillmore's birthplace was a log cabin, scantily furnished, in which the only tools of education were a Bible and a hymnbook. In later years the President said that he was nineteen before he saw a copy of Shakespeare or a *Robinson Crusoe*, or even a map of the United States. Perhaps because of this early literary starvation he later became a discriminating bibliophile, for he amassed a private library of about five thousand volumes, and also secured an appropriation from Congress to stock the empty bookshelves of the White House.

Young Millard had little time for schooling, being fully occupied with farm chores. At the age of fifteen he was apprenticed to a clothier and fuller, from whom he was expected to learn the trade of dressing cloth and dyeing and carding wool. Fired with ambition, before his apprenticeship was finished he bought its remainder from his master with a promissory note, and taught school while he studied law. In 1823 he was admitted to the New York Bar, where his success steadily increased until he became one of its leaders. At the age of twenty-six he married Abigail Powers, the daughter of a Baptist clergyman of Saratoga County, New York, and herself a schoolteacher.

On their joint professional income they set up a modest establishment in a home built by his own hands, and within a few years he attained political recognition by being elected to the State Assembly on a anti-Mason ticket. Thurlow Weed, Van Buren's archenemy, was attracted by the young man, who possessed most agreeable and courteous manners, and sponsored his candidacy for the national House of Representatives on an anti-Jackson ticket. He was elected and served four terms in Congress, first as an anti-administration man, then as a Whig. In the Twenty-seventh Congress he was Chairman of the Ways and Means Committee.

While in the House, he favored a protective tariff and internal improvements. He joined John Quincy Adams in the fight to maintain the right to present antislavery petitions, and advocated the exclusion of slavery from the District of Columbia. He also championed Morse, the inventor of the telegraph, sponsoring an appropriation to enable him to carry on his work.

When Fillmore preened his feathers for higher flight and tried to become Whig Governor of New York he was defeated, but received a consolation prize three years afterwards by being chosen Comptroller of the state.

Upon Taylor's nomination as President, it seemed advisable to the Whig leaders to secure the second position on the ticket for a New Yorker. The affable Fillmore, who could be relied upon to say or do nothing untoward, was their successful choice. The Clay faction had supported him for the nomination, having refused to accept Lawrence, a New England textile manufacturer, saying "they would not have cotton at both ends of the ticket."

Fillmore was not renominated to succeed himself as President. Soon after his retirement his wife died of a chill contracted during Pierce's inaugural procession. They had been a devoted couple, and he suffered keenly from her death. "For twenty-seven years," he said, "my entire married life, I was always greeted with a happy smile." He, too, was of a happy and benevolent temperament. His kind blue eyes were indicative of his good disposition, his politeness was the offspring of his natural sweetness. His person was massive, but handsome and impressive. Within a year of his wife's death he also lost his daughter Abigail, who had taken her invalid mother's place as the hostess of the White House. His other child, a son, Millard Powers Fillmore, is notable for his vandalism in having prescribed that upon his own death all his father's letters and papers should be destroyed. This mandate was unfortunately obeyed. In 1858, Fillmore married for a second time; his wife was Mrs. Caroline C. McIntosh, a widow from Albany, who survived him seven years.

Fillmore retained little political prominence after his retirement from the presidency. He refused a proffered degree from Oxford University on the ground that his scientific and literary attainments did not entitle him to the honor. In 1856, while traveling abroad, he was nominated for President by the American, or Know-Nothing, party. The nominee attracted the remnants of the moribund and disorganized Whig Party, but at the election he carried only the state of Maryland. This contest marked the demise of the American as well as of the Whig party. The former had its origin in a secret society called the "Supreme Order of the Star Spangled Banner," a nativist movement, strongly anti-Catholic, and anti-foreigner. There was a great deal of hocus-pocus connected with its flummeries. Its operations in local elections had been effective and secret: if one of its members was questioned as to his affiliation with it, the indicated answer was, "I know nothing," from which it derived its popular name.

The great issue during Fillmore's administration was, of course, the perennial agitation over slavery. Shortly after being elected Vice-President, Fillmore had written: "I regard this election as putting an end to all ideas of disunion. It raises up a national party, occupying a middle ground, and leaves the fanatics and disunionists, North and South, without the hope of destroying the fair fabric of our Constitution." Alas for his predictions! Although the Wilmot Proviso, prohibiting slavery in the territories which might be acquired from Mexico, had never been approved, it remained a pregnant source of mischief. Calhoun had countered it by claiming that the right to hold slaves was guaranteed by the Constitution, that slaveowners could take their Negroes into the territories, where their ownership must be recognized, and that Congress had no authority to legislate on the subject for the territories. Things were at a stalemate, with the Southerners refusing to allow Congress to organize the territories, when California, with the approval of President Taylor, applied directly for admission to the Union as a state, with a Constitution prohibiting slavery within its limits. This fabulous land, where eggs sold for ten dollars a dozen, became during 1849 alone the haven of over one hundred thousand immigrants, and the voice of its people resounded in Washington.

With Taylor and the Northern and Western Whigs insisting on the admission of California and the preservation of the Union, with Southern fire-eaters opposing admission and clamoring for secession, the prospect for harmony was dark indeed. The difference in character between the population and the problems of the North and South were basic. In the North slavery was an uneconomic institution, while in a large part of the South it was considered an economic necessity. Moreover, the sentimental attitude of the two sections toward those enslaved was radically different.

Actually, in the South, there had always existed a strong aversion on the part of most of its greatest leaders to slavery. George Washington, Thomas Jefferson, James Madison, James Monroe, John Marshall and Patrick Henry, to name only a few distinguished Virginians, were all in favor of eventual emancipation.

However, the culture of cotton had made the Deep South increasingly dependent upon slave labor and Calhoun voiced the social and political attitude of extremists in that section when he asserted: "We see it [slavery] now in its true light, and regard it as the most safe and stable basis for free institutions in the world."

But Calhoun did not represent the more enlightened thought of Virginia statesmen. Virginia had always been in the forefront of movements for emancipation. Almost from the arrival of the first Negro, on a Dutch ship in 1619, her foremost men had protested against the slave trade. Their dislike of George III's tyrannical rule was partially based on that monarch's refusal to listen to the requests of the colony for the abolition of the traffic in human beings. Until the very outbreak of the Civil War the best public opinion in Virginia regarded the institution of slavery with distaste. Robert E. Lee had emancipated his own slaves before that conflict, Confederate Generals J.E.B. Stuart, Fitzhugh Lee, Stonewall Jackson, Joseph E. Johnston and A. P. Hill, all Virginians, had either never owned slaves or had freed them.

To some extent the position of Virginia was different from that of the cotton states, but everywhere throughout the South there existed a strong unionist and antislavery sentiment. If left to her own devices, without outside interference, there is little doubt that Virginia would in time have emancipated all her slaves, under the pressure of the moral objections of her own people. Where Virginia led, the other border states would quickly have followed. In due course the rest of the South might have fallen into line. The real cause of the South's opposition to emancipation did not lie only in the determination of the Southerners to preserve slavery, but was also due to other and broader reasons.

The fact is that two distinct political and social philosophies were struggling for survival. The south, Nordic in blood, agrarian in economy, aristocratic in its views, was opposed in its whole conception of living to Northern industrialism, which was fast becoming dependent upon imported labor, and the democracy of which, logically applied, would have reduced the white Southerner to the level of his own black servants. The civilization of the South was constantly attacked and vilified by Northern abolition writers who pictured a plantation owner leering at his female slaves while he threatened the males with a whip in one hand and a dagger in the other.

In turn, the Southern planters, who gave the tone to the political thought of their section, grew to hate the whole North because of the scurrilities of its extreme abolition writers. In addition they felt that a government administered in behalf of Northern banking and industrial requirements would be destructive of their interests, which were based on the production of raw materials. In contrasting the lot of their own Negroes, most of whom were moderately well fed and clothed, with the condition of sweated Northern factory laborers, they may indeed have believed that slavery was a more humane system than was provided in industrial centers for those whom Shakespeare termed "greasy mechanicks." There was no social legislation to protect the factory worker, whereas a slaveowner, no matter how unsentimental, cared for the health of his human property for the most practical reasons.

As far back as 1831, when William Lloyd Garrison started his paper, the *Liberator*, he had enunciated the policy thereafter followed by the extreme abolitionists. "I shall strenuously contend," he wrote, "for the immediate enfranchisement of our slave population. . . . On this subject I do not wish to write, or speak, or think with moderation! No! No! Tell a man whose house is on fire to give an immediate alarm; tell him to moderately rescue his wife from the hands of the ravisher; tell the mother to gradually extricate her babe from the fire into which it has fallen; but urge me not to moderation in a cause like the present. I am in earnest—I will not equivocate—I will not excuse—I will not retreat a single inch—and *I will be heard.*"

In spite of strong opposition to these utterances by many Northern leaders, such as Webster, the abolitionists would not heed any counsel of moderation. They clamored for immediate emancipation without compensation, which, if effected, would have meant the economic ruin of a great section of the country. Also the proposed enfranchisement of the Negro would have resulted in the destruction of that Southern white political supremacy which the South, not unjustly, considered had contributed most of the leadership in national affairs. From a social aspect, emancipation without any simultaneous arrangement for Negro colonization conjured up a spectacle of horror among planters who lived in remote and sparsely settled counties, and who had never forgotten the tales of the bloody slave insurrections in Santo Domingo and in Haiti, as well as in Virginia and other Southern states.

Faced by what seemed the implacable hostility of the North, aimed at the destruction of all it held dear, sentimentally and financially, the South retreated into its shell. By 1850 the influence of external thought had almost ceased to have currency within its borders. Poetry, literature and art became sterile. Daydreaming and romantic illusions replaced reality. It is significant that the novels of Walter Scott at this period were the favorite possessions of Southern libraries. Slavery was now openly justified on moral and religious grounds; Southern politicians defended the institution as being the cornerstone of their civilization. Secession was discussed as the only remedy for their differences with the North; most Southerners believed that it would be peaceably permitted if the South finally decided it was necessary.

Moreover, the planting aristocracy, although comprising a small minority of the Southern population, had by mid-century consolidated its hold on the machinery of the Democratic party. Calhoun had taken over the leadership of the South from the more moderate Virginians. His followers had become increasingly sympathetic to the interests of the slaveholders of the Deep South.

Calhoun and the planting aristocracy made the fatal mistake of allowing the issue of slavery alone to dominate the discussion of all the sources of conflict existing between the industrial North and the agrarian South. It is highly possible the Civil War would have been avoided had they been willing, before bitterness between the two sections became ineradicable, to sponsor a national program of compensated emancipation. The Calhounites and abolitionists together forced the South into a position where it was eventually to fight a war presumed by the Western world to be waged solely on behalf of an institution that most Europeans and Northerners, as well as many Southerners, regarded with abhorrence.

Except for statesmen and abolitionists, the North was too absorbed in its own restless energies to envisiage an approaching crisis. Many Northerners had devoted Southern friends, and there was considerable contact between the upper classes of both sections, at universities, at watering places and even on the Continent of Europe. Nevertheless, the still inadequate transportation and publicity facilities of the South made a real understanding of plantation life impossible at the North.

Especially in the Deep South the plantation owners were as far removed from any close association with commercial centers as if they had been Ivanhoes or Quentin Durwards. All their available capital was invested in more land and more slaves, to make more cotton. As they looked further Southward, they imagined a great Nordic slave empire, embracing Cuba, Texas, Mexico, Central America and perhaps even fabled Brazil. They would turn their backs on the Northern moneygrubbers and extend their territories toward the Southern Cross. The successful outcome of the Mexican War seemed the first link in the forging of this chain of imperialism. It was with a real sense of betrayal and frustration that slavery protagonists witnessed the improbability of their securing any benefits for their institution from the acquisitions of the war in which they had gallantly participated.

By the unanimous vote of the Kentucky legislature Henry Clay, "the Great Pacificator," had, after an absence of seven years, been sent back to the Senate, where it was believed he could conjure up a compromise to save the Union from disruption. In spite of age and debility his old fires of eloquence blazed again.

On February 5, 1850. he addressed the Senate, saying: "I consider our country in danger, and if I can be the means of in any measure averting that danger, my health and life are of little consequence." For two days he pleaded for a comprehensive settlement of factional and sectional differences on slavery. To the Southerners he frankly announced that the West would never permit secession and the consequent influence of another government over any part of the Mississippi River. Indignantly he retorted to the charge of having forsaken the cause of the South: "Sir, I know no South, no North, no East, no West to which I owe any allegiance. I owe allegiance to two sovereignties, and only two: one is to the sovereignty of this Union, and the other is to the sovereignty of the State of Kentucky. My allegiance is to this Union and to my State; but if gentlemen suppose they can exact from me an acknowledgment of allegiance to any idea of future contemplated confederacy of the South, I here declare that I owe no allegiance to it."

On March 4, Calhoun's speech was read for him by Senator Mason of Virginia. Calhoun himself was in his Senate seat, but was too feeble to stay long upright. His six feet two inches were slouched in his chair, he was wrapped in flannels, a large sheet of paper covered his chest, from which an occasional hacking cough originated. Bushy brown brows almost obscured those wonderful gray eyes which were so striking a feature of his physiognomy. His thin, small hands rested motionless as he followed intently the words of Mason. He had welded the South together in opposition to the Hamiltonian program of the North, but he had broken away from his Jeffersonian moorings and was adrift in what he never recognized as a reactionary tide. Public opinion thoughout the world had condemned the institution he so passionately defended. In asking for Southern rule in perpetuity coequally with the North, he was fighting against insuperable odds of population and wealth.

The South, said Calhoun, had no concession to make. State rights had been swept away. The general government had been transformed from a federal republic into a national consolidated democracy. The North must put an end to agitation over the slavery question; she must admit slavery in New Mexico and California; she must observe a stringent law for the return of fugitive slaves; she must consent to the amendment of the Constitution, so as to restore to the South the equilibrium of federal power formerly shared with the North.

This last object was to have been attained, as an examination of Calhoun's posthumous papers disclosed, by the election of two Presidents, one from the slave states and one from the free states, each with a veto on legislation. In the absence of such action secession from the Union was the only honorable course for the South to follow. Ironically enough, this was the same remedy proposed by the abolitionists, but for entirely different reasons.

On March 31, Calhoun died. On March 7, Daniel Webster came to Clay's assistance. Both of them had only two years to live and were beyond the reach of purely temporal ambitions. The Jovelike head of the Northern orator, more suited for display on a pedestal in a sculpture gallery than to rest on mortal shoulders, attracted all eyes. The thunder of his eloquence intimidated, overbore, fascinated and beguiled his hearers. For days his life had been preserved by administrations of oxide of arsenic and other medical prescriptions, but his voice was vigorous, his manner firm, though grave.

"I wish to speak today," he said, "not as a Massachusetts man, nor as a Northern man, but as an American. . . . I speak today for the preservation of the Union. Hear me for my cause." He denounced the abolitionists and pleaded fervently for the preservation of the Union. It was a "taunt and reproach" to slaveholders, he said to ban their institution by law from New Mexico and California, since nature's law had already accomplished this. "I would not take pains uselessly to reaffirm an ordinance of nature, nor to re-enact the will of God," he declared. He advocated mutual tolerance and conces-sion, and held himself ready to vote for a drastic fugitive slave law. It was an effective speech and a brave one, for it cost him the sup-port of many old admirers.

Senator William H. Seward, of New York entered the lists against Calhoun and ably criticized his contentions. The debate was acri-monious, and a civil war, with words for weapons, was daily waged in the senate chamber. President Taylor's death on July 9 was helpful to the cause of the compromise toward which he had adopted a contemptuous attitude. Fillmore strongly favored it. After Clay had declined his offer to become Secretary of State, he appointed Web-ster to that position, rejecting the advice of Seward, who had been largely responsible for Taylor's intransigence on the subject of slavery. One by one the various compromise measures passed by Congress were signed by the President, until their tale was com-plete. They provided for: (1) the adjustment of the Texan bound-aries, and the assumption by the national government of the Texan debts; (2) the organization of the territories of New Mexico and Utah, with or without slavery as their future Constitutions might decree at the time of their admission to the Union as states; (3) the abolition of the slave trade—not slavery itself—in the District of Columbia; (4) the immediate admission of California as a free state; and (5) the application of a new and severe fugitive slave law.

This last law was too stringent to be enforceable. It allowed an owner even without an affidavit, to recapture an alleged fugitive, through an agent or attorney. The fugitive could be brought before a federal Commissioner, where he was denied the right of trial by jury and was not permitted to give evidence on his own behalf or to summon witnesses. The measure was retroactive. If a Commis-sioner decided in favor of the defendant his fee was five dollars; if he decreed the return of the Negro to the claimant his fee was doubled. There were large penalties imposed for sheltering and abetting the escape of fugitives.

On September 18, 1850, Fillmore signed this act and committed political suicide. It was a courageous proceeding on his part, for without it the South could not have been conciliated or the Union saved. But Ralph Waldo Emerson represented the considered thought of many individuals, both North and South, when he wrote in his journal: "This filthy enactment was made in the nineteenth century, by people who could read and write. I will not obey it, by God." *Uncle Tom's Cabin,* published in 1852, aroused tremendous feeling over the issue, and the "Underground Railway" by which fugitives were transported from the South to Canada soon became a highly perfected system of bootlegging.

The passage of the compromise was the last important legislative act of the Whig party, which was already in a state of slow dissolution. The remainder of Fillmore's term contained no exciting domestic incidents, except the visit of Louis Kossuth to the United States. Congress had passed a resolution authorizing the President to secure, if possible, the release of the Hungarian patriot from exile, and his transportation to the United States on an American man-of-war. Webster, Secretary of State, was sufficiently infected by the Kossuth fever to write to Austria, in the course of a diplomatic dispute over its rebellious subject: "The power of this republic at the present moment, is spread over a region one of the richest and most fertile on the globe, and of an extent in comparison with which the possessions of the house of Hapsburg are but as a patch on the earth's surface." Having thus officially defied Austria, Webster was further emboldened and when Kossuth actually arrived in Washington to be the guest of honor at a congressional dinner the Secretary offered the toast: "Hungarian independence, Hungarian control of her own destinies, and Hungary as a distinct nationality among the nations of Europe."

Fillmore was wiser than his Secretary of State. Although he received Kossuth cordially at the White House, he made it clear to his visitor that the United States would not intervene in European affairs in his favor. In the field of foreign relations Fillmore's term was notable for his having ordered the penetration into Japan's forbidden waters of the expedition led by Commodore Matthew C. Perry. In his last message he departed from Polk's ambition and expressed his opposition to the idea of securing Cuba as a state of the Union.

Fillmore was a commonplace President, though an adequate one. Fortune had been kind to him beyond his deserts, but he had attracted her attention by his industry, his scrupulous honesty and his sound patriotism. He died on March 8, 1874, and was buried in Buffalo. But he had long been a political corpse.

Franklin Pierce

Born: November 23, 1804.
Graduated from Bowdoin College: 1824.
Admitted to Bar: 1827.
State House of Representatives: 1829-33.
Married: 1834.
United States House of Representatives: 1833-37.
United States Senator: 1837-42.
Brigadier General in Mexican War: 1847.
President of the United States: 1853-57.
Died: October 8, 1869.

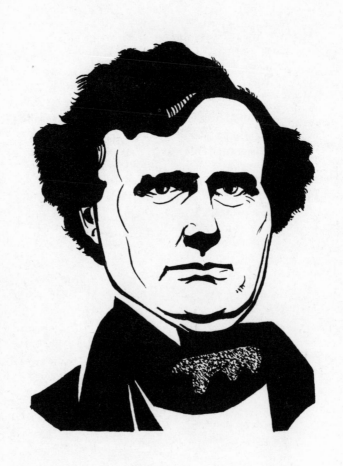

FRANKLIN PIERCE

THE career of Franklin Pierce was fundamentally tragic. Nature herself seemed to have intended his life to be happy. He was gifted with a charming manner and an exceptionally handsome appearance, his disposition was friendly and affectionate, his abilities were not negligible. But there had been bad fairies too at his christening. His convivial tendencies led him into a course of dissipation which racked his health and undermined his moral balance. His attitude on the slavery question was in accord with his settled convictions on the subject, but caused him to be hated in his own section of the country and by his own people, who anathematized him as a "Northern man with Southern principles." His domestic life, in which he might have found a solace from worldly cares, was marked by extreme disappointments. In his last years there was almost none so poor as to do him reverence. Even his death did not moderate the animosity of his enemies; it was over half a century before a monument was erected to his memory in his native state.

His marriage and its consequences were unfortunate. At the age of thirty he espoused Jane Means, daughter of a former President of Bowdoin College, at which Pierce had matriculated. Her skin was too tender to withstand the ordinary buffets of life, and in the company of strangers she was morbidly diffident. She shrank from crowds and unfamiliar human contacts with an almost psychopathic aversion. Political controversies were abhorrent to her, the very discussion of political topics distasteful. Her poor health was aggravated by neurasthenia. In her husband's career she was not merely a cipher but a liability. Yet he loved her, as she did him; he was undeviatingly faithful to her and sacrificed much for her sake. It was probably due to her dislike of Washington that he resigned his seat in the United States Senate, and later refused an appointment to that body, as well as declining an invitation from President Polk to become Attorney General.

Her tribulations had been great. Two sons in their infancy had been lost by the Pierces, and though her religious faith to some extent sustained her, her nerves were weakened by these misfortunes. Her outlook on life was narrow, her interests limited. These last became concentrated on her remaining son. After Pierce's election, and only two months before his inauguration, the future Chief Executive, his wife and their child were on a train journey when the axle of a passenger coach broke and the cars fell down an enbankment. The parents were badly bruised, and the boy was killed. Mrs. Pierce expressed shortly afterwards the belief that their son had been taken from them because of her husband's election as President, and that God thereby intended to keep his mind from being distracted from the nation's business. This gnarled reading of the Almighty's purposes was a source of the deepest distress to Pierce, who gave some credence to it.

Franklin Pierce was born at Hillsborough, New Hampshire, on November 23, 1804, in a county celebrated as having nurtured Daniel Webster and General Stark. His father was General Benjamin Pierce, a veteran of the Revolutionary War, a native of Massachusetts who after moving to New Hampshire served thirteen years in the legislature of that state and was twice its Governor. The General's first wife died after twelve months of marriage, leaving a daughter. His second wife, Anna Kendrick, had eight children, of whom Franklin was the sixth.

While Frank was attending a local academy, two of his brothers were fighting in the War of 1812. After a course of schooling at Hancock, Francestown, and Exeter the lad entered Bowdoin College in 1820, where he was remembered as having been "a very small, slight and apparently frail boy of sixteen." The discipline there was strict, and since young Pierce was unusually carefree he was often in trouble with the authorities. Soon after the beginning of his third year he was so neglectful of the curriculum that his standing as a scholar was the lowest in the class. His father wrote him the customary parental advice to avoid vices which "kreep in unexpectedly and become confirmed when there is no such thing as aradacating them." There is no indication that Pierce was ever a great reader, though he spelled better than his father, nor were the college rules as favorable as they might have been to the pursuit of knowledge. The library was open only from noon to one o'clock daily, and no student could borrow books more than once in three weeks. However, the boy at least improved his comparative scholastic position before graduation, for he then stood fifth in a class numbering about a dozen students.

Pierce became a lawyer after studying at Northampton, Massachusetts. With the political influence of his father at his disposal, he was elected to the legislature, at that time called the Great and General Court. At the age of twenty-six he was chosen its Speaker and bought a frock coat to serve as his badge of office.

In 1833 he was elected to the national House of Representatives. His father had been a disciple of the political school of Jefferson and Madison, and the son readily embraced Jacksonianism. A strict party man, he voted against the Bank of the United States. He expressed himself on the slavery question as favoring the enforcement of the rights vested in the South by the Constitution and was inflexibly opposed to the policy of internal improvements constructed at federal expense.

The Congressman's personal magnetism was great. It was later said of him that he could concentrate his personality to the point of its becoming an almost hypnotic power. He pleased the people of New Hampshire by his career in the House sufficiently for them to select him as one of their national Senators. When he took his seat at the beginning of Van Buren's term, he was the youngest member of the United States Senate. When he resigned his post before the expiration of his term to return to his home and his profession he did not leave behind him any reputation as a statesman. However, he had established himself in national Democratic circles as a dependable party man and a pleasant companion.

After his retirement from Washington, Pierce plunged into the practice of law but remained active in Democratic state politics. His first case at the Bar was a miserable failure. Undiscouraged, he said: "I will try nine hundred and ninety-nine cases, if clients continue to trust me, and if I fail just as I have today, I will try the thousandth. I shall live to argue cases in this court-house, in a manner that will mortify neither myself nor my friends." This determination, which reminds one of Disraeli's statement following his maiden speech in the House of Commons, enabled Pierce to become a very successful lawyer. He was not especially conversant with the traditions and lore of his profession, but he had a fine voice, a facile delivery and a way of persuading juries to adopt his views. President Polk named him a federal District Attorney, and in that capacity he was an efficient government officer.

After war was declared against Mexico, Pierce, over his wife's opposition, enlisted as a private in the army. His promotion was magically rapid. On February 15, 1847, he was appointed a Colonel, on March 3, he was commissioned a Brigadier General. The good ladies of Concord buckled a fine sword on him, his friends contributed a black horse. Sped by the enthusiastic acclaim of all New Hampshire, he sailed from Newport on March 27, 1847, and arrived a month later at Vera Cruz.

Brigadier General Pierce's conduct in Mexico was honorable, although not spectatcular. His men liked him, and he genially shared their privations and hardships. Before the final attack on Mexico City he was chosen by General Scott as one of a commission of three to arrange an armistice.

In 1850 he was named a member of a convention to redraft the obsolete state Constitution. In this connection he unsuccessfully advocated the removal of restrictions on office-holding by Roman Catholics.

His nomination for President on the Democratic ticket was a great surprise to him, but a greater one to his wife, who fainted when she heard the tidings. William R. King of Alabama had been named as his running mate. Pierce's selection was made on the forty-ninth ballot, after it was apparent that the two-thirds rule would make impossible the nomination of either Case or Buchanan, the early favorites.

Since the time of John Quincy Adams, no New Englander had received a presidential nomination. The party managers had finally chosen Pierce in the belief that he would attract a large Northern following because of his antecedents, his vote-getting ability, his place of residence and his personal popularity, and would hold the South because of his sympathetic slavery views. As both the Whig and Democratic parties had ratified the Compromise of 1850, there was no choice between them on that score. However, the platform of the Democrats made assurance doubly sure in this regard by pledging specifically: "Resolved, that the Democratic party will resist all attempts at renewing in Congress, or out of it, the agitation of the slavery question, under whatever shape or color the attempt may be made."

The Whigs nominated General Winfield Scott. That remarkable person was a better soldier than politician. An Admirable Crichton, he could do all things except captivate a public gathering. If he had merely shown himself, without speaking, he might have been elected. He was handsome in a superb way, his six feet four of stature being nobly proportioned. He wrote well, and the matter of his speeches was good. However, he was tactless and invariably gave his audience the impression—a true one—that he was consummately and inordinately vain. Meanwhile Pierce, who had been brightly christened "Young Hickory of the Granite Hills," was touted as a second Andrew Jackson.

In the midst of the campaign Clay and Webster died, and the Whig Party was further weakened. The result of the election was a great victory for the Democrats. Pierce lost only four states and had 254 electoral votes to 42 for Scott, although Scott had received 1,386,578 popular votes to 1,601,474 for Pierce. John P. Hale, the Free-Soil Democratic candidate, had been given 156,149 popular votes; only in New York, Ohio and Massachusetts did his party poll over ten thousand ballots per state.

The fourteenth President took his oath on March 4, 1853. His Cabinet remained intact throughout his term and consisted of William L. Marcy of New York, Secretary of State; James Guthrie of Kentucky, Secretary of the Treasury; Jefferson Davis of Mississippi, Secretary of War; Caleb Cushing of Massachusetts, Attorney General; James Campbell of Pennsylvania, Postmaster General; James C. Dobbin of North Carolina, Secretary of the Navy; and Robert McClelland of Michigan, Secretary of the Interior. Vice-President King had been in Cuba during the inauguration, for the sake of his health. He took his oath there, but did not long survive his return to the United States, dying in Alabama on April 18, 1853.

In his inaugural address Pierce said: "With the Union my best and dearest earthly hopes are entwined. . . . I believe that involuntary servitude as it exists in different states of this Confederacy, is recognized by the Constitution. I believe that it stands like any other admitted right, and that the states where it exists are entitled to enforce the constitutional provisions. I hold that the laws of 1850, commonly called the 'compromise measures', are strictly constitutional, and to be unhesitatingly carried into effect. . . . I fervently hope that the question (of slavery) is at rest, and that no sectional or ambitious or fanatical excitement may again threaten the durability of our institutions or obscure the light of our prosperity."

It had become a matter of course to reward the spoilsmen. When the Whigs entered into possession of the national government, they proscribed the Democrats; when the Democrats overturned the Whigs, they reversed the process. Pierce's manner toward applicants for public positions seemed to hold out to them hopes of success that were often not realized. He wanted intensely to be liked and admired by everybody; this together with his poor judgment of men, his obstinacy, his vanity and his reluctance to deny any importunity, were his greatest weaknesses as a statesman. It was not long before Jefferson Davis perceived his susceptibility to flattery and to influence. Pierce had always hated the abolitionists, and it was not difficult to induce in him an attitude favorable on most points to Southern slavery doctrine. In addition he was personally more inclined to friendly intercourse with Southern leaders than with Northern ones. His gaiety and gregariousness found a ready counterpart in the geniality that marked the social life of the South, and many Southern statesmen were well disposed toward him, not only because they found him sympathetic to their political aspirations, but also because they were genuinely fond of him as a man.

Throughout the country the auguries were favorable to the success of his administration. A popular mandate had indicated that the people had tired of the contentious subject of slavery and wished it to lie quietly under the tombstone of the Compromise of 1850. This tranquility, however, was soon rudely disturbed. Stephen Arnold Douglas, Democratic Senator from Illinois, allowed his ambition to overreach his judgment and conceived a measure, later known as the Kansas-Nebraska Bill, fated to wreck Pierce and his administration. Douglas was not yet forty. Called "the Little Giant," he combined the powers of a fine orator with a veritable genius for parliamentary management. Looking forward to the next presidential nomination, he may have thought that he could gain it by adding to his present supporters a large Southern following. Interested as an investor in Western lands and desirous of a railroad to the Pacific, the idea occurred to him to foster his political ambitions without harming his private investments by a congressional enactment opening up the great Nebraska Territory to rapid colonization.

In spite of these selfish motives Douglas, a true patriot, also wished to throw the protection of organized Government over the hardy individuals who had pushed forward into the prairies, for he was an enthusiastic advocate of the development of the West. He baited his hook to catch Southern votes by advocating the principle of applying popular sovereignty, or as it came to be derisively called, "squatter sovereignty," to the proposed territory. This principle was that the settlers in a territory should be free to admit or banish slavery within its limits, as they should themselves elect.

The Nebraska Territory included the present states of Nebraska, Kansas, North Dakota, South Dakota, Montana and portions of Wyoming and Colorado. It had formed part of the Louisiana Purchase, and lay altogether north of the Missouri Compromise line, extending northwest from Missouri to Canada. Although there were less than one thousand white inhabitants in this huge area, an attempt to organize it as a territory had been submitted to the preceding Congress. Neither then nor at any future date was the fact that its ownership had been solemnly guaranteed to the Indians considered any bar to its pre-emption by American settlers.

When Douglas, as Chairman of the Committee on Territories, submitted his plan in January 1854 to the Senate, certain Southern members promptly requested that it be amended to repeal the Missouri Compromise, which had already been breached as a result of the permission given in 1850 to the territories of Utah and New Mexico to allow or deny slavery as they saw fit. This request brought Douglas in hot haste to the White House on a Sunday—a day upon which Pierce, a strict Sabbatarian, normally refused to discuss any business. Through the mediation of Jefferson Davis the President acquiesced in Douglas' proposals, and the plot so fatal to the Chief Executive's career was hatched. The very proponents of the plan differed regarding its implications. Some held there could be no prohibition of slavery in a territory by its inhabitants, for this right could exist only after it had become a state. Others maintained the converse. Still others belonged to the school that had always considered the Missouri Compromise an unconstitutional act.

The bill as finally passed divided Nebraska into two parts, the northern, Nebraska, and the southern, Kansas. The Missouri Compromise was declared "inoperative and void." In the Senate the vote was 37 for the act, and 14 opposed to it. In the House the contest was closer, but after Douglas applied the whip and spur there were 113 affirmative to 100 negative ballots.

The result of this enactment was astonishing. The sleeping dog of slavery had been awakened. Pierce and Douglas, according to the famous editor Greeley, had created more abolitionists almost overnight than the foremost antislavery leaders could have in five decades. The Fugitive Slave Law became a dead letter in the North, only enforceable by the use of police and soldiery. In 1854 a new party—the Republican—sprang into being, dedicated to fight the extension of slavery. Anti-Nebraska Democrats, Free-Soilers, Whigs, Know-Nothings and Abolitionists hastened to join it. In large portions of the country Pierce's popularity descended to the nadir of detestation. In 1852 he had carried every Northern state except two; in 1854 the Democrats lost every free state except California and New Hampshire. Douglas fared even worse. A group of women in Ohio sent him thirty pieces of silver. He said that he "could travel from Boston to Chicago by the light of his own effigies."

In the South, the bill increased the ambitions and swelled the arrogance of the Hotspurs. Suggestions were made that the importation of slaves be revived and legalized. In 1855 Governor Adams informed the legislature of South Carolina: "The world owes its civilization to slavery. It exists with us in its most desirable and enduring form. 'It is the corner stone of our republican edifice.'"

It was at once apparent that Nebraska was certain to become a free state, but the Southerners hoped to offset this by the eventual admission of Kansas as a slave state. To effect this purpose a few planters emigrated to Kansas, taking their slaves with them. The free states countered this action by organizing Emigrant Aid Societies, and sending free settlers into the territory. The pro-slavery advocates were soon outnumbered. Since the greater part of the property of Southern slaveholders consisted of nonliquid assets, it was obviously impossible to balance the influx of Northern settlers to Kansas by an equivalent representation from the slave states. However, the slave state of Missouri adjoined Kansas, and bands of border ruffians made frequent forays into the territory, terrorizing the free settlers. On the day of the election of the territorial legislature about five thousand Missourians, armed with bowie knives and pistols, led by a United States Senator, took possession of the polling places and proceeded to cast twice as many votes as there were voters in Kansas. Although an overwhelming majority of the population was opposed to slavery, the belligerent minority enforced its wishes. The legislature passed laws Draconian in their severity. Among others it was provided that any free person who by speaking, writing or printing should advise or induce slaves to rebel should suffer death. Death or ten years' imprisonment was to be meted out to anyone who enticed a slave to leave his master.

The pro- and antislavery factions each appointed a delegate to the national Congress, each was refused the privileges of the House. Both factions held conventions and applied for the admission of Kansas into the Union, one as a free and the other as a slave state. The President, favoring the cause of slavery proponents, characterized the Topeka free-state legislature as being engaged in rebellion. He announced his intention "to exert the whole power of the Federal Executive to support public order in the Territory and to vindicate its laws, whether federal or local, against all attempts of organized resistance." The census of 1855 showed that out of a total population of eighty-six hundred persons in the territory there were fewer than two hundred slaves. Sentiment in the South was mirrored in the statement of the Charleston *Mercury* that the struggle in Kansas was "between fanatical hirelings and noble champions of the South," and "the cause of Kansas is the cause of the South."

The territory was soon the scene of civil war. Bloodshed and assassinations were so widespread that the area was called "Bleeding

Kansas." The fanatic, John Brown, in retaliation for the murders of five free-state men deliberately caused the mutilation and massacre of five proslavery settlers at Pottawatomie Creek. Men went armed to till their fields. Guerrilla bands roamed the country. The President, having espoused the proslavery cause, found himself unable to bring its designs to fruition, thereby further diminishing his own prestige. The problem of Kansas was not destined to be solved during his administration and was left by him as an embarrassing legacy to his successor.

The focus of the attention of the country was Kansas, but the Chief Executive and his Cabinet were also kept occupied with other problems. The era was one of railroad building, and Pierce once complained to an importunate promoter that he had thought he had been elected President of the United States and not of a railroad company. Jefferson Davis wished the government to use its war powers to construct a Southern transcontinental line, while the Northerners advocated three separate routes to connect the East with the shores of the Pacific. In pursuance of Southern ambitions the Executive arranged to buy from Mexico the Messilla Valley, in what is now southern Arizona, consisting of about forty-five thousand square miles, for the sum of ten million dollars. This acquisition, handled through the mediation of Captain Gadsden, was called the Gadsden Purchase. It was proposed to run the Southern railroad route through this region.

Pierce's insistence on the observance of the Fugitive Slave Law further inflamed public opinion against him at the North. A critic addressed him as "the chief slave catcher of the United States," and continued: "You damned infernal scoundrel, if I only had you here in Boston I would murder you."

When Pierce became President, the national debt amounted to about seventy million dollars; before he left office it had been reduced to about thirty million dollars. At a cost of eleven millions, a hundred and seventy-four million acres of Indian lands had been acquired by the customary dishonest treaties. The President was a low-tariff man and a strict constructionist. He vetoed a bill for public works and an act to donate ten million acres of public lands to the states for the relief of indigent insane persons.

In the field of foreign affairs the administration was kept incessantly busy. One of the most interesting foreign appointments was that of Nathaniel Hawthorne as Consul at Liverpool. The President and he had been lifelong friends; to the day of his death the great writer never traveled without a photograph of Pierce. During the dark period of the Civil War, when the ex-President was discredited at the North, Hawthorne, then a literary lion, dedicated his book, *Our Old Home,* to him. The publishers objected, and Hawthorne replied: "If Pierce is so exceedingly unpopular that his name is enough to sink the volume, there is so much the more need that an old friend should stand by him. I cannot, merely on account of pecuniary profit or literary reputation, go back from what I have deliberately felt and thought it right to do; and if I were to tear out the dedication, I should never look at the volume again without remorse or shame."

James Buchanan was appointed to the Court of Saint James, and James Y. Mason of Virginia to Paris, where his habit of expectorating tobacco juice in drawing rooms was a source of mingled amusement and disgust to his French hosts and hostesses. But it was Spain which received our most remarkable minister, in the person of Pierre Soulé, a Louisianian. He was at once the most tactless and the most bellicose of men. His darling project, which coincided with the wishes of the administration, was to purchase Cuba from Spain. While he was waiting for the possible opportunity to broach the subject at the Court of Madrid, he became embroiled in a duel with the French Ambassador, the Marquis de Turgot, and shot his colleague in the thigh, permanently laming him.

On top of this incident the affair of the *Black Warrior* was superimposed. This American merchant vessel was detained at the port of Havana and her cargo confiscated. The circumstances of the case were sufficient, if Pierce had so desired, to warrant his forcing a war on Spain. Fortunately the President and Secretary of State Marcy procrastinated and finally the Spanish government apologized for the ill-timed zeal of its Cuban officials. The President was equally discouraging to those elements in the South which were abetting filibustering expeditions against Cuba. Quitman, the leader of one such enterprise and a friend of Jefferson Davis, was arrested in full career by order of the government and made to promise to observe his country's neutrality laws.

But the administration had by no means abandoned its aspiration to own Spain's rich Caribbean possession. In August of 1864 the Secretary of State suggested that Messrs. Buchanan, Mason and Soulé convene and study the question of the acquisition of Cuba. They met at Ostend, then adjourned to Aix-la-Chapelle, whence they sent home the draft known as the Ostend Manifesto. This egregious document informed Marcy that its signers favored the immediate purchase of Cuba for one hundred and twenty million dollars.

Soulé was once described as a "perfect bird charmer," and the manifesto was undoubtedly the product of his enthusiasm. When Marcy poured cold water on the project, Soulé, disgruntled, resigned his post as Minister.

During Pierce's administration one of those periodic disputes arose over our diplomatic uniform that have, from that time to this, provided joy to cartoonists. Secretary Marcy ordered our representatives abroad to appear at official functions, if practicable, in "the simple dress of an American citizen." Mr. Buchanan was especially embarrassed by these instructions, for in his attempt to obey them he ran full tilt into the strict protocol of Queen Victoria's court. The London *Chronicle* did not ease his difficulties by stating: "There is not the least reason why her Majesty . . . should be troubled to receive the 'gentleman in the black coat' from Yankee-land. He can say his say at the Foreign Office, dine at a chop-house in King Street, sleep at the old Hummums, and be off as he came, per liner, when his business is done." Mr. Buchanan finally compromised by appearing in the "very dress which you have often seen me wear at the President's levees, with the exception of a very plain black-handled and black-hilted dress sword." His wearing of the sword he said was prompted by his desire to distinguish himself from the upper court servants.

During Pierce's term the British Minister at Washington, Mr. Crampton, was handed his passports, for although he was personally popular he had been found guilty of soliciting recruits for the British army on American soil.

Pierce and Marcy actively engaged in a variety of foreign negotiations. They decided to make an annexation treaty with the monarch of Hawaii, and evinced our willingness to buy Alaska from Russia. When William Walker had established his dominion over

Nicaragua, they recognized the Minister whom he sent to Washington. This professional filibusterer had invaded Lower California and the state of Sonora. Unsuccessful there, he had concentrated his attention on Nicaragua, where he succeeded in having himself elected President. To the delight of his Southern sympathizers, he repealed all laws against slavery. A quarrel with the doughty Commodore Vanderbilt, who was deeply engaged in Central American shipping operations, led to his return to his native country. Once again he landed in Nacaragua but was forced to flee. His last escapade was an essay against Honduras, in the course of which he was surrendered to the Honduran authorities and executed at the age of thirty-six.

The Mission of Perry to Japan was successfully concluded during Pierce's occupancy of the White House, and that ancient kingdom opened to a limited American trade.

While he was Chief Executive, Pierce found time for a certain amount of relaxation. He rode horseback—and he adored horses—for exercise, and gave dinners for pleasure. Such functions were short in the duration; the guests assembled at six in the evening and took their departure at eight-thirty. As the President trusted and liked everybody, he was frequently imposed upon, but his credulous faith in the sublimity of human nature was never completely shaken by the disillusions he experienced.

It was evident long before the convocation of the Democratic Convention that Pierce could not be renominated. The Kansas-Nebraska Bill had alienated Northern sentiment from him, and he was considered there to be hand-in-glove with the secessionists. On the first ballot he received 122 votes to 135 votes for Buchanan, and 33 for Cass, but on the seventeenth Buchanan was unanimously nominated. When it was realized he would not succeed himself, the rats left the sinking ship.

Pierce went abroad after the inauguration of Buchanan, and later visited the island of Nassau. Refusing to have his name used for the presidential nomination in 1860, he favored the selection of Jefferson Davis. Constant in his convictions, he opposed the Emancipation Proclamation, although he never embraced the doctrine of secession. He publicly spoke of the War between the States as "this fearful, fruitless, fatal civil war." It can be imagined that his position in his own state was almost untenable. His wife died in 1863, and his own health began to fail thereafter. Only children continued to love him; to them he had always been a fascinating friend. A lonely, despised figure, his once powerful frame bent and crippled with dropsy, he went to his final rest on October 8, 1869.

James Buchanan

Born: April 23, 1791.
Graduated from Dickinson College: 1809.
Admitted to Bar: 1812.
Member of Pennsylvania House of Representatives:
    1814-16.
United States House of Representatives: 1821-31.
Minister to Russia: 1832-33.
United States Senator: 1834-45.
Secretary of State: 1845-49.
Minister to Great Britain: 1853-56.
President: 1857-61.
Died: June 1, 1868.

JAMES BUCHANAN

PRESIDENT POLK once made the observation, regarding his Secretary of State: "Mr. Buchanan is an able man, but is in small
matters without judgment and sometimes acts like an old maid."
Later critics of the fifteenth President have not hesitated to impeach
his judgment in great matters. That James Buchanan was vacillating
in some of his opinions is manifest. Fearful at one period of the
consequence of attempts to acquire Cuba, he later coveted acquisition of that island. Having coquetted with the idea of being named
a Supreme Court Justice, he could not bring himself to accept the
nomination he had so ardently desired. His stand on the Oregon
boundary controversy was mercurial. In the matter of annexing
Mexican territory he first boggled over acquiring even a small slice
of it, then resented not being permitted to swallow the whole.

Faced with the threat of civil war, Buchanan sought refuge not
in action but in discourses on the strict constuction of the Constitution, in prayers, in tears and, according to an enemy, in whisky.
Whether, under the circumstances, another attitude would have been
successful will remain a disputed point. His inertia, as states seceded
from the Union like autumn leaves dropping from a tree, at least
preserved the possibility of a compromise between the contending
factions. Many who have criticized him for not employing the
ridiculously inadequate armed forces of the national government to
coerce wayward South Carolina forget that Lincoln pursued for
some weeks the same policy as his predecessor. The struggle during
Buchanan's administration over secession was so complex that Solomon in all his wisdom could have done little to resolve it.

But calumny itself cannot accuse Buchanan of any marked faults
of character other than vacillation and timidity. Had his career

ended before his election as President, he would have been remembered as a statesman who had conscientiously served his country for
more than four decades. He early entered the Pennsylvania House
of Representatives, and after an interval was sent to the National
House, where remaining ten years he headed the powerful Judiciary
Committee. A term as Minister to Russia preceded his election to
the United States Senate, to which body he was twice re-elected.
He quitted his seat there to become Polk's Secretary of State. During and after the Taylor-Fillmore interregnum he was politically
quiescent until Pierce appointed him to the Court of Saint James.

Presidents valued his counsel, women relished his social attractions, men enjoyed his urbane conversation. His outward casing was
most impressive. Six feet tall, his frame was broad and massive. The
pink cheeks and white hair of the Chief Executive, coupled with his
old-world, stately demeanor, made him appear singularly sedate.
There was no frivolity in his attire. He always affected a white
stock, carefully and neatly swathed about a high and well-starched
collar. His black coats would have befitted a Presbyterian divine.
By a peculiarity of nature he was equipped with a contradiction in
eyes, for one was blue and the other dark, one far and the other
nearsighted, which probably accounted for his habit of carrying
his head inclined to one side. They were however unusually keen,
and he reconciled their differences without the use of glasses, except for reading small print in his old age. His hearing was always
unusually acute. Rather small feet supported his bulky body, and
he walked lightly and quickly. His manners were courteous, cordial
and dignified.

His White House hostess was his niece, Miss Harriet Lane. Only
envy could cavil at her charms and accomplishments. Her beauty
was notable. Buchanan permitted no dancing in his official mansion,
not because he had a personal aversion to that amusement but on
the score that many Americans objected to it. Except for dancing,
the President's house was the center of the most attractive social
life in Washington. Jefferson Davis, while imprisoned at Fortress
Monroe, had occasion to remark: "The White House, under the administration of Buchanan, approached more nearly to my idea of a
Republican Court than the President's house had ever done before
since the days of Washington."

James Buchanan was of Scotch-Irish Presbyterian stock. He was
born in a log cabin, located in a mountain gorge near Cove Gap in
the state of Pennsylvania, on April 23, 1791, the second of eleven

children. His father, for whom he was named, a native of County Donegal in Ireland, had emigrated to the United States in 1783. His mother, Elizabeth Speer, had a liking for poetry, and won from her son the heartfelt tribute: "Under Providence, I attribute any little distinction which I may have acquired in the world to the blessing which He conferred upon me in granting me such a mother."

The father, a farmer, also engaged in various mercantile enterprises. Young James attended school at Mercersburg, then became a student at Dickinson College, situated in Carlisle, Pennsylvania. In addition to his scholastic triumphs he had proved himself to be a good athlete and a fine shot.

Admitted to the practice of law in 1812, the young barrister, after the capture of Washington by the British, joined the army and marched to the defense of Baltimore, but was not brought under fire. In 1814 he was elected to the Pennsylvania legislature, from Lancaster County, and was re-elected for a second term.

Applying himself assiduously to his profession, he was soon successfully established in it; his cash fees for the year ending April 1, 1819, amounted to $7,915.92. This year, so propitious in pecuniary fortune was fatal to his sentimental happiness; he had become engaged to Anne C. Coleman, of Lancaster, an attractive and wealthy girl; her parents had consented to the match, but a lovers' quarrel, based apparently on a minor misunderstanding, estranged the couple. During a visit to Philadelphia the young lady suddenly died at the age of twenty-two. It was hinted, but never proven, that she had committed suicide.

Buchanan was distraught with grief over this occurrence. He wrote her father a letter, couched in pathetic terms, begging to be allowed to see her body and follow it to the grave. The letter was returned to him unopened. Whether or not he then vowed to remain unmarried is unknown, but he became the first and only bachelor President.

His friends supported him in a campaign for a seat in the national House, and as a Federalist he was elected. A few years later he was to express his considerations on slavery as follows: "I believe it to be a great political and a great moral evil. I thank God, my lot has been cast in a State where it does not exist. But, while I entertain these opinions, I know it is an evil at present without a remedy. . . . There are portions of this Union, in which, if you emancipate your slaves they will become your masters." But he joined John Quincy Adams in defending the "sacred right of petition."

Buchanan embraced Democracy in the person of Andrew Jackson, and was appointed by Old Hickory Minister to Russia, to replace John Randolph of Roanoke. The practice of law had made Buchanan independently wealthy, and his money was wisely invested. He was therefore able to surround himself with some luxuries at St. Petersburg, the lack of which had irritated his predecessors there. The negotiation of a commercial treaty was successfully accomplished by him. He noted the scarcely concealed Russian habit of opening foreign diplomats' mail, but enjoyed his sojourn.

Buchanan's election by the Pennsylvania legislature to the United States Senate plunged him into the turmoil of Jackson's second term. A stout advocate of the President's financial measures he voted in favor of Benton's "expunging" resolution. He became the Chairman of the Committee on Foreign Relations and a frequent, though not brilliant, speaker.

His firmest conviction was his almost idolatrous belief in the merits of the federal Constitution and a corresponding concern for the reserved rights of the states.

Buchanan declined an invitation from Van Buren to become Attorney General but acceded to Polk's request to fill the position of Secretary of State. In that office he displayed a great deal of ability in the drafting of diplomatic instructions. On the subject of expatriation the Secretary of State instituted a precedent of considerable importance when he maintained that "naturalization in the United States not only clothes the individual with a new allegiance, but also absolves him from the obligations of the old."

After Zachary Taylor, the Mexican War hero, had been elected President by the Whigs, Buchanan retired to his twenty-two-acre farm near Lancaster and cultivated his Pennsylvania political connections, holding court there under the appellation of "the Sage of Wheatland." Since 1844 he had been the favored son of his own state delegation for the presidency, and when Franklin Pierce came into office the new President persuaded his erstwhile rival to go abroad as Minister to Great Britain.

Buchanan's absence from the United States during the bitter disputes over the Kansas-Nebraska Bill had much to do with his nomination by the Democratic party for President. It was felt he would be the strongest candidate available to his party since he had not been involved in recent sectional bitterness, and though a Northern man had always shown a friendly spirit to the South. His platform condemned slavery agitation and approved the Compromise of 1850.

J. C. Breckinridge, of Kentucky, aged thirty-five, fresh from a brilliant four years in the House at Washington, was nominated as Vice-President. He was later to become a member of the United States Senate, to be expelled from that body for treason during the Civil War, to attain the rank of Major General in the Confederate Army, and to serve for a time as the Confederate Secretary of War.

Meanwhile the Whig Party, split into many factions, came to an inglorious end. Its official fragments endorsed the American Party candidacy of Millard Fillmore and stated in dirge-like words: "The Whigs . . . have no new principles to announce, no new platform to establish, but are content to broadly rest—where their fathers rested —upon the Constitution of the United States, wishing no safer guide, no higher law." In that same year, the new Republican party held its first national convention—its members, because of their antislavery sentiments, were called "Black Republicans" by the Southerners.

The Republican platform was frankly sectional and belligerent. It denied the "authority of Congress, of a Territorial Legislature, or any individual or association of individuals to give legal existence to slavery in any territory of the United States, while the present Constitution shall be maintained." The Republicans were "opposed to the repeal of the Missouri Compromise, to the policy of the present Administration, to the extension of slavery into free territory; in favor of admitting Kansas as a free State." The Church of the Latter-day Saints was included in a fulmination: "That the Constitution confers upon Congress sovereign power over the Territories of the United States, for their government, and that in the exercise of this power it is both the right and duty of Congress to prohibit in the Territories those twin relics of barbarism, polygamy and slavery."

After considerable jockeying for position, John C. Frémont was nominated by the Republicans for President and William L. Dayton, of New Jersey, for Vice-President, for which latter office Abraham Lincoln, the rising Illinois politician, received 110 votes. The choice of the head of the ticket was not especially fortunate. Frémont's dashing career on the West Coast, his marriage with Senator Benton's daughter and the romantic elements in his personality made him a vivid figure. However, many men instinctively distrusted him. Ulysses S. Grant, upon being asked why he had voted for Buchanan, observed succinctly: "I knew Frémont."

When the election took place, Buchanan received 1,838,169 votes to 1,341,264 for Frémont, and 874,534 for Fillmore. The vote in the electoral college was 174 for Buchanan, 114 for Frémont, and 8 for

Fillmore. The new President had been carried in by the votes of Pennsylvania and Indiana, New Jersey, California, Illinois and the Southern states. "Buck and Breck" had triumphed over the slogan of "Free Labor, Free Speech, Free Men, Free Kansas, and Frémont." In the whole South, Frémont had received less than one thousand votes.

Unconscious of how temporary his triumph was to be, Buchanan appointed as members of his Cabinet: Lewis Cass of Michigan, Secretary of State; Howell Cobb of Georgia, Secretary of the Treasury; John B. Floyd of Virginia, Secretary of War; Isaac Toucey of Connecticut, Secretary of the Navy; Aaron V. Brown of Tennessee, Postmaster General; Jacob Thompson of Mississippi, Secretary of the Interior; and Jeremiah S. Black of Pennsylvania, Attorney General.

The inauguration ball was a splendid affair. Fifteen thousand tickets were sold for it. The President's carriage headed a procession including a 'Liberty car," with "the Goddess of Liberty, magnificently attired, supported by a liberty pole fifty feet high, drawn by six horses."

Buchanan's inaugural address was mild as milk. He specifically announced his determination not to become a candidate for re-election. He further said: "A difference of opinion has arisen in regard to the point of time when the people of a territory shall decide this question [of slavery] for themselves. This is happily a matter of but little practical importance. Besides it is a judicial question, which legitimately belongs to the Supreme Court of the United States, before whom it is now pending, and will, it is understood, be speedily and finally settled. To their decision, in common with all good citizens, I shall cheerfully submit, whatever this may be, though it has ever been my individual opinion that, under the Kansas-Nebraska act, the appropriate period will be when the number of actual residents in the territory shall justify the formation of a constitution with a view to its admission as a State into the Union." He continued: "The whole territorial question being thus settled on the principle of popular sovereignty—a principle as ancient as free government itself—everything of a practical nature has been decided. . . . May we not, then, hope that the long agitation on this subject [of slavery] is approaching its end, and that the geographical parties to which it has given birth, so much dreaded by the Father of his country, will speedily become extinct."

The President's reference to his willingness to abide by the forth-

coming decision of the Supreme Court was, as it transpired many
years later, a disingenuous promise, for he had, contrary to all precedent, been already advised of the import of that decision. The
court was composed of five Justices from the slave states and four
from the free states. Mr. Justice Grier had informed Buchanan that
the Missouri Compromise would be declared invalid, saying "though
contrary to our usual practice, we have thought it due to you to state
in candor and confidence the real state of the matter." Two days
after the inauguration, Chief Justice Taney delivered his famous
Dred Scott opinion. If the conclusions reached were no surprise to
the President, their effect on the country was cataclysmic. The Supreme Court had been asked to decide the free or slave status of an
individual, illiterate Negro. Taney's opinion went far beyond a decision on this point. Scott, who had claimed that he had become free
as a result of a stay with his owner in a territory dedicated to freedom by the Missouri Compromise, was remanded to slavery. The
Missouri Compromise was declared null and void. A Negro under
the Constitution could not become a citizen.

This decision therefore gave a slaveholder the right to take his
bondsmen into the territories and hold them there despite any congressional or territorial legislation to the contrary, until such time
as the territories might become states. A paean of praise for the
Court's reasoning arose in the South, but the North and West were
sullen and resentful. Lincoln voiced the sentiment of the Republicans when he said: "We think its [the Supreme Court's] decisions
on Constitutional questions, when fully settled, should control not
only the particular cases decided, but the general policy of the country, subject to be disturbed only by amendments to the Constitution.
. . . More than this would be revolution. But we think the Dred
Scott decision is erroneous. We know that the court that made it
has often overruled its own decisions, and we shall do what we can
to have it overrule this. We offer no resistance to it." Plainly enough,
Lincoln was ready to let time do its work, hoping a change in administration might enable a new President, through the power of
appointment, to change the complexion of the Supreme Court.

The slavery element was now predominant in the national government. It controlled the President, one of whose most influential ad-
visers was Jefferson Davis. It controlled the Cabinet, the Supreme
Court, the Senate, and was powerful in the House. However it did
not control the public opinion of the country or of the world. Everywhere, except in the Southern states, which numerically had a min-

ority of the population of the United States, a strong tide was running against it, and each victory gained by it only stiffened the ranks of the opposition.

Buchanan had long wanted to tranquilize Kansas, and favored its admission to statehood under the Lecompton (proslavery) Constitution, declaring that Kansas is "at this moment as much a slave state as Georgia or South Carolina." Meanwhile, in Kansas, the free-state men who undoubtedly constituted a majority in the territory, had refused to vote for delegates to the Lecompton Convention. The President's situation was embarrassing. He fell back upon the letter of the law, accusing the Free-Soilers of establishing "a revolutionary government, under the so-called Topeka Constitution." To complicate matters further the Constitution, as submitted to Kansas voters, gave them no opportunity to declare their outright and unequivocal opposition to slavery.

Stephen Douglas, denouncing this fraud, broke with the chieftains of his party and patriotically caused the defeat of the President's recommendations regarding Kansas. For this action he remained unforgiven, either by Buchanan or by the South. His opposition was the more powerful because it was based not on high moral grounds, but on the proviso that the people of the territory should settle the question of slavery by a fair vote. "You have no more right," he said, "to force a free-State constitution on Kansas than a slave-State constitution. . . . It is none of my business which way the slavery clause is decided. I care not whether it be voted down or voted up. . . . I take it for granted that it will be voted out." The eventual outcome was the admission of Kansas as a free state in 1861, during the Buchanan Administration.

Other clouds now gathered about the President's head. Gold from California had inflated values, notes of wildcat banks had been loosed on the country, large debts had been contracted in Europe, speculation in railroads, in land and in industrial enterprises had been rife. In 1857 the natural consequence—a panic—ensued.

As if economic disorder were not enough, Fate, in the form of John Brown, cast more fuel on the slavery flames. In October 1859 the old fanatic led eighteen men, five of whom were Negroes, against the federal arsenal at Harpers Ferry and murdered a few peaceful citizens. It was apparently, his original intention to set up a free commonwealth in the near-by Virginia mountains, whence he might liberate slaves and extend his operations throughout the South. Colonel Robert E. Lee, with a company of United States marines, cut short his delusions of successful rebellion by assaulting the engine house in which the band had sought refuge. Ten conspirators were killed, four escaped, and five including John Brown were taken prisoner. The chief prisoner was indicted by a grand jury, convicted, sentenced and executed. The cause of freedom now had a martyr.

The great presidential campaign of 1860 confronted a divided and bittered country. Buchanan was not a candidate, and favored the nomination by the Democrats of Vice-President Breckinridge. Douglas, however, always an aspirant for the office, had strong support from Northern Democrats but was unacceptable to the slaveholding oligarchy of the South. His prestige, sharply diminished there by his opposition to the admission of Kansas as a slave state, had been still further impaired by his debates with Lincoln. The latter had driven "the Little Giant" into an admission—the so-called Freeport Doctrine—that "slavery cannot exist a day or an hour anywhere, unless it is supported by local police regulations," which meant that a territorial legislature could, in effect, deny the rights granted to slaveholders under the Supreme Court decision in the Dred Scott case.

The South was determined and implacable. Its leaders announced that it would never permit a Black Republican President to rule it. Jefferson Davis, its keynoter in the United States Senate, warned the Free-Soilers in that body: "It is not humanity that influences you in the position which you now occupy before the country. . . . It is that you may have an opportunity of cheating us that you want to limit slave territory within circumscribed bounds. It is that you may have a majority in the Congress of the United States and convert the Government into an instrument of northern aggrandizement. It is that your section may grow in power and prosperity upon treasures unjustly taken from the South, like the vampire bloated and gorged with the blood which it has secretly sucked from its victim. . . . You desire to weaken the political power of the southern states; and why? Because you want, by an unjust system of legislation, to promote the industry of the New England states, at the expense of the South and their industry."

Buchanan, isolated, blamed all slavery agitation on the abolitionists, and sympathized openly with the spokesmen of the South. In 1860, Senate resolutions were adopted, stating slavery to be lawful in all territories under the Constitution, and that neither Congress nor a local legislature could abolish it. In the same year the Covode Committee attempted but failed to impeach the President.

Breckinridge was finally nominated by the ultraslavery wing of the Democratic party, while Douglas was nominated by the more moderate Democrats, who relied on the doctrine that territorial legislatures possessed the power to impair the ownership of slaves by passing unfriendly legislation. The Constitutional Union party selected John Bell of Tennessee, and Edward Everett of Massachusetts as their candidates. This was called the "Kangaroo ticket," on the charge that "the hinder part was stronger than the head," and it stood on the vague platform of the preservation of the Constitution. The Republicans had held a sort of revivalist convention, from which Abraham Lincoln of Illinois and Hannibal Hamlin of Maine emerged as the nominees.

The presidential campaign of 1860 advanced ominously to its climax. Lincoln was elected by a minority vote. Of the total ballots cast, he had received 1,857,610; Douglas, 1,291,574; Breckinridge, 850,082; and Bell, 646,124. Lincoln obtained 180 electoral votes; Breckinridge, 72; Bell, 39, and Douglas, 12.

The election was over, but Buchanan's Calvary had just begun. His strongest sentiment was for the maintenance of the Union, yet on December 20, 1860 South Carolina passed an ordinance of secession. In his annual message on December 5, 1860, Buchanan had stated his explicit denial of the right of secession, while admitting if a state should secede he believed the federal government was without constitutional authority to coerce her into remaining in the Union. He asserted however the undeniable right of the central government, in such a case, to enforce the execution of federal laws and to preserve federal property. "Our Union rests upon public opinion," he said, "and can never be cemented by the blood of its citizens shed in civil war. If it cannot live on the affections of the people, it must one day perish. Congress possesses many means of preserving it by conciliation; but the sword was not placed in their hand to preserve it by force."

Congress had been careful not to place any sword in the President's hand or in its own. The federal military establishment was an empty shell. The regular army numbered only eighteen thousand men when recruited to full strength. Compromise measures were pending, and Congress would grant the President no powers. Even such a fire-eater as Jefferson Davis desired to give the Lincoln Administration a period of grace before deciding on hostilities against it. The influential Horace Greeley had at first wished to say to seceding states: "Wayward sisters, depart in peace."

Agitation throughout the country was intense, but the slavery question had been settled several times before by adroit compromises, and many persons reasoned it would be again. Buchanan decided to execute the revenue laws and protect federal property, meanwhile considering, ostrich-like, that the seceded states were still within the Union. The North despised him for his lack of aggressive firmness, the South because he attempted, though vainly, to reinforce a fort at Charleston. The aging President took frequent refuge in prayers and tears.

Uncertain whether to commit the country either to war or peace, Buchanan was derisively called "the Property Man of the United States." His Cabinet was disintegrating. On December 2, 1860, Cobb had resigned because of the President's refusal to recognize the alleged right of secession. Ten days later Cass resigned in dudgeon because the Charleston forts had not been reinforced. On December 29 Floyd, who had been the subject of ugly rumors, severed his connection with his associates.

Meanwhile the conciliators had not been idle. Crittenden, of Kentucky, the Nestor of the Senate, had given his name to a compromise measure calculated to appease all warring elements. This resolution proposed, in brief, the restoration of the Missouri Compromise line of 36° 30′ if the project were approved by a direct vote of the people. There were other minor provisions. Buchanan recommended this measure in a special message on January 8, 1861, but it was summarily rejected by Lincoln and the Republicans in Congress. Its rejection meant that war was inevitable. On January 15, Isaac Hayne went as a Special Commissioner from the Governor of South Carolina to negotiate at Washington for the purchase of federal property in that state. He was received by the President in his personal, but not his accredited official capacity. On February 4, 18 1, the Peace Convention sponsored by Virginia convened, under the direction of ex-President Tyler, but its efforts ended in nullity.

On February 8, 1861, the Confederate States of America came into being. Jefferson Davis of Mississippi was named their Provisional President, and Alexander H. Stephens of Georgia, Vice-President. The hope of Calhoun had been realized, but not in the manner envisaged by him. There were two Presidents in the United States— one in the North and one in the South—but instead of working in harmony they were at loggerheads.

Jefferson Davis, the youngest of nine children, had been born, like Lincoln, in Kentucky, under the humblest circumstances. Due to the great success and generosity of his oldest brother Joseph, who became a millionaire planter, he was enabled to attend West Point. After his marriage to Zachary Taylor's daughter and her untimely death, he retired from the army to his farm. The call of his country drew him back into military life during the Mexican War, wherein he acquired renown as a military hero. Returned again to civil life, he married the beautiful Varina Howell, led the life of a rural philosopher on his Mississippi plantation. He and his brother Joseph were responsible, according to Ulrich Phillips, for the most thorough-going application on record of self-government by slaves. "The slaves were not only encouraged," said Phillips, "to earn money for themselves in every way they might, but the discipline of the plantations was vested in courts composed wholly of slaves, proceeding formally, and imposing penalties to be inflicted by slave constables, except when the master intervened with his power of pardon." It is interesting to know that after the Civil War the brothers' slaves were model freemen.

As secretary of War in the Pierce Administration, Davis had dominated the government. He was in appearance and manner the perfect aristocrat. A close friend of Buchanan, he sincerely desired to avert war. After Lincoln's election he openly opposed secession, and even as President of the Confederacy continued for a time to work for a peaceful settlement of the national difficulties, basing his opposition to the North more on economic and political lines than on the subject of slavery *per se*.

The last month of Buchanan's term was passed in watchful waiting, and at last he was free of the burdens of office. He retired to Wheatland, whence he gave the North his loyal support and wrote a history of his administration. Exhausted by rheumatic gout, he died in his seventy-eighth year and was buried near Lancaster. His last words were: "O Lord, God Almighty, as Thou wilt."

In no measure can Buchanan be considered a great man, but he possessed many fine qualities. He was generous and kindly. His ample fortune was the result of his prudence and his wisdom in investment; at the time of his death it amounted to three hundred thousand dollars. His honesty was unimpeachable.

He was profoundly religious and a confirmed student of the Bible. His imagination was limited, his intellectual culture commonplace. He had neither the fire of genius nor the temerity of talent. He was in an eminent degree "a safe man."

Abraham Lincoln

Born: February 12, 1809.
Illinois House of Representatives: 1834-41.
Married: November 4, 1842.
United States House of Representatives: 1847-49.
President: 1861-65.
Outbreak of Civil War: April 12, 1861.
Died: April 15, 1865.

ABRAHAM LINCOLN

T HE UNKNOWN Lincoln is as incomprehensible to posterity as he was to his own intimates. Despite his lifelong brooding over the perplexities of human existence he left behind him no revelation by which his innermost feelings can be interpreted. His record abounds in contradictions. One of the most amusing storytellers of his time was the prey of ineradicable melancholy. The Great Emancipator of Negro slaves publicly declared that he cared little whether or not the slaves should be freed if the Union could be preserved. The statesman whose craft as Chief Executive saved the Union had never previously occupied a public office with any measure of success. The man who abhorred war made it almost inevitable by summarily rejecting the Crittenden Compromise, the only probable means of averting it.

There was nothing simple about Lincoln's character except his love of mercy, truth and honesty. "Politics," said Herndon, "were his life, newspapers his food, and his great ambition his motive power." Yet Herndon thought him "the best man, the kindest, tenderest, noblest, loveliest since Christ."

In spite of the manifold inconsistencies in Lincoln's thoughts and actions, he is one of the most striking personages in American history. He was not a truly great statesman, he was not a great political philosopher, but he was a great leader and, essentially, a great man. He was also the man of the hour, attuned to the particular emergency that confronted him as President. His sad heart overflowed with a genuine sympathy for all those in distress. He was compassionate and merciful in the highest degree, and remarkably free from preconceived prejudices. He was unwearying in the search for truth. His ability to interpret the aspirations of the average man was perfect. "I claim not," he once said, to "have controlled events, but confess plainly that events have controlled me. . . . With public sentiment," he declared, "nothing can fail, without it nothing can succeed"; and he was the ideal diviner of underlying public sentiment.

His integrity inspired universal confidence. Though remarkable for his ugliness, there was that in his face which drew men to him. He had a keen sense of justice and a broad tolerance for the weaknesses to which flesh is heir. He had little intuitive sense—his mind labored to reach wise and sound conclusions. Herndon thought that "the natural bias of his qualities was towards the negative side."

This outwardly unromantic figure had rare quality. His defects were as apparent as the mole on his cheek, his virtues were of a more elusive nature. He won the unstinted admiration and affection of such fastidious judges of character as Seward, Sumner and Stanton. On the morning of Lincoln's death it was the usually acidulous Stanton who pronounced his real epitaph: "Now he belongs to the ages."

He was six feet four inches in height and weighed one hundred and eighty-five pounds. His frame was spare but sinewy. His arms and legs were uncommonly long and seemed ill articulated with his body. His feet and hands were immense. He walked with a stoop that accentuated his flat chest. His clothes did not appear to fit him but gave the impression of having been dropped hastily upon him, like harness on a fire-engine horse. His small gray eyes were set deep in his skull. His nose was large, his cheekbones high. His chin was powerful, and his mouth full and sensual. His ears were large and protruding, as was his Adam's apple. A shock of coarse black hair surmounted his fine forehead. After his nomination as President he grew a beard saying he wished to please a young girl who had written him on the subject. His skin, yellow, tough and leathery, was seamed with furrows. His physical health was good. At the age of forty-seven he bought his first spectacles—they cost thirty-seven cents.

His mastery of the spoken and the written word was one of his greatest sources of power. His memory was magnificent. As he once said: "My mind is like a piece of steel—very hard to scratch anything on it, and almost impossible after you get it there to rub it out." He could repeat hymns, doggerel and other poetry interminably. His favorite poem was Knox's, "Oh! Why should the Spirit of Mortal be Proud," and he was likewise fond of "The Last Leaf," by

Oliver Wendell Holmes. His familiarity with the Bible largely influenced his style. "The Dream," by Byron, pleased him greatly. When asked for a toast to Burns, he wrote: "I can not frame a toast to Burns; I can say nothing worthy of his generous heart and transcending genius; thinking of what he has said I cannot say anything which seems worth saying. A. Lincoln." He preferred gloomy poetry, but at the same time rejoiced in the work of such humorists as Artemus Ward and Petroleum V. Nasby. While riding circuit, he read and mastered Euclid. The works of Thomas Hood, Bryant and Whittier interested him. In a desultory way he liked science and once patented an invention. The poet he most often quoted was Shakespeare.

Herndon states that Lincoln never read anything through, and was without interest in or knowledge of most of the great literary classics. However he developed a beautiful prose style.

His letter to Mrs. Bixby, of Boston, who was then believed to have lost five sons in the Union service, is a fine example of his humanity.

Dear Madam [he wrote]: I have been shown, in the files of the War Department, a statement of the Adjutant-General of Massachusetts, that you are the mother of five sons who have died gloriously on the field of battle. I feel how weak and fruitless must be any words of mine which should attempt to beguile you from a loss so overwhelming. But I cannot refrain from tendering to you the consolation that may be found in the thanks of the Republic that they have died to save. I pray that our Heavenly Father may assuage the anguish of your breavement, and leave you only the cherished memory of the loved and lost, and the solemn pride that must be yours to have laid so costly a sacrifice upon the altar of freedom.

Yours very sincerely and respectfully,
ABRAHAM LINCOLN

His speech at Gettysburg, on November 19, 1863, was of course, his most famous piece of writing, as it is one of the greatest prose expressions in our language. These were his words:

Four score and seven years ago our fathers brought forth on this continent a new nation, conceived in liberty and dedicated to the proposition that all men are created equal. Now we are engaged in a great civil war, testing whether that nation, or any nation so conceived and so dedicated, can long endure. We are met on a great battlefield of that war. We have come to dedicate a portion of that field as a final resting place for those who here gave their lives that this nation might live. It is altogether fitting and proper that we should do this. But, in a larger sense, we cannot dedicate —we cannot consecrate—we cannot hallow—this ground. The brave men, living and dead, who struggled here have consecrated it far above our poor power to add or to detract. The world will little note nor long remember what we say here, but it can never forget what they did here. It is for us, the living, rather to be dedicated here to the unfinished work which they who fought here have thus far so nobly advanced. It is rather for us to be here dedicated to the great task remaining before us—that from these honoured dead we take increased devotion to that cause for which they gave the last full measure of devotion; that we here highly resolve that these dead shall not have died in vain; that this nation, under God, shall have a new birth of freedom; and that government of the people, by the people, for the people, shall not perish from the earth.

As an orator, Lincoln's matter was better than his manner. His voice was high-pitched, shrill and harsh, but became more agreeable as he settled down to his discourse. In his early years he gesticulated freely and awkwardly. He probably acquired this habit from watching speakers at revivalist meetings. "When I hear a man preach, I like to see him act as if he were fighting bees," he once said. As he grew older, his platform manner became composed and dignified.

His farewell remarks at Springfield, when he left to take his oath as President, had a solemn ring. "My friends," he spoke, "no one, not in my situation can appreciate my feeling of sadness at this parting. To this place, and the kindness of these people, I owe everything. Here I have lived a quarter of a century, and have passed from a young to an old man. Here my children have been born, and one is buried. I now leave, not knowing when or whether ever I may return, with a task before me greater than that which rested upon Washington. Without the assistance of that Divine Being who ever attended him I cannot succeed. With that assistance I cannot fail. Trusting in Him who can go with me, and remain with you, and be every where for good, let us confidently hope that all will yet be well. To His care commending you, as I hope in your prayers you will commend me, I bid you an affectionate farewell."

The end of his first inaugural address was a plea to the South for Union. He said: "I am loath to close. We are not enemies, but friends. We must not be enemies. Though passion may have strained, it must not break our bonds of affection. The mystic chords of memory, stretching from every battlefield and patriot grave to every living heart and hearthstone all over this broad land, will yet swell the chorus of the Union, when again touched, as surely they will be, by the better angels of our nature."

Four years later his second inaugural address closed with passages that might have sprung from the pen of an Old Testament prophet: "Both read the same Bible, and pray to the same God; and each invokes his aid against the other. It may seem strange that any men should dare to ask a just God's assistance in wringing their bread from the sweat of other men's faces; but let us judge not, that we be not judged. The prayers of both could not be answered—that of neither has been answered fully. The Almighty has his own purposes. 'Woe unto the world because of offences! for it must needs be that offences come; but woe to that man by whom the offence cometh.' If we shall suppose that American slavery is one of those offences which, in the providence of God, must needs come, but which, having continued through his appointed time, he now wills to remove, and that he gives to both North and South this terrible war, as the woe due to those by whom the offence came, shall we discern therein any departure from those divine attributes which the believers in a living God always ascribe to him? Fondly do we hope—fervently do we pray—that this mighty scourge of war may speedily pass away. Yet, if God wills that it continue until all the wealth piled by the bondman's two hundred and fifty years of unrequited toil shall be sunk, and until every drop of blood drawn with the lash shall be paid by another drawn with the sword, as was said three thousand years ago, so still it must be said, 'The judgments of the Lord are true and righteous altogether.'

"With malice toward none; with charity for all; with firmness in the right, as God gives us to see the right, let us strive on to finish the work we are in; to bind up the nation's wounds, to care for him who shall have borne the battle and for his widow, and his orphan —to do all which may achieve and cherish a just and lasting peace among ourselves, and with all nations."

Lincoln's great talent was as a storyteller. In that capacity he was almost unique. "He can make a cat laugh," said one of the companions of his boyhood. The recounting of anecdotes was a relaxation for him; it relieved the spells of melancholy and gloomy abstraction to which he was subject.

Lincoln's habits were temperate. He never smoked and, except on a few occasions, never drank. He took no pride, however, in refraining from drink. He said: "I am entitled to little credit for not drinking, because I hate the stuff. It is unpleasant to me, and always makes me feel flabby and undone." He did, however, serve wine at the White House. Regarding drunkards he remarked: "Indeed, I believe, if we take habitual drunkards as a class, that their heads and their hearts will bear an advantageous comparison with those of any other class." He was almost entirely indifferent to food except that he liked apples and hot coffee.

During Lincoln's administration, there was little social life at the White House. He held a few public receptions and gave the necessary state dinners. The only White House ball was bitterly criticized as evidencing a lack of sensibility on the part of the President and his wife for the hardships being suffered by Union soldiers in the field. When his son Willie died shortly afterwards, malicious gossips said it was a judgment of God upon the Lincolns for sponsoring frivolities.

The President was a poor sleeper and an early riser. His habits were irregular and unmethodical. He got to his desk at eight o'clock but paid little attention to correspondence. He read few letters and wrote fewer. Most of his office time was spent in conversation, and he permitted an incessant stream of visitors to have access to him. Although he was an impolite listener, he was extremely amiable and hated to say no to any petition; "I shudder to think," he commented, "what would have happened to me if I had been a woman, but I suppose my ugliness would have been a shield." He was once involved in the preliminaries of a duel, having insulted a neighbor by anonymous satirical attacks in a newspaper. When asked, as the challenged party, what weapons he would choose, he is supposed to have answered: "How about cow dung at five paces?" He finally selected broadswords and practiced with them, but the duel was called off.

Lincoln was almost as indifferent to money as he was to food. When he entered the White House, he was worth about ten thousand dollars. "Wealth," he said, "is simply a superfluity of what we don't need."

In some respects he was humble. When campaign biographers

wanted to describe his early environment, he told them: "The story of my life is the short and simple annals of the poor. That's all you or anyone else can make out of it." On the other hand, he was intellectually proud, and fully conscious of his powers. He rarely asked for other persons' opinions.

He was accused, during the war, of granting too many pardons for military offenses. "You do not know," he retored, "how hard it is to let a human being die, when you feel that a stroke of your pen will save him." A Congressman burst into the President's bedroom in the middle of the night to present some additional evidence in favor of a convicted deserter. "Well," decided the President, "I don't see that it will do him any good to be shot." He telegraphed to General Meade: "I am unwilling for any boy under eighteen to be shot." To Colonel Mulligan he wired: "If you haven't shot Barney D. yet, don't."

He was the embodiment of personal democracy. "As I would not be a slave," he once wrote, "so I would not be a master. This expresses my idea of democracy. Whatever differs from this, to the extent of the difference, is no democracy."

Lincoln was not irreligious in the broad sense, but cared nothing for the forms or denominations of religion. He attended church services and said prayers. The year before his death he wrote to his friend Speed: "I am profitably engaged in reading the Bible. Take all of this book upon reason that you can, and the balance upon faith, and you will live and die a better man."

He was a pessimist and a fatalist. He frequently quoted Shakespeare's lines:

> There's a divinity that shapes our ends,
> Rough-hew them how we will.

He visited a voodoo fortuneteller, and was superstitious. "I fear that I shall meet with some terrible end," he once observed.

Students of heredity would find it difficult to trace the greatness in Abraham Lincoln's character to ancestral sources. From the time that one of his forebears emigrated to New England, from Old England, in the early part of the seventeenth century to his own birth, none of his direct lineage had achieved any particular measure of distinction, although his collateral Lincoln relatives in Massachusetts had produced some noteworthy public characters.

Abraham's grandfather, after whom he was named, was a Virginian and had owned a farm in the Shenandoah Valley. During the Revolutionary War he decided to remove to Kentucky, where he was killed by Indians. His son Thomas, who had been born in Virginia, grew up to prefer the hunting of game to any other pursuit. At times he plied the trade of a carpenter and almost always owned an unproductive farm in one or the other states to which his wandering feet transported him.

Abraham's mother, Nancy Hanks, died in October 1818 when her boy was nine years old, but he retained a tender recollection of her kindness and love. She was completely illiterate yet intelligent, and evidently superior to her husband in initiative and manners. She was the illegitimate child of Lucy Hanks, and was supposed to have been the fruit of a romance between her mother and a Virginia planter.

The first child of Thomas and Nancy Lincoln was a daughter, Sarah, who later married Aaron Grigsby and died in childbirth before her brother reached his majority. On February 12, 1809, their second child, Abraham, was born on a bed of cornhusks and bearskins, in a rude, dirt-floored log cabin at Sinking Spring Farm, in Hardin County, Kentucky, a place for which his father had paid two hundred dollars. Near his birthplace the youngster spent the first seven years of his life and learned to read and write at a backwoods school, before his vagabond parent set forth with the family for the Indiana wilderness. This move did not improve the material condition of the Lincolns. They merely exchanged a moderately comfortable log cabin in a settled community for a lean-to (later replaced by a cabin) in a rough forest country that had begun to attract pioneers.

In 1819, Thomas went back to Kentucky and there married a former friend, the widow Sarah Bush Johnston. To his own brood and inadequate stock of furniture she added her three children and a wagonload of household conveniences. Under her close supervision the cabin was immaculately clean, and she encouraged Abraham to read the books she had brought with her, *Robinson Crusoe, Pilgrim's Progress, Sindbad the Sailor,* and *Aesop's Fables.* Between her own and her husband's children she drew no distinction. Although unable to read, she approved highly of book learning. Long afterwards her famous stepson said of her that she had been his best "Friend in this world, and that no Son could love a Mother more" than he loved her.

There was little time or opportunity for Abe to attend school. He afterwards said that his entire youthful schooling did not amount to twelve months of instruction. But he learned to write a good hand

and to spell correctly. In addition to his father's Bible and his stepmother's books, he read Grimshaw's *History of the United States* the
Revised Laws of Indiana, Parson Weem's *Life of Washington* and
Life of Franklin, and *Lessons in Elocution.* His cousin Dennis Hanks
once commented: "We lived the same as the Indians, 'ceptin' we
took an interest in politics and religion." Abe was remarkable however, among his companions for his love of reading. As Dennis
Hanks said: "There's suthin' peculiarsome about Abe."

While helping his father, Abe made a little money for himself.
At the age of seventeen he helped operate a ferry across the Ohio
River, at a wage of thirty-seven cents a day, and was paid thirty-one
cents a day for his services during hog-killing time.

Even this early his physical strength was noteworthy. He was
said to be able to carry a six-hundred-pound chicken house, or to
lift a barrel of whisky over his head. He was not only a champion
"rassler" but was distinguished in jumping and weight-lifting contests. Much of his early political popularity was due to the reputation he acquired as a rough-and-tumble fighter.

In 1828, Abe was employed by James Gentry to take a boatload
of produce to New Orleans. This was his first glimpse of the outside
world, and he thoroughly enjoyed it. The journey covered one thousand miles, and when he returned home after three months, he had
earned twenty-four dollars. A few years later he made a second trip
to the Queen City by flatboat.

Impatient of the growing population of Indiana, Thomas Lincoln,
in 1829, pushed on with his family to Illinois. Almost two years
later Abe left his father and stepmother and settled in New Salem,
in Sangamon County, Illinois, then a village of fifteen houses, about
the size of Chicago.

Here he found himself in a brave new world. There were a general store, companionship and opportunities to take part in the
political discussions for which he already showed a preference. A
Whig and a confirmed admirer of Henry Clay, he cast his first vote
in a presidential campaign for that statesman instead of for Andrew
Jackson.

Abe's first occupation was as clerk in the store of Denton Offutt.
In 1833 he was made village postmaster and carried the weekly mail
in the lining of his hat. With no previous training, he became assistant to the county surveyor and learned the rudiments of that profession. During the Black Hawk War he volunteered, to quote one
of his fellow soldiers, "to Serve his Cuntry with the Ballance of the

Patriotick Boys to Defend the frontier settlers . . . from the Savages Tomihack and Skelping Knife." Abe was elected a Captain by the troops, but his forces never saw the enemy.

His military service had greatly enlarged the circle of his acquaintances. "I desire to live, and I desire place and distinction as a politician," he asserted. True to that impulse, he ran for a seat in the state legislature. His campaign speech was brief. "Fellow Citizens," he said, "I presume you all know who I am—I am humble Abraham Lincoln. I have been solicited by many friends to become a candidate for the Legislature. My politics are short and sweet, like the old woman's dance. I am in favor of a national bank. I am in favor of the internal improvement system, and a high protective tariff. These are my sentiments and political principles. If elected I shall be thankful; if not it will be all the same." He was defeated, but had carried his own precinct by 205 of its 208 votes. He was once selected as a Clerk of Election, to replace a man who had suddenly been taken ill. Upon being asked by the other Clerk whether he could write, Lincoln answered, "I can make a few rabbit tracks," and thereupon was promptly sworn into office.

He engaged in a mercantile partnership with W. F. Berry, under the firm name of "Berry and Lincoln." Berry spent a certain portion of each day in consuming the firm's stock of liquor, and Lincoln, in intervals between waiting on customers, lay on his back upon the notions counter and read newspapers or books. This idyllic way of doing business terminated in bankruptcy. Berry died, and Lincoln was left with eleven hundred dollars of debts. It took him two decades to pay them, but he satisfied them in full. "That debt," he once commented to a friend, "was the greatest obstacle I have ever met in my life; I had no way of speculating and could not earn money except by labor, and to earn by labor eleven hundred dollars, besides my living, seemed the work of a lifetime. There was, however, but one way. I went to the creditors and told them that if they would let me alone I would give them all I could earn over my living as fast as I could earn it."

During his storekeeping career Lincoln not only greatly augmented his fund of anecdotes but read omnivorously, especially newspapers. A peddler sold him a barrel of mixed trash for fifty cents; at the bottom of it was a legible copy of Blackstone's *Commentaries*. This book inspired Lincoln as Chapman's *Homer* did Keats, and he chewed and digested parts of it, determining when chance offered to become a lawyer. Meanwhile he browsed through

Gibbon's *Decline and Fall of the Roman Empire,* Rollin's *Ancient History,* Burns and Shakespeare. His favorite historical character was George Washington, for whom he had unbounded admiration. At this period he read Voltaire, Paine and Volney. Their example influenced him toward skepticism regarding religion.

In 1834 he realized his ambition to enter the state legislature. There he supported the Internal Improvement Bill, a measure that had disastrous consequences to the finances of the state. At this and at all other periods in his career Lincoln was ignorant of the general principles of public and private finance, nor did he have either curiosity or interest in the subject. During his eight years in the Illinois House his most important achievement was effecting the removal of the state capital from Vandalia to Springfield. For several sessions he was the Whig floor leader in the legislature, as well as the unsuccessful Whig candidate for Speaker. Among other measures he advocated the distribution of the proceeds of the sale of public lands to the states, and a limited woman's suffrage. He was also friendly to the idea of a national bank. On March 3, 1837, he supported resolutions declaring that he and a colleague believed "that the institution of slavery is founded on both injustice and bad policy, but that the promulgation of abolition doctrines tends rather to increase than abate its evils; . . . [that] Congress . . . has not power under the Constitution to interfere with the institution of slavery in the different States."

In 1837, Lincoln was admitted to practice as a member of the Illinois Bar. He had previously appeared, in an informal way, in several minor cases at the New Salem Court, but now resolved to move to Springfield and hang out his shingle there.

Before, however, Lincoln took up his residence in Springfield, he had undergone a sad experience in New Salem, in the death of Anne Rutledge, the girl he loved, who fell ill and died, on August 25, 1835, of a brain fever. Her death was said by his friends to have reduced Lincoln to a condition of acute prostration. Legend has it that, in speaking of her grave, he proclaimed: "My heart lies buried there"; and that he also said: "The thought that the snows and rains fall upon her grave fill me with indescribable grief."

Mary Todd, who eventually became his wife, was from Lexington, and was sprung from good Revolutionary stock. Her grandfather was prominent and wealthy; her father had served in both branches of his state legislature and was President of the Bank of Kentucky for more than twenty years. Mary was born on December

13, 1818, and at the time that Lincoln met her was not beautiful, but handsome in a stern way. She was rather short and weighed about a hundred and thirty pounds, being already inclined to stoutness. Her temper was quick, violent, uncontrollable and easily provoked. She was very sensitive, spirited, proud and unduly sarcastic. Among her accomplishments was a good working knowledge of the French language. She was abnormally ambitious. During her prolonged stays with her married sister in Springfield, she became the center of a lively social circle. Stephen A. Douglas often called her, but is not known to have offered her marriage. Lincoln became engaged to her, but tortured her and himself by alternately thinking himself in and out of love with her. A date was finally fixed for the wedding. On January 1, 1841, the feast was set. Mary Todd waited in her wedding dress for the bridegroom, but he never arrived. What actually happened is shrouded in mystery. There was no explanation forthcoming. Perhaps in shame and despair at his conduct, "Lincoln went as crazy as a loon." His friends took razors and knives away from his presence fearing lest he kill himself. He forsook the halls of the legislature. Three weeks after he had escaped marriage, he wrote: "I am now the most miserable man living. If what I feel were distributed to the whole human family there would not be one cheerful face on the earth. Whether I shall ever be better, I cannot tell; I awfully forbode I shall not. To remain as I am is impossible; I must die or be better, it appears to me."

On November 4, 1842, Lincoln married Miss Todd. Inside the wedding ring were engraved the words, "Love is eternal." Friends had brought about their reconciliation. His best man said that at the wedding "Lincoln looked and acted as if he were going to the slaughter." While he was dressing for the ceremony, a little boy at his boardinghouse asked where he was going. "To hell, I reckon," was the gloomy answer. Afterwards, in a letter to a friend, he commented: "Nothing new here, except my marrying, which, to me, is a matter of profound wonder."

The couple went to live at the Globe Tavern, where their room and board cost four dollars a week. In 1844, Lincoln bought a house for fifteen hundred dollars, and in it, with their son, Robert Todd, they made their first real home. The Lincolns cannot be viewed as having been a well-suited or happily married couple. Although Herndon's judgment that Mary Lincoln was a "shewolf" is overharsh, she was a perfect termagant. The only thing in the world that she feared was a thunderstorm, which her temper closely resembled. Servants could not abide her, nor could most of her husband's friends. She was something of a snob, and Lincoln, when asked why the Todd name was spelled with a double *d*, is said to have answered that he guessed one *d* was good enough for God, but the Todds needed two. She liked entertaining, but during their long residence in Springfield, Lincoln scarcely ever asked anyone to his home for a meal. Visitors were sometimes surprised, and his wife annoyed, by his opening the door to callers while clad in bedroom slippers, with his collar laid aside and his suspenders sliding off his shoulders. What happened between them in the way of disagreements can only be surmised. His attitude toward her is probably well summed up in a quotation that he often used in relation to other matters: "My old father used to have a saying, 'If you make a bad bargain, hug it all the tighter.'" It was noticed that when he was riding circuits as a lawyer he never displayed any eagerness to return home, and, indeed, absented himself from Springfield for almost six months in the year. On one occasion Mrs. Lincoln pursued him outdoors, waving a butcher knife. As the neighbors were coming from church, Lincoln turned on her, so it is said, and propelled her through the kitchen door, giving her a sharp slap on the seat, and exclaiming, "There now, stay in the house, and don't be a damned fool before the people." Once a man who thought he had been unjustly berated by her sharp tongue sought out her husband and complained to him of the incident. "My friend," Lincoln sadly replied, "I regret to hear this, but let me ask you in all candor, can't you endure for a few moments what I have had as my daily portion for the last fifteen years?"

Nevertheless, it would be erroneous to think of the Lincoln's married life as representing a prolonged period of misery. She was not only greatly interested in his political career, but her judgment on political matters was often valuable to him. After he became habituated to her peculiarities, he was careful not to provoke her anger.

The Lincolns had four children. Robert Todd, born August 1, 1843, graduated from Harvard University, was a staff officer during the Civil War, Secretary of War under Presidents Garfield and Arthur, Minister to England under President Benjamin Harrison, for many years President of the Pullman Car Company. He died in Washington in 1926. Edward Baker, born March 10, 1846, died in infancy. William Wallace, born December 21, 1850, died in the White House, February 20, 1862. Thomas, commonly called "Tad," born April 4, 1853, died in Chicago on July 15, 1871.

During the Civil War, Mrs. Lincoln loyally supported her husband and his policies, although she had come from a slaveholding family and had no personal dislike for the institution of slavery. Three of her brothers were killed in as many different battles, fighting on the Confederate side, and two of her sisters were wives of officers in the Confederate army.

After the assassination of the President, Mrs. Lincoln's behavior became very eccentric. Her closest friend for a time was probably Elizabeth Keckley, a colored seamstress and ex-slave whose memoirs make interesting reading. Mrs. Lincoln had always been excessively fond of dress and it was only by chance that she was dissuaded from selling at public auction her personal belongings, which were for a while on display in a Broadway shop. A cerebral disease, no doubt present in her system for many years, became swiftly accentuated after her husband's death. For a considerable period she was an inmate of an insane asylum. She used to complain that hot wires were being drawn through her eyes and nails hammered into her head. Dr. Thomas W. Dresser, who attended her during her last illness, said: "In the late years of her life mental peculiarities were developed which finally culminated in a slight apoplexy, producing paralysis of which she died. Among the peculiarities alluded to, one of the most singular was the habit she had during the last year or so of her life of immuring herself in a perfectly dark room and, for light, using a small candlelight, even when the sun was shining bright out of doors. No urging would induce her to go out into the fresh air. Another peculiarity was the accumulation of large quantities of silks and dress goods in trunks and by the cartload, which she never used and which accumulated until it was really feared that the floor of the store-room would give way." Although she had sufficient means for her support, she lived in fear of starvation and importuned Congress for pecuniary assistance. This was tardily granted. Her tragic life came to a close at Springfield, Illinois, on July 16, 1882.

Lincoln served in the national House of Representatives from 1847 to 1849 as the only Whig representative from Illinois. He had won his election over a strong Democratic candidate, Peter Cartwright, a circuit-riding evangelist, by a vote of 6340 to Cartwright's 4829; an Abolitionist, Walcott, ran a poor third with 249 votes. Lincoln's electioneering expenses amounty to seventy-five cents for the purchase of cider. There were no vital issues involved in the campaign, except that of the Mexican War which Lincoln mildly supported.

On the floor of Congress, Lincoln soon took issue with the Polk Administration and, as a good Whig, denounced its conduct of the war, though voting for necessary supply bills. He fathered the Spot Resolutions, calling for an explanation of where initial hostilities had taken place and contrary to his campaign declarations, spoke of the war as having been unnecessarily and unconstitutionally begun.

In a speech on his resolutions he advanced a theory of revolution entirely at variance with his later stand as President on the subject. "Any people anywhere," he said, "being inclined and having the power have the right to rise up and shake off the existing government, and form a new one that suits them better. This is a most valuable, a most sacred right—a right which we hope and believe is to liberate the world. Nor is the right confined to cases in which the whole people of an existing government may choose to exercise it. Any portion of such people that can may revolutionize and make their own of so much of the territory as they inhabit. More than this, a majority of any such portion may revolutionize, putting down a minority, intermingled with or near about them, who may oppose this movement. Such minority was precisely the case of the Tories of our own Revolution. It is a quality of revolutions not to go by old lines or old laws; but to break up both and make new ones."

Lincoln was assigned to the Committee on Expenditures in the War Department, and to the Committee on Post Offices and Post Roads. He favored a protective tariff and internal improvements but took no strong position on slavery matters, except to vote several times for the principle of the Wilmot Proviso. Before being elected he had announced that he would not run for re-election, a decision which he regretted. However, it is fortunate that he was not a candidate to succeed himself, for his attitude toward the war had rendered him extremely unpopular in his district. The Whigs now lost his constituency.

In 1848 he spoke in the North for the Taylor ticket. He wished an appointment from the new President as Commissioner of the General Land Office. Instead Taylor offered to make him Secretary of the Oregon Territory. Mrs. Lincoln strongly opposed the acceptance of this position, feeling that it would hinder his future political preferment, and he wisely declined it, as well as a tentative offer to become Governor of the same territory.

His standing at the Illinois Bar during the next ten years was a high one. His business was large, both in the state and federal courts. His first partner was John T. Stuart. Their fees amounted to about sixteen hundred dollars a year. Their charges were small and often were paid in produce, such as vegetables or chickens. In 1841, Lincoln entered into partnership with Stephen A. Logan. Their respective political ambitions made this alliance an unhappy one, and in 1844 Lincoln dissolved the firm and started a new one, under the name of "Lincoln and Herndon." William (Billy) H. Herndon played an important part in Lincoln's life. His feelings on the subject of slavery were strong enough to make him an abolitionist. Moreover, he idolized his senior partner and played Boswell to him, his material for a biography being the most valuable that we have regarding the early life of the President.

This partnership only ended with Lincoln's death. During its active continuance Lincoln's income from his legal practice for many years varied from two to three thousand dollars. Their office was a room of moderate size, so ill kept that seeds sprouted out of the piles of dirt in its corners. But much of the time Lincoln was absent on circuit. Sometimes on horseback, sometimes in a buggy, he attended the courts. The accommodations and fare were rough, but Lincoln never noticed them. He delighted in this type of life, for it afforded him constant companionship. After court adjourned, he would fore-gather with other famous storytellers in a hospitable tavern, and they would swap yarns far into the night.

As a lawyer Lincoln acquired his name of "Honest Abe." He discouraged contention, saying: "Point out to them [clients] how the nominal winner is often a real loser—in fees, expenses, and waste of time. As a peacemaker, the lawyer has a superior opportunity of being a good man. There will still be business enough. Never stir up litigation. A worse man can scarcely be found than one who does this." He was persuasive with a jury and prepared his cases with great care. In spite of his natural laziness and disorderly way of doing things, he was painstakingly thorough in his investigation of legal decisions bearing on cases in which he was interested. He won ninety-six out of one hundred and seventy-five suits tried by him before the Supreme Court of Illinois. His best clients were railroad companies—from the Illinois Central he once received a fee of five thousand dollars. He had no antipathy toward representing corporations. Regarding one such client, he observed: "But our client is but a conventional name for thousands of widows and orphans whose husbands' and parents' hard earnings are represented by this defendant." Occasionally lawyers from Chicago or the East, when first brought into contact with him, underrated his abilities. His appearance was uncouth, and his rusty stovepipe hat, shabby frock coat and too short trousers (which may have gained for him his nickname of "Long Shanks") did not impress strangers favorably. At bedtime, clad in a long yellow flannel nightshirt, his appearance was said to have been grotesque in the extreme. But, upon further acquaintance, they were forced to recognize his ability. He was especially gifted in seizing upon the essence of any involved legal complication and separating it from its surrounding unessentials. He was one of the leaders at the Bar of his state.

The repeal of the Missouri Compromise awakened Lincoln to a new interest in politics. With timely judgment he espoused the principle of limiting the extension of slavery, and confined most of his speeches to an elaboration upon that subject. In 1855 he unsuccessfully attempted to be named to the United States Senate. In 1856 he definitely abandoned the dying Whig cause and joined the Republican party. He soon became one of its most active members, receiving 110 votes for the vice-presidency at the Frémont Convention. In 1858 he was nominated by the Republicans for the Senate, and carried on his famous debates with the Democratic incumbent, Stephen A. Douglas.

Reading these debates today, one is not especially impressed by them. Lincoln was never a profound political thinker in the same sense as Jefferson. He accepted the Hamiltonian doctrines without close scrutiny, and derived strength from his single-minded purpose to neglect discussion except that of slavery. In fact, all through his career, it is notable how little independent political thinking was done by Lincoln. During his presidency his mind was entirely concentrated on preserving the Union.

Contemporary interest in the Lincoln-Douglas debates was enormous. They toured the state, Douglas in a special train, to which was attached a flatcar carrying a brass cannon. They debated from the same platforms. Douglas was a magnificent stump speker, but Lincoln proved his equal as a campaigner. Lincoln's platform manner was quiet compared with that of Douglas. The latter in speaking, according to one observer, "lashed himself into such a heat, that if his body had been made of combustible matter, it would have burnt out."

Lincoln pierced the Achilles' heel of his opponent's doctrine of

popular sovereignty by asking the question: "Can the people of a
United States Territory, in any lawful way, against the wish of any
citizen of the United States, exclude slavery from its limits prior to
the formation of a State Constitution?" When his friends advised
him that his insistence on a answer to this question would not win
the election, he replied: "I am killing larger game; if Douglas an-
swers he can never be President, and the battle of 1860 is worth a
hundred of this."

Douglas did answer, and stated that slavery could not exist in any
place where the people were opposed to it, for it required local
police regulations for its protection. Lincoln won a majority of the
popular vote, but the legislature, by a strict party division, re-elected
Douglas to the Senate. The defeated candidate, however, was right
in one respect. Douglas, in enunciating the Freeport Doctrine, made
it impossible for the Republicans to choose him as their candidate,
in 1860, for the presidency, while the ardent, proslavery Democrats
of the South became embittered against him because he had, in
effect, declared that it was lawful for a territorial legislature to make
slaveowning practically impossible.

The result of the debates, although adverse to Lincoln, established
his position as a potential choice of the Republican party for the
presidency. He was now a national figure. A visit to New York and
a fine speech delivered by him there at Cooper Union, made him
known personally to many of the Eastern antislavery leaders. When
the Republican Convention met, he was the logical compromise
candidate of his party and, as such, was nominated and elected.

The new President had carried every Northern state except New
Jersey. In ten Southern states he had not received a single vote. It
is to Douglas' honor that he bore no rancor against his successful
antagonist. During the President's inaugural speech Douglas held
the orator's hat and cane. On the day that Sumter fell he called at
the White House. After a long conversation with Lincoln he thenceforth stood patriotically for the defense of the Union. His death took
place shortly afterwards.

Lincoln's opinions and utterances on the subject of slavery are
most interesting. He was in no sense a crusader. In spite of Herndon's pleadings he never joined the Abolitionists. "If slavery is not
wrong, nothing is wrong," he once said: "I cannot remember when
I did not think so and feel so." But during the Douglas debates he
stated: "That I am not, nor ever have been, in favor of bringing
about in any way the social and political equality of the white and

black races; that I am not, nor ever have been in favor of making voters of the free negroes, or jurors, or qualifying them to hold office, or having them marry with white people. I will say in addition that there is a physical difference between the white and black races which, I suppose, will forever forbid the two races living together upon terms of social and political equality; and inasmuch as they cannot so live, that while they do remain together there must be the position of the superiors and the inferiors; and that I, as much as any other man, am in favor of the superior position being assigned to the white man."

He continued to insist that the real issue between the South and the rest of the country was confined to the territorial extension of slavery. In the Buchanan-Frémont campaign, when questioned as to the difference between the two parties, he answered: "Simply this. Shall slavery be allowed to extend into United States territories now legally free? Buchanan says it shall, and Frèmont says it shall not. That is the naked issue and the whole of it." He held that slavery in the states had been guaranteed to those states favoring it by the federal Constitution, and this privilege could only be taken away by an amendment to the Constitution. Slaveholders should not be blamed for their adherence to their institution.

In 1854 he said: "I have no prejudice against the Southern people. They are just what we would be in their situation." He confessed himself perplexed as to how slavery could be eliminated. "When the Southern people," he stated, "tell us they are no more responsible for slavery than we are, I acknowledge the fact. When it is said that the institution exists, and that it is very difficult to get rid of it, in any satisfactory way, I can understand and appreciate the saying. I surely will not blame them for not doing what I should not know how to do myself. If all earthly power was given me, I should not know what to do as to the existing institution. My first impulse would be to free all the slaves, and send them to Liberia, to their own native land."

His "House Divided" speech, delivered on June 16, 1858, enunciated views that many of his friends advised him were too extreme to be politically expedient. He could not be dissuaded from his position. In this oration he said: "In my opinion it [slavery agitation] will not cease until a crisis shall have been reached and passed. 'A house divided against itself cannot stand.' I believe this government cannot endure permanently half slave and half free. I do not expect the Union to be dissolved—I do not expect the house to fall—but I do expect it will cease to be divided. It will become all one thing, or all the other. Either the opponents of slavery will arrest the further spread of it, and place it where the public mind shall rest in the belief that it is in the course of ultimate extinction; or its advocates will push it forward till it shall become alike lawful in all the States, old as well as new, North as well as South."

In September 1859, Lincoln stated: "I say that we must not interfere with the institution of slavery in the States where it exists, because the Constitution forbids it, and the general welfare does not require us to do so. We must not withhold an efficient fugitive slave law, because the Constitution requires us, as I understand it, not to withhold such a law. But we must prevent the outspreading of the institution, because neither the Constitution nor general welfare requires us to extend it. We must prevent the revival of the African slave-trade, and the enacting by Congress of a territorial slave code. We must prevent each of these things being done by either congresses or courts. The people of these United States are the rightful masters of both congresses and courts, not to overthrow the Constitution, but to overthrow the men who pervert the Constitution."

The John Brown raid met with his condemnation. "That affair," he said, "in its philosophy, corresponds with the many attempts related in history at the assassination of kings and emperors. An enthusiast broods over the oppression of a people till he fancies himself commissioned by Heaven to liberate them. He ventures the attempt which ends in little else than his own execution. Orsini's attempt on Louis Napoleon and John Brown's attempt at Harper's Ferry were, in their philosophy, precisely the same."

In fact Lincoln's moral indignation over the institution of slavery has probably been exaggerated in the popular estimation of his character. Always the issue of slavery was subordinate in his judgment to that of Union.

It was as a Unionist that Lincoln performed his greatest service to the country. Although we have noted one of his early utterances on the right of revolution, he later became a confirmed Unionist and never wavered in his convictions. "If I could save the Union," he declared, "without freeing any slaves I would do it; and if I could save it by freeing all the slaves I would do it; and if I could save it by freeing some and leaving others alone, I would also do that."

When the Crittenden Compromise was pending in Congress in December 1860, Lincoln was responsible for defeating it and thereby more or less responsible for causing the ensuing war between the states. He firmly advised the Republicans against entering into any compromise, the effect of which would be to extend slavery; acting on this advice they rejected the salient features of the Crittenden proposal. About this time he told a friend that he could not in his heart believe "that the South designed the overthrow of the Government."

From the outbreak of the war there was a strong Northern, as well as Southern, antislavery element that insisted the slaves should be immediately emancipated. The President refused to listen to the exhortations of these partisans. Before his inauguration he had said: "My policy is to have no policy," and afterwards he shaped his actions toward slavery as circumstances dictated. "What good," he once complained, "would a proclamation of emancipation do especially as we are now situated? I do not want to issue a document that the whole world will see must necessarily be inoperative like the Pope's Bull against the comet."

In his annual message of December 1862 the President proposed that a constitutional amendment be referred to the voters, providing, in substance, "first, that compensation should be given in United States bonds to any State, whether now in rebellion or not, which should abolish slavery before the year 1900; secondly, that the slaves who had once enjoyed actual freedom through the chances of the war sould be permanently free, and that their owners should be compensated; thirdly, that Congress should have authority to spend money on colonization for negroes." Little was done in regard to this proposal. On March 6, 1862, he sent a message to Congress, outlining a plan for compensated emancipation. It came to nothing. On September 22, 1862, he issued the famous preliminary Emancipation Proclamation, announcing "That, on the first day of January, in the year of our Lord one thousand eight hundred and sixty-three, all persons held as slaves within any State, or designated part of a State, the people whereof shall then be in rebellion against the United States, shall be then, thenceforward and forever free."

On January 1, 1863, the definitive proclamation was promulgated. The Emancipation Act, it will be noted, applied only to slavery in the rebellious states, and it was not until December 1865, after Lincoln's death, that the passage of the Thirteenth Amendment to the federal constitution sounded the death knell of slavery and involuntary servitude in the United States. Lincoln evidently cared little for emancipation for its own sake, but advocated it as a war measure designed to be helpful to the Union cause.

His slow progress to the issuance of any such decree had been politically wise. He knew the importance of not antagonizing the Unionists who remained slaveowners or who were proslavery in their opinions. Any premature action would have alienated their support of his administration. It was, therefore, only when public opinion was ripe for the change that he advocated it, and sugared the pill for slaveholders in the loyal states by not including them in the edict.

Those Southerners who realized that secession would mean war, and still advocated secession, committed an irreparable error of judgment, for they misjudged the extent and strength of Unionist sentiment. Alexander Stephens, Vice-President of the Confederacy, had rightly estimated the situation when he said: "I consider slavery much more secure in the Union than out of it if our people were but wise." But the fire-eaters and the bigoted economists in the South had their way. The one group believed the Yankees would not, and could not, fight, but felt secure that if they should one Southerner could whip three Northerners. The other group's attitude was typified by the utterance of Senator J. H. Hammond, of South Carolina, who predicted: "Without firing a gun, without drawing a sword, should they make war on us, we could bring the whole world to our feet. . . . No, you dare not make war on cotton. No power on earth dares make war upon it. Cotton is King."

Alas for Senator Hammond, the English mills at the commencement of war possessed a great surplus of cotton, and the English mill operatives rapidly became so Northern in their sentiments that they would rather have gone without work than assist the Southern cause. The Northern blockade soon became effective enough to halt large shipments of cotton abroad. The King lost his crown, and his subjects lost their wealth.

Lincoln's induction into the presidential chair came at a most critical time. The Democrats still controlled Congress and the Supreme Court. Washington was filled with Southern sympathizers occupying high offices. The idea of secession did not then, in many minds, have the ugly connotations it now possesses. The right of a state, or states, to secede from the Union was admitted even by some prominent antislavery constitutional lawyers. Many Republicans realized that war between the two sections of the country would result either in the complete disruption of the nation or else in the annihilation of one or the other cultures that distinguished the respective antagonists. There was a general disposition in the North to avoid hostilities. Horace Greeley declared that even the opponents of slavery "would not be citizens of a Republic of which one part was pinned to the other part with bayonets." To a Northern banker however who predicted that grass would grow in the streets if war were declared, Lincoln answered: "I registered an oath in heaven to protect and preserve this Union, and to maintain it against all manner of assault, even if we must go to war—let the grass grow where it will."

Conservative Southern leaders were willing to oppose the attempt to extend slavery, and wished to maintain their institution under the preferred status guaranteed by the federal Constitution. Numbers of them loathed the institution itself. Robert E. Lee, who freed his slaves before the war began, was for a long time a Unionist at heart; he once wrote to his son: "I can contemplate no greater calamity for the country than a dissolution of the Union."

At the time of Lincoln's nomination his managers had, without his authority, in order to win doubtful delegates to their cause, made certain promises regarding cabinet appointments. Lincoln disavowed this procedure but nevertheless resolved to satisfy these pledges. The Cabinet, as finally constituted, consisted of William H. Seward of New York, Secretary of State; Simon Cameron, of Pennsylvania, Secretary of War; Caleb B. Smith of Indiana, Secretary of the Interior; Gideon Welles of Connecticut, Secretary of the Navy; Salmon P. Chase of Ohio, Secretary of the Treasury; Edward Bates of Missouri, Attorney General; and Montgomery Blair of Maryland, Postmaster General. His private secretaries, who proved of the greatest assistance to him and later wrote a monumental biography of him, were John G. Nicolay, a German immigrant, and John M. Hay, of Indiana, afterwards famous as statesman and author. The appointment of Cameron evoked a considerable degree of disapproval. The bitter-tongued Thaddeus Stevens, when questioned by the President as to whether he thought Cameron would steal, replied: "No, I don't think he would steal a red-hot stove." Cameron was later replaced by Edwin M. Stanton, in spite of Stanton having repeatedly referred to Lincoln as "an imbecile."

This selection of cabinet members was dictated entirely by political considerations. Several of them had been Lincoln's rivals for the presidential nomination. One of them, Chase, was a perennial candidate for the next nomination. With rare magnanimity Lincoln, when the opportunity offered, made Chase Chief Justice of the Supreme Court of the United States. Personal feeling among members of the Cabinet was often bitter, and it required a very unusual degree of tact on the President's part to keep them working harmoniously together. In the beginning Seward was inclined to view himself as a Prime Minister and hoped to treat the President as a nonentity. Lincoln quickly squelched these pretensions and made Seward not only a useful subordinate but a firm friend.

For a time after his inauguration the policy of the new President toward the secession movement seemed to be as invertebrate as that of his predecessor. Seward, with misguided enthusiasm, proposed a foreign war or wars as a possible way to reconcile internal factions. Lincoln vacillated between a desire to strengthen Fort Sumter or to evacuate it. The Confederates cut the Gordian knot and fired upon it. The war was on.

Lincoln took an active part in military operations. He named and dismissed generals, read books on strategy and haunted the war office. He seldom interfered with the decisions of his commanders and supported them in the most loyal way. When McClellan was unbearably rude to him, his only comment was: "Never mind, I will hold McClellan's horse if he will only bring us success."

Lincoln possessed no military talents. Sometimes, after a Union defeat he was oppressed by melancholy, but his will to win never faltered. Gradually his determination infected the people of the North. They began to put almost as much faith in "Father Abraham" as in the armies. Had he possessed better military judgment, the duration of the conflict might have been materially shortened. Had his judgment been worse or his fortitude less, the Union cause might well have been lost. His heavy responsibilities brought out all his latent powers. The rail splitter was revealed to be a man of true genius. He grew continually to match the needs of his country. He seemed almost to have been especially produced to meet such a crisis as confronted him.

During the war he indulged in no bitterness toward the Confederate cause but treated its protagonists as if they were merely temporarily estranged fellow countrymen. It is true that he sanctioned Sherman's march to the sea, an event which was to leave behind it generations of bitterness, but he probably did not realize the possibilities of rapine in such an operation.

When hostilities ceased, his treatment of the vanquished was marked by a deep humanity. He ordered the immediate release of General Lee's two sons, whom some of his supporters wished to execute. Elizabeth Keckley recounts that on the morning of his father's assassination Captain Robert Lincoln came into the room carrying a photograph of Robert E. Lee. Lincoln took the picture, laid it on the table before him, scanned the face thoughtfully and said: "It is a good face; it is the face of a noble, noble, brave man."

On the Northern side there was no such galaxy of military genius as the South produced. But, more important, the North had the assistance of wealth and the census returns. General after General was promoted to the chief command and found wanting. Finally, Sherman, Sheridan, Thomas and, above all, Grant supplied the leadership so anxiously desired by the President. But Lincoln himself was the Strong Man of the Union. His tall, gaunt form, his homely features, his moth-eaten hat, his shabby clothes, the tattered gray shawl that often served him instead of an overcoat, his torn cotton umbrella, his awkward gestures, his shambling gait, even the melancholy "that dripped from him as he walked," had become throughout the North the symbol and the hope of the Union.

Although Lincoln had entertained doubts of his re-election, the verdict of his countrymen was a sweeping mandate to him. He ran on a National Union ticket, with Andrew Johnson, a Democrat from Tennessee, as the candidate for the vice-presidency. His chief argument on his own behalf was that "it is bad policy to swap horses while crossing a stream." He interposed no alibi to the threat of defeat. When advised that Grant might wish to take his place, he replied: "If he takes Richmond, let him have it." He made plans to co-operate with his opponent, McClellan, if that gentleman should be nominated. But he need have had no misgivings about the result. Only three Northern states—one of them Illinois—voted against him.

During his administration countless foreign problems, in addition to grave domestic ones, pressed for his attention. He had disapproved of the French invasion of Mexico and the erection of an empire there. But in that case, as in others, he did not beard the lion, thinking one war at a time was enough. With his assistance and advice Seward competently managed the foreign relations of the Union. When England, in warlike terms, demanded the surrender of Mason and Slidell, the Confederate Commissioners who had been forcibly removed by a Yankee captain from the British mail steamer *Trent,* the administration did not stand on false pride but gave them up. Abroad, the President's prestige waxed steadily greater. His diplomatic achievements were of the highest rank. The failure of the Southern hope of foreign intervention was chiefly attributable to him.

Aside from war measures, the history of his presidency is not noteworthy for constructive policies. The tariff of 1864 was high beyond all precedent and was a landmark of extortionate rates in our economic history. Profiteers and grafters ran amuck and unchecked. The buccaneers took possession of the citadels of finance; Lincoln apparently neither knew nor cared. The President openly used patronage to strengthen his position. Even government advertising was placed in newspapers whose support was deemed advisable. Wealth at the North increased greatly. The national debt in August 1865 reached $2,845,000,000, and the South was bankrupt, but the national income was growing by leaps and bounds.

Victory did not fill Lincoln with exultation, but deepened his sense of responsibility and melancholy. Those who looked to him to impose harsh terms upon the defeated South were soon disillusioned. The close of his second inaugural address gave notice to the fanatical proponents of revenge upon the conquered that they must first reckon with his powerful opposition.

A fanatic of another stripe was to disappoint his dreams of binding up a nation's wounds. On April 14, 1865—Good Friday—the President went to Ford's Theatre in Washington to see *Our American Cousin,* with Laura Keene playing the lead. An actor, John Wilkes Booth, brother and son of famous Thespians, crazed by drink and infatuation for the Confederacy, had conceived with some associates the grandiose scheme of murdering the chief officers of the administration. To others was delegated the duty of despatching the subordinates; Seward was visited, and stabbed. But Booth reserved for himself the chief role. Appearing behind the President in his box, he shot him through the back of the head. Then, jumping onto the stage, brandishing a knife and yelling, *"Sic semper tyrannis,"* the assassin made his escape. A few days later he was apprehended and killed.

The President never regained consciousness. He lingered through the night but did not survive the morning. Lincoln was dead, the Lincoln myth was born. An outburst of almost universal grief in the North acknowledged his passing. Most Southerners were shocked and apalled at his tragic death. They had reason to be. Ten years later Jefferson Davis said: "Next to the destruction of the Confederacy, the death of Abraham Lincoln was the darkest day the South has ever known."